Cornbread Nation 5

The Best of Southern Food Writing

Cornbread Nation 5

The Best of Southern Food Writing

Edited by Fred W. Sauceman
General Editor, John T. Edge

Published in association with
The Southern Foodways Alliance
at the Center for the Study of Southern Culture
at the University of Mississippi

The University of Georgia Press ■ Athens and London

Published by the University of Georgia Press
Athens, Georgia 30602
www.ugapress.org
© 2010 by the Southern Foodways Alliance,
Center for the Study of Southern Culture, University of Mississippi
All rights reserved
Designed by Anne Richmond Boston
Set in 10.5 Adobe Minion
Printed and bound by Sheridan Books
The paper in this book meets the guidelines for permanence and durability of the Committee
on Production Guidelines for Book Longevity of the Council on Library Resources.

Printed in the United States of America
14 13 12 11 10 P 5 4 3 2 1

Library of Congress Cataloging-in-Publication Data
Cornbread nation 5 : the best of Southern food writing / edited by Fred W. Sauceman.
        p.   cm.
    ISBN-13: 978-0-8203-3507-0 (pbk.)
    ISBN-10: 0-8203-3507-x (pbk.)
    1. Food writing. 2. Food habits—Southern States. I. Sauceman, Fred William.
    TX644.C69 2010
    394.1'20975—dc22
                                                2009032881

British Library Cataloging-in-Publication Data available

Underwritten, in part, by a gift from the Atticus Trust.

The recipes in this book have not been kitchen tested for this publication.
Acknowledgments for previously published material appear on pages 308–311,
which constitute a continuation of this copyright page.

Contents

ACCENTS

THE LIQUID SOUTH

A BENEDICTION

Foreword

John Egerton

When the Southern Foodways Alliance was still in the full-throated rambunctiousness of its infancy, a few of its more hyperkinetic activists decided—in the course of a single one-hour meeting—to publish a yearly anthology of exemplary writing about the object of our affections, Southern food. The meeting took place during our annual symposium at the University of Mississippi's Center for the Study of Southern Culture, under whose umbrella we had first gathered in the fall of 1998, almost a year before the formal birthing of the SFA.

I remember that little ad hoc caucus as if it were yesterday. Every man and woman among us was stoked with high-octane enthusiasm and conviction, as if we had just invented sliced bread and confidently expected to feed the world with it. We had drawn more than two hundred people (and turned away others) to a three-day communion over Southern food and culture. We had set out to prove that the path to social advancement and regional equality ran straight through the kitchen, and when the hunch turned out to be correct, you would have thought we had struck a vein of gold. "Let's do a book, an anthology of great food writing! . . . In time for the next symposium, and every year from then on! . . . How hard is that? Piece-a-cake!"

Reminiscent of an old cereal commercial on television—the punch line of which was "Let's give it to Mikey: he'll eat anything!"—my nervy colleagues offered me the editorship of that freshly conceived volume, and, like Mikey, I wolfed it down.

It was not a mere six months but more like two years later that the first edition of *Cornbread Nation: The Best of Southern Food Writing* finally made its appearance. Approximately every second year since then another has followed, so that now, a decade hence, we welcome volume five, proving, if proof were needed, that nothing having to do with books is ever as fast and easy as it promises to be when you first think it up.

But the good news is that the evolving *Cornbread Nation*, with its succession of editors, has more than made up in quality for whatever it first lacked in ease and speed. Lolis Eric Elie put the second volume together, Ronni Lundy edited the third, and the fourth was the work of John Shelton Reed and Dale Volberg Reed, each building on the achievements of the previous volume. Far from reinventing the wheel, these discerning and skillful editors—bolstered by the in-house oversight of SFA staffers John T. Edge and Mary Beth Lasseter, who have given continuity to the project from the first—managed slowly but surely to fashion a first-class anthology of great food journalism, essays, and poetry.

Now comes the aptly named Fred Sauceman, who not only knows gravy from grease (as my father was fond of saying) but also knows writing from typing (as Truman Capote once declared). His talents as an editor, writer, diplomat, and two-fisted food handler make Sauceman the main man for this all-new fifth edition of *Cornbread Nation*—and as you will quickly discover, the anthology continues to improve with age as surely as a country ham, or a hoop of farm-made cheddar, or a bottle of aged-in-the-wood sipping whiskey.

Just take a glance at some of the writers and the variety of things they're writing about. Among the familiar bylines are those of Roy Blount Jr., the late-great Edna Lewis, Scott Peacock, Brett Anderson, Kathleen Purvis, Corby Kummer, Robert St. John, Ben Barker, Julia Reed, Sara Roahen, Amy Evans, Dan Huntley, Martha Stamps, Robb Walsh, John Martin Taylor, and Ari Weinzweig.

And these are a few of the titles and topics: fried Coke (!), Delta hot tamales, Spartanburg's Beacon Drive-In, funeral food, "Corn as a Way of Life," a fond farewell to the White Lily Flour plant in Knoxville, "Opinion Stew," Southern caviar and truffles, "Poor Man's Pâté," Juneteenth Jamboree in Texas, a piece called "Demystifying Grits for the Northern Palate," and my personal favorite, "A Jewish Yankee's Quest for the Last Great Country Hams of Western Kentucky."

There you have a mere sampling of the stars and stories to be found in *Cornbread Nation* 5. So take out and help yourself from this all-you-can-eat buffet, remembering that while it may be only virtual eating, swept clean of calories, hangovers, indigestion, and guilt, it's almost as memorable and soul-satisfying as the real thing.

Cornbread Nation 5

The Best of Southern Food Writing

Introduction

Fred W. Sauceman

In his classic study first published in 1987, *Southern Food: At Home, on the Road, in History,* John Egerton asked readers to consider whether Southern food was endangered or enduring. If written material about the subject is any clue, consider the fact that John's book is still in print, still quoted from, still authoritative. The book is a living resource, not a nostalgic relic. And consider the fact that over twenty years later, we're still asking that same question: Is Southern food endangered or is it enduring?

Fertilized largely by the Southern Foodways Alliance at the University of Mississippi, the genre of Southern food writing has grown substantially since that organization's first gathering in the late 1990s, making a collection such as this one, subtitled *The Best of Southern Food Writing,* especially difficult to assemble. And it is in the struggle to decide what finally gets published in this compendium that I find what I think, and hope, is the answer to John's fundamental question.

Southern food endures like the perfume of garlic in the wooden salad bowls rubbed down by Aunt Florence Signa at Doe's Eat Place in Greenville, Mississippi. Southern food endures in the churches of Watkinsville, Georgia, where a stew called Chicken Mull is thickened with crushed saltine crackers. Southern food endures as long as we argue over vinegar versus tomatoes in barbecue sauce and bifurcate a state along lines of whole hog or pork shoulder.

Southern food endures as long as Alabama singers cool throats strained by Sacred Harp harmonies with bowls of fresh peach ice cream, its fruit flavor bolstered with Nehi. Southern food endures as Greeks serve red snapper throats in Alabama and Chinese stir-fry collard greens in woks in Mississippi.

Southern food endures in the revival of tomato soup aspic and tea cakes, and in a renaissance of red velvet cake. It survives in the gritty glory of livermush in North Carolina and the smell of ribs rubbed with tequila on Juneteenth in Texas. Southern food endures through the inheritance of cushaws, crook-necked squash in Tennessee.

The scenes, scents, and stories that have been selected for inclusion in *Cornbread Nation 5* depict an evolving South, a South of ever-changing ethnicities and attitudes, yet a South still rooted in the everlasting truth of corn and beans.

Setting the Table

Why Study Southern Food?

Marcie Cohen Ferris

As a scholar of food, I often find myself defending why it is important to study the subject. In spite of front-page news and Internet stories that deal with international food shortages, genetically modified crops, and food scares, the study of food is still viewed with some skepticism in the academy. How does it contribute to the quest for greater knowledge? What new theories or analytical interpretations can be gained? Food provides a more nuanced reading of the texture of daily life in the past, but is that *all* there is?

I call these the "so what?" questions. Because my academic home is the field of American studies, my answer to these questions lies in the relationship between food and the construction of regional and national identity, which has much to do with the concept of difference. How can we understand our own experience without contrasting it to the experience of others? Boundaries are critical to identity formation.

Food reflects both our national and regional culture as surely as do the fields of art, folklore, geography, history, literature, music, politics, and religion. The problem with the study of food is food itself. If only food were more arcane, less accessible, less *popular*, not so sensual or comforting, even divisive, its study would surely find a place in the hallowed halls of the academy.

The "so what?" question is the wrong one. The real question is what can the "small things forgotten," the detail, the texture of everyday life—pigs smoked, oysters shucked, tamales shaped, cakes baked, cocktails imbibed, the *foods shared at a common table*—tell us about who we are, where we come from, and where we're going.

When my dear brother-in-law, Grey Ferris, died after a long fight with cancer, we went back to my husband Bill's home in Vicksburg, Mississippi, to be with family and to attend Grey's funeral. As family and friends gathered, food arrived in an elaborate display of community organization and love. Emily Compton and her daughter Danny brought Bill's mother Shelby's homemade Vicksburg tomato sandwiches, stuffed eggs, tomato aspic, and a beautiful congealed salad of brandied peaches and ginger that glistened like amber. Each night, Bobby Ferguson, a talented carpenter and friend of the family, came by with a casserole prepared by his wife Elaine, who told us, "I just made what my family loves."

There were stiff drinks of bourbon enjoyed with cheese straws, platters of fried chicken and pulled pork, and delicacies brought from New Orleans by Grey's mother-in-law, Mittie Terral, whose weekly visits from Louisiana revived the family with her gumbos and étouffée. Dr. Eddie Lipscomb, a veterinarian from nearby Port Gibson, Mississippi, brought a pecan-smoked brisket he had lovingly prepared for the family. There were strawberry cakes, blueberry pound cakes, caramel cakes, and double fudge brownies baked by Mary Bell Gibbs, whose mother was famous for her brownies, too.

While we attended Grey's funeral in town, Story Stamm Ebersole, a talented Vicksburg caterer, laid out supper for the family—platters of Mrs. Compton's tomato sandwiches and big bowls of chicken salad. Food never tasted as good as it did that day. We ate and drank in small groups and later gathered in a large circle around Shelby Ferris, telling family stories until late in the night. If ever there was an answer to the "so what?" of why we study food, the answer lay in the food served that week and how it poignantly expressed Southern community, memory, and tradition.

What Is Southern?

Edna Lewis

How did Southern food come into being? The early cooking of Southern food was primarily done by blacks, men and women. In the home, in hotels, in boarding-houses, on boats, on trains, and at the White House. Cooking is hard and demanding. It was then, and it still is now. What began as hard work became creative work. There is something about the South that stimulates creativity in people, be they black or white writers, artists, cooks, builders, or primitives that pass away without knowing they were talented. It is also interesting to note that the South developed the only cuisine in this country. Living in a rural setting is inspiring: Birds, the quiet, flowers, trees, gardens, fields, music, love, sunshine, rain, and the smells of the earth all play a part in the world of creativity. It has nothing to do with reading or writing. Many of those cooks could not read or write.

I grew up among people who worked together, traded seed, borrowed setting hens if their own were late setting. Early hatched chickens were like a prize. Neighbors would compete to see who would serve the first spring chickens pan-sautéed. The first spring greens, lettuce, scallions in a vinegar dressing with salt, pepper, and sugar—no oil. They shared favors of all kinds, joined in when it came to planting or harvesting a crop, wheat threshing, hog butchering, and cutting ice on the ponds to store for the summer in the community icehouse.

I grew up noticing the food feasts, picnics, church revival dinners with long white tablecloths. Families put out warm fried chicken, braised leg of mutton, thin slices of boiled Virginia ham. Green beans cooked in pork stock, beets in a vinaigrette sauce. English peas in cream. Baked tomatoes with crusty squares of bread on top. Fragrant corn pudding. Potato salad with a boiled dressing.

Watermelon and cantaloupe pickles and relishes, preserves and jellies, and iced tea.

Southern is an early spring morning shrouded in a thick mist. The warmth of a bright sunrise reveals shimmering, jewel-like dewdrops upon thicket and fence. A large spider web glistens, a spider trying desperately to wind its prey into the web. My father set out to prepare for planting corn. The first day, I walked behind him while he was plowing and singing one of his favorite hymns. For me, it was a great moment. Walking along, pressing my bare feet against the warm plowed earth. All of the chickens were behind me, picking up the earthworms and bugs. He turned up roots of sassafras bushes, which we took to the house for the next morning.

Southern is a spring breakfast of herring with its roe. It is the most delicious of the first-caught of spring. Shad is more advertised. They both are spring fish, then they disappear until the next spring. Herring roe is of a finer quality than the shad and wonderful sautéed in garlic, lemon juice, butter, and herbs.

Southern is a meal of early spring wild greens—poke sallet before it is fully uncurled, wild mustard, dandelion, lamb's-quarter, purslane, and wild watercress. These are greens that are looked for as the first taste of spring, boiled in pork stock and served with cornmeal dumplings. The next delightful green vegetable is wild asparagus, delicious and tender, found around fence posts where birds drop the seed. They are picked at the right time, steamed and served on toast, with a rich cream sauce spooned over. Southern is a midday dinner of potted squab, tossed until done in a covered iron pot. Served with those first wild greens, a casserole of white potatoes baked in chicken stock, and a delicious strawberry shortcake of biscuit dough.

Southern is an evening of turtle soup. We would find the turtle, having been washed out of the stream in a thunderstorm, crawling toward the house, so we would pick it up, keep it for a few days, then clean and cut it up. There would be great excitement if it contained eggs, which we would add to the stew. After cooking the turtle slowly for hours, we would strain the broth, season it well, add good Sherry, chop up some of the meat, and make dumplings to add to the soup with the eggs.

Southern is Truman Capote. When dining at Café Nicholson, he would request that I make him some biscuits. Southern is a guinea hen, a bird of African origin. They live in trees around the house and make a big noise if strangers come around. Like any game bird, they have to be aged before cooking. They have a delicious flavor and are best when cooked in a clay pot with butter, herbs, onions, and mushrooms.

Southern is Bessie Smith. Give me a pig foot and a bottle of beer. Southern is a great yeast roll, the dough put down overnight to rise and the next morning shaped into rolls and baked. Served hot from the oven, they are light as a dandelion in a high wind.

Southern is a mint julep. A goblet of crushed ice with a sprig of mint tucked in the side of the glass, a plain sugar syrup the consistency of kerosene poured over the ice, then a jigger of bourbon. Stir and bruise the mint with a silver spoon. Sip and enjoy. Southern is a hot summer day that brings on a violent thunderstorm, cooling the air and bringing up smells of the earth that tempt us to eat the soil. Southern is Tennessee Williams and *Streetcar*. Southern is a springhouse filled with perishables kept cool by a stream running through. And a spring keeper—a salamander—is there, watching over.

Southern is Bourbon Street and Louis Armstrong. Southern is a seafood gumbo of crab, okra, tomatoes, scallions, onions, green pepper, bacon, garlic, and herbs. Southern is fresh-made corn fritters, light and crisp enough to fly away. Southern is an okra pancake in a cornmeal batter. Southern is a platter of deviled crabs prepared with soaked slices of white bread torn and mixed with chopped onion, fine-cut scallions, melted butter, fresh-ground black pepper, cayenne, eggs, and the best crabmeat. Baked in the oven, served hot, a morsel to die over. Southern is a pitcher of lemonade, filled with slices of lemon and a big piece of ice from the icehouse, and served with buttermilk cookies. Southern is a delicious chicken salad at a bride's luncheon.

Southern is a bowl of shrimp paste, rich in butter, shrimp, Sherry, spices, and lemon juice. Blended to a soft consistency and served over a plate of grits, a delicious breakfast treat. Southern is a barbecued pig that was cooked for hours and served with a tomato- or vinegar-based sauce, as well as coleslaw, potato salad, baked beans, hush puppies, and iced tea. Southern is a bowl of homemade peach ice cream, served during the peach season. Southern is Richard Wright and his "Bright and Morning Star." Southern is an oyster roast. Guests are presented with white gloves for shucking and pots of melted butter. Southern is leftover pieces of boiled ham trimmed and added to a saucepan of heavy cream set on the back of the stove to mull and bring out the ham flavor, then served spooned over hot biscuits, with poached eggs on the side.

Southern is hunting season, a time that men take off to hunt rabbits, squirrel, opossum, deer, quail, partridge, plover, and dove. We used to trap snowbirds and enjoy a pan of them baked. Southern is a Brunswick stew of squirrel or rabbit, beans, corn, tomatoes, onions, herbs, fresh-ground black pepper, and salt. Long cooking results in a great stew. Southern is a wild pig served with pork liver sauce, peanut sauce, rice for spooning the sauces over, and spicy sauces for the sliced pork.

Southern is Thomas Wolfe and *Of Time and the River*. Southern is Craig Claiborne, for more than twenty-five years the distinguished food critic of the *New York Times*. Southern is a country steak smothered with onions on a Sunday morning, with gravy and spoon bread to spoon the gravy over. Southern is she-crab soup, thick with crab eggs and crabmeat, served with benne biscuits. Southern is a lemon-flavored pound cake served with brandied peaches and homemade blackberry wine.

Southern is a moss rose, a camellia, a buttercup, a tea olive tree sending its fragrance through the air and into the kitchen. Southern is the call of the whip-poor-will at midnight. Southern is Reynolds Price discussing his mother's cooking. Southern is a pot of boiling coffee sending its aroma out to greet you on your way in from the barn. Coffee was always served piping hot, so much so that if someone talked too much, they were told, "Save your breath to cool your coffee."

Southern is a walk along the streams in September to find out if the fox grapes are ripening. Southern is Scott Peacock, one of the South's most creative young chefs. Southern is weeks of canning, pickling, and preserving—cucumber pickle, artichoke pickle, pear pickle, tomato pickle, watermelon rind pickle, citron preserves, green tomato preserves, fig preserves, cherry preserves, grape conserve, crab apple jelly, wild blackberry jelly, fox grape jelly, quince jelly, guava jelly, wild plum jelly, wild strawberry preserves (the best).

Southern is Christmas, a wonderful time of the winter. In the early history of the South, there was no Christmas tree. Beautiful flowers such as camellias were used in Charleston. And it was a German professor—a refugee—who, while boarding with a family in Williamsburg, brought them stories of Christmas decorations in his native Germany.

Our house was decorated with running cedar branches with juniper berries. Red tissue-paper bells were hung throughout the house, lending a festive air. On the sideboard were the Christmas foods such as fruitcake, homemade candies—divinity, peanut brittle, and ribbon squares—nuts, oranges, and coconut made into confections.

Christmas was ushered in before daylight with the thunderous noise of Roman candles—our father waking the community from its sleep. Southern is a delicious oyster stew of sautéed oysters, cream, Sherry, salt, cayenne, fresh-ground black pepper, salsify, a spoon of butter in the bottom of the bowl, and a garnish of chervil. Southern is hoppin' John—black-eyed peas cooked in hog's-head stock—served with a dish of greens on New Year's Day. This to bring good luck in the new year to come. Southern is Dr. Martin Luther King Jr., with a dream.

Southern is William Faulkner, *Intruder in the Dust*. I met him in Café Nicholson. Upon our meeting, he wanted to know if I had studied cooking in Paris. Southern is a beautiful dish of fried chicken, cooked carefully in home-rendered lard and butter with pieces of country ham added, then served with a brown gravy spooned over spoon bread. Southern is Elizabeth Spencer's writing in *The Light in the Piazza*.

Southern is desserts galore—coconut cake, caramel layer cake, black walnut whiskey cake, groom's wedding cake, fig pudding, mincemeat pie, lemon meringue pie, fried apple pies, damson plum pie, rhubarb pie with orange zest, peach cobbler, blackberry cobbler, blackberry roly-poly with blackberry sauce.

Southern is Eugene Walter, deep in Alabama, a Renaissance man, a gourmet, always with a brilliant thought. Southern is Marie Rudisill, author of a cookbook that emulates the friends she grew up with, cooked with, and loved. Southern is Carson McCullers in *The Member of the Wedding*. Southern is all the unsung heroes who passed away in obscurity.

So many great souls have passed off the scene. The world has changed. We are now faced with picking up the pieces and trying to put them into shape, document them so the present-day young generation can see what Southern food was like. The foundation on which it rested was pure ingredients, open-pollinated seed—planted and replanted for generations—natural fertilizers. We grew the seeds of what we ate, and we worked with love and care.

Simmered Greens with Cornmeal Dumplings
Serves 6.

1 1-pound piece slab bacon	2 teaspoons packed brown sugar
3 quarts water	1 teaspoon baking powder
3 pounds mixed greens such as	1 tablespoon unsalted butter
collard, mustard, and turnip	½ cup whole milk
⅔ cup all-purpose flour	Salt and pepper
⅓ cup yellow cornmeal	

Score bacon 2 or 3 times (do not cut all the way through), then simmer in water in a wide 6-quart pot, covered, 1 hour. Discard any coarse stems from greens and coarsely chop leaves. Add greens, 2½ teaspoons salt, and 1 teaspoon pepper to bacon and cook, uncovered, stirring occasionally, 25 minutes.

Meanwhile, whisk together flour, cornmeal, brown sugar, baking powder, and ¼ teaspoon salt, then blend in butter well with your fingertips. Stir in milk until just combined. Let dough stand 5 minutes.

With wet hands, roll rounded tablespoons of dough into balls. Gently place dumplings on top of greens. Cook, covered and undisturbed, over low heat until greens are very tender and silky and dumplings are puffed and cooked through, about 20 minutes. Discard bacon. Season with salt and pepper.

The Grace before Dinner

Jennifer Justus

When the pastry chef behind Princess Diana's wedding confections shows up for dinner, it's not a night you'd want the cake to fall. But when eighty-two-year-old Phila Hach put the finishing touches on a spread for the chef—along with a room full of other international pastry experts visiting Nashville for a world competition—it became clear she knew her grandmother's recipe for custard pie would suit the group just fine.

"I hope you'll enjoy some good country cooking," she said to them as the meal began. She kept a close eye on the contents of each plate to make sure nobody left hungry.

"You didn't get enough chicken," she told Louise Hoffman, a New York chef.

"I've been eating desserts all day," the woman asserted.

"Well, that's why we did chicken," Hach said, as she scooped another helping onto the woman's plate.

So how does a humble country cook entice a collection of renowned chefs to her bed-and-breakfast inn in Joelton, Tennessee? Don't let the tight bun of white hair and old-fashioned apron fool you. Hach has Southern roots in the area for sure, having grown up near her Hachland Hill Inn, but she's traveled and cooked with chefs the world over.

While working for American Airlines, she created an early catering manual for the airline industry and hosted a TV cooking show in the 1950s, sharing her table with June Carter, Minnie Pearl, Julia Child, and a certain man by the name of Duncan Hines. As a young woman in her twenties, she even met Albert Einstein once and, in a moment of awe, recalls blurting out: "I love your theory of relativity."

But even after meeting and cooking for so many famous faces—or perhaps because of that—Hach knows the importance of keeping it real in the kitchen, and in life. Mealtime doesn't have to be a place to show off; rather, it's a place to share during the holidays or any time of year.

"There's something about sitting around the table," she said. "It feeds our soul and our heart and brings back memories."

At her dinner party for the visiting pastry chefs, guests from around the world were seated along two tables the length of the long dining room. Hach lured them like trout from behind rocks as they crowded toward her end of the table, savoring every word of the catering stories she has collected from sixty years in the business. They listened as she relayed her memories about serving country ham and other Southern delicacies to former Secretary of State Henry Kissinger and about eighteen hundred dignitaries at a United Nations dinner.

"Did Kissinger eat the ham?" one of the chefs asked as her story came to a close.

"Honey, there were Muslims there who ate the ham," she said.

Hach, of course, means no disrespect. After her experiences, she well knows that sharing a meal connects all walks of life to their common humanity, encouraging appreciation for cultural differences without losing a special place for one's own.

"Now you can go back and be professional. You do what you do, and I do what I do," she said, sending the guests off. "The pleasures of the table will always be there."

Phila Hach began cooking at just three years of age, making mud pies decorated with daisies for her father. But it wasn't long before he went to Hach's mother with a plea: "For goodness sakes," she recalled him saying, "get that child some flour, sugar, and eggs if I'm going to have to eat it."

Hach inherited an early love for cooking from her mother, a home demonstrator.

"She empowered me to have a passion for entertaining and life and good health and cheer," Hach said.

By the time she was thirteen, Hach was spending her summers learning from master chefs at the former Lookout Mountain Hotel in Chattanooga when she traveled there with her father, an entrepreneur and "visionary," as she called him.

Hach earned a degree in music from Ward-Belmont College, but it was her bachelor's degree from Vanderbilt University in foods and nutrition that shaped her career.

Her cooking repertoire took on a more worldly note when she began a career as a flight attendant with American Airlines in the early 1940s. Back when attendants stayed in fine hotels such as the Savoy in London or the Georges V in Paris, she spent her layovers popping into famous kitchens learning foreign techniques.

An upscale Parisian hotel was also the setting where Hach met her future husband, Adolf Hach, a Sorbonne-educated businessman who offered to help with her luggage. She didn't accept his aid but remembers having just a quick chat.

"That's what flight attendants do," she said. "Speak to everybody."

Two years after their meeting, the man from that hotel recognized Hach on WSM-TV, now Nashville's WSMV-Channel 4, while working in Tennessee as a tobacco exporter. It was the early '50s and Hach was hosting *Kitchen Kollege*, the first cooking show in the South. Adolf began to write her letters, which she'd promptly toss in the trash, until finally she relented for a date.

"I never saw another man," she said.

The couple put their careers on hold to honeymoon for a year. The first of their two children was born eleven months later. They settled in Clarksville, Tennessee, near Fort Campbell, and began an inn together there.

In 2004, Hach moved back near her old homeplace. The author of seventeen cookbooks, she still caters for flights, working closely with the military, and still welcomes guests into her country inn. She takes no medicine, doesn't make regular jaunts to the doctor, doesn't wear glasses, and rises often before the sun, sleeping only about four hours per night. In 2008, she delivered the keynote address to six thousand high-end caterers at a Las Vegas conference.

"With my little, very simple business, they asked me to speak. Because I don't care what you do in life, to enjoy that life, you have to have passion for it, and then it isn't work. I have a passion for the things we eat."

But surely after collecting all these experiences, she has one to name as tops.

"Today is my favorite day," she said. "It's amazing."

Even when Hach isn't hosting the United Nations or international pastry chefs, a night at her Sunday suppers guarantees good food and conversation. When she recently fêted one of the few men to cultivate truffles in the United States—he was visiting Nashville from East Tennessee—among the guests were a local chef, a socialite, a high-profile photographer, and even a clairvoyant.

"She meets no strangers at all," said longtime friend Margaret Parker, who worked for the parent company of WSM-TV. "She collects people from wherever. She just has entertained the world, literally."

And after hosting a recent Sunday supper, an event that might cause cooks fifty years her junior to stagger with exhaustion, Hach's cheeks stay rosy and her steps lively as she slips second helpings onto the edges of her guests' plates. It's only when car keys begin to jangle and guests begin to leave that she seems to get anxious. You imagine she'd just as soon have everyone stay the night with the food and conversation flowing until morning.

"I'm just intoxicated with life," she said. "I believe in Santa Claus. I believe in life, and goodness, and everything."

Chocolate Fudge Pie
Serves 6 to 8.

½ cup melted butter	1 cup sugar
4 whole eggs	1 teaspoon vanilla
¼ teaspoon salt	1 unbaked pie shell
⅓ cup cocoa	

Mix all ingredients quickly. Put in pie shell and bake in 350-degree oven until firm, about 30 minutes. Do not overcook. This pie has a custard texture. Serve warm with ice cream.

Recipe adapted from Southern Heritage Recipes *by Phila Hach, special edition published by Phila Hach, 2007.*

Gardens, Fields, and Forests

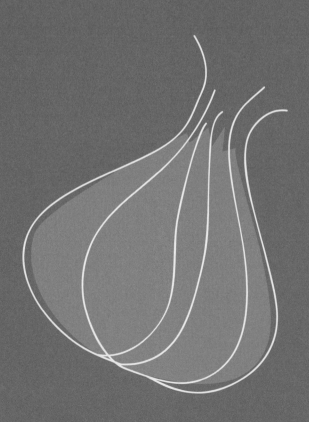

Gratitude
May

Barbara Kingsolver

On Mother's Day, in keeping with local tradition, we gave out tomato plants. Elsewhere this may be the genteel fête of hothouse orchids, but here the holiday's most important botanical connection is with tomatoes. Killing spring frosts may safely be presumed behind us, and it's time to get those plants into the garden.

We grow ours from seed, so it's not just the nursery-standard Big Boys for us; we raise more than a dozen different heirloom varieties. For our next-door neighbor we picked out a narrow-leaved early bearer from the former Soviet Union with the romantic name of "Silvery Fir Tree." Carrying the leggy, green-smelling plant, our family walked down the gravel driveway to her house at the bottom of our hollow.

"Oh, well, goodness," she said, taking the plant from us and admiring it. "Well, look at that."

Every region has its own language. In ours, it's a strict rule that you *never* say "Thank you" for a plant. I don't know why. I was corrected many times on this point, even scolded earnestly, before I learned. People have shushed me as I started to utter the words; they put their hands over their ears. "*Why* can't I say thank you?" I've asked. It's hard. Southern manners are so thoroughly bred into my brain, accepting a gift without a thank-you feels like walking away from changing a tire without washing my hands.

"Just don't," people insist. If you do say it, they vow, the plant will wither up straightaway and die. They have lots of stories to back this up. They do not wish to discuss whether plants have ears, or what. Just *don't*.

So we knew what our neighbor was trying not to say. We refrained from saying "You're welcome," had a nice Sunday afternoon visit, and managed not to jinx this plant—it grew well. Of all the tomato plants that ultimately thrived in her garden, she told us the Silvery Fir Tree was the first to bear.

On the week of May 9 we set out our own tomatoes, fourteen varieties in all: first, for early yields, Silvery Fir Tree and Siberian Early, two Russian types that get down to work with proletarian resolve, bred as they were for short summers. For a more languid work ethic but juicy mid-season flavor we grow Brandywines, Cherokee Purples, orange Jaune Flammes, and Green Zebra, which is lemony and bright green-striped when fully ripe. For spaghetti sauces and canning, Martino's Roma; Principe Borghese is an Italian bred specifically for sun-drying. Everything we grow has its reason, usually practical but sometimes eccentric, like the Dolly Partons given us by an elderly seed-saving friend. ("What do the tomatoes look like?" I asked. She cupped her hands around two enormous imaginary orbs and mugged, "Do you have to ask?") Most unusual, probably, is an old variety called Long Keeper. The fruits never fully ripen on the vine, but when harvested and wrapped in newspaper before frost, they slowly ripen by December.

That's just the tomatoes. Also in the second week of May we set out pepper seedlings and direct-seeded the corn, edamame, beets, and okra. Squash and cucumber plants went into hills under long tents of row-cover fabric to protect them from cool nights. We weeded the onions, pea vines, and potatoes; we planted seeds of chard, bush beans, and sunflowers, made bamboo tepees for the pole beans, and weathered some spring thunderstorms. That's one good week in food-growing country.

By mid-month, once warmth was assured, we and all our neighbors set out our sweet potato vines (there was a small melee down at the Southern States co-op when the management underordered sweet-potato sets). We also put out winter squash, pumpkins, basil seedlings, eggplants, and melons, including cantaloupes, honeydews, rock melons, perfume melons, and four kinds of watermelons. Right behind planting come the weeding, mulching, vigilance for bugs and birds, worry over too much rain or not enough. It so resembles the never-ending work and attention of parenting, it seems right that it all should begin on Mother's Day.

For people who grow food, late spring is the time when we pay for the relative quiet of January, praying for enough hours of daylight to get everything done. Many who farm for a living also have nine-to-five jobs off the farm and *still* get it done. In May we push deadlines, crunch our other work, borrow time, and still end up parking the tractor with its headlamp beams pointed down the row to finish getting the last plants heeled into place. All through May we worked in rain or under threat of it, playing chicken with lightning storms. We worked in mud so thick it made our boots as heavy as elephant feet. On work and school days we started pre-dawn to get an early hour in, then in the late afternoon picked up again where we'd left off. On weekends we started at daybreak and finished after dusk, aching hungry from the work of making food. Labors like this help a person appreciate why good food costs what it does. It ought to cost more.

In the midst of our busy spring, one of us had a birthday. Not just a run-of-the-mill birthday I could happily ignore, but an imposing one, involving an even fraction of one hundred. We cooked up a party plan, setting the date for Memorial Day so out-of-town guests could stay for the long weekend. We sent invitations and set about preparing for a throng of guests, whom we would certainly want to feed. Our normal impulse would have been to stock up on standard-issue, jet-propelled edibles. But we were deep enough into our local-food sabbatical by now, that didn't seem entirely normal.

Something had changed for us, a rearrangement of mindset and the contents of our refrigerator. Our family had certainly had our moments of longing for the illicit: shrimp, fresh peaches, and gummy worms, respectively. Our convictions about this project had been mostly theoretical to begin with. But gradually they were becoming fixed tastes that we now found we couldn't comfortably violate for our guests, any more than a Hindu might order up fast-food burgers just because she had a crowd to feed.

It put us in a bit of a pickle, though, to contemplate feeding a huge crowd on the products of our county this month. If my mother had borne me in some harvest-festival month like October, it would have been easy. But she (like most sensible mammals, come to think of it) had all her children in the springtime, a fact I'd never minded until now. Feeding just my own household on the slim pickings of our local farms had been a challenge in April. The scene was perking up in May, but only slightly. Our spring had been unusually wet and cool, so the late-spring crops were slow coming in. We called a friend who cooks for a living, who came over to discuss the game plan.

Apparently, the customary starting point for caterers in a place that lacks its own food culture is for the client to choose a food theme that is somebody else's land-based food culture. Then all you have to do is import the ingredients from somebody else's land. Mediterranean? A banquet of tomato-basil-mozzarella salads, eggplant caponata, and butternut ravioli—that's a crowd pleaser. And out of the question. No tomatoes or eggplants yet existed in our landscape. Our earliest of early tomatoes was just now at the blossom stage. Mexican? Enchiladas and chipotle rice? Great, except no peppers or tomatillos were going to shine around here. Siberian Tundra was maybe the cuisine we were after. We began to grow glum, thinking of borscht.

Not to worry, said Kay. A good food artist knows her sources. She would call the farmers she knew and see what they had. Starting with ingredients, we'd build our menu from there. As unusual as this might seem, it is surely the world's most normal way of organizing parties—the grape revels of Italy and France in September, the Appalachian ramp hoedowns in April, harvest festivals wherever and whenever a growing season ends. That's why Canadian Thanksgiving comes six weeks before ours: so does Canadian winter. We were determined to have a feast, but if we meant to ignore the land's timetable of generosity and organize it instead around the likes of birthdays, a good travel weekend, and the schedules of our musician friends, that was *our* problem.

Kay called back with a report on our county's late May pantry. There would be asparagus, of course, plus lots of baby lettuces and spinach by then. Free-range eggs are available here year-round. Our friend Kirsty had free-range chicken, and the Klings, just a few miles from us, had grass-fed lamb. The Petersons had strawberries, Charlie had rhubarb, another family was making goat cheese. White's Mill, five miles from our house, had flour. If we couldn't pull together a feast out of that, I wasn't worth the Betty Crocker Homemaker of Tomorrow Award I won in 1972. (Kind of by accident, but that is another story.)

The menu wrote itself: Lamb kabobs on the grill, chicken pizza with goat cheese, asparagus frittata, an enormous salad of spring greens, and a strawberry-rhubarb crisp. To fill out the menu for vegan friends we added summer rolls with bean sprouts, carrots, green onions, and a spicy dipping sauce. We had carrots in the garden I had nursed over the winter for an extra-early crop, and our daughter Camille ordinarily grew bean sprouts by the quart in our kitchen windowsill; she would ramp up her production to a couple of gallons. We might feed our multitudes after all.

As the RSVPs rolled in, we called farmers to plead for more strawberries, more chickens. They kindly obliged. The week of the party, I cut from our garden the first three giant heads of Early Comet broccoli—plants we'd started indoors in February and set out into nearly frozen soil in March. Without knowing it, I'd begun preparing for this party months ago. I liked seeing now how that whole process, beginning with seeds, ending with dinner, fixed me to some deeper than usual sense of hospitality. Anyone who knows the pleasure of cooking elaborately for loved ones understands this. Genesis and connection with annual cycles: by means of these, a birthday could be more than a slap on the back and jokes about memory loss.

On Tuesday, four days pre-party, Camille and I hoed weeds from around corn seedlings and planted ten hills of melons for some distant, future party: maybe we'd have corn and cantaloupe by daughter Lily's birthday in July. By dusk the wind was biting our ears and the temperature was falling fast. We hoped the weather would turn kinder by this weekend. We expected well over a hundred people—about thirty spending the weekend. Rain would wreck any chance for outdoor dancing, and camping in the yard would be grim.

We scowled at the clouds, remembering (ruefully) the cashier who'd jinxed the rain in Tucson. We weren't in drought here, so we decided we could hope with impunity. And then take what came.

On Wednesday we checked the bean sprouts Camille had started in two glass gallon jars. Their progress was unimpressive; if they intended to fill out a hundred fat, translucent summer rolls in three days, they had some work to do. We tried putting them in a sunnier window, but the day was cloudy. Suddenly inspired, we plugged in a heating pad and wrapped it around the jars. Just an hour did the trick. I'm sure we violated some principle of Deep Ecology, but with just a quick jolt from the electric grid our sprouts were on their way, splitting open their seeds and pushing fat green tails into the world.

On Thursday I went to the garden for carrots, hoping for enough. With carrots you never know what you've got until you grab them by the green hair and tug them up. These turned out to be gorgeous, golden orange, thicker than thumbs, longer than my hand. Shaved into slivers with green onions and our indolent sprouts, two dozen carrots would be plenty. I could only hope the lambs and chickens were cooperating as well. I stood for a minute clutching my carrots, looking out over our pasture to Walker Mountain on the horizon. The view from our garden is spectacular. I thought about people I knew who right at that moment might be plucking chickens, picking strawberries and lettuce, just for us. I felt grateful to the people involved, and the animals also. I don't say this facetiously. I sent my thanks across the county, like any sensible person saying grace before a meal.

Guests began to trickle in on Friday: extended family from Kentucky, old college friends from South Carolina, our musician friends John, Carrie, and Robert. I was bowled over by the simultaneous presence of so many people I care about, from as far away as Tucson and as near as next door. We made all the beds and couches, and pitched tents. We walked in the garden and visited. All those under age twelve welded into a pack and ran around like wild things. I overheard a small platoon leader in the garden command: "You, whatever your name is, go down that way and I'll hide and we'll scare the girls." I only made two rules: Don't injure each other, and don't flatten the crops. With the exception of one scraped finger and the tiniest mishap with a Dolly Parton, they obliged.

We set up a sound system on the back patio, dragged bales of straw into benches, and eyed the sky, which threatened rain all day Saturday but by later afternoon had not delivered. We carried a horse trough out of the barn and filled it with ice to chill our Virginia Chambourcin and Misty River wines, and beer from a nearby microbrewery. The lamb kabobs on the grill made all our mouths water for an hour while Kay and her helpers worked their mojo in our kitchen. The food, when it came out, was applauded: the summer rolls were saucy, the lamb succulent, the frittata puffy and light. The strawberry-rhubarb crisp vanished into thin air. Here's what we *didn't* have: the shrimp arranged in a ring like pink poker chips; those rock-hard broccoli wedges and lathed carrots surrounding the ubiquitous white dip; the pile of pineapple and melon chunks on a platter. Nobody seemed too disappointed.

Some of us were in fact sticking our fingers into the rhubarb-crisp pans to lick up crumbs when the music started. The three-year-olds were the first ones out on the flagstone dance floor, of course, followed closely by my seventy-five-year-old parents, the teenagers and the elders and the middle-aged, recklessly dancing across age categories. And it still didn't rain. Nobody fell in the creek, nobody went hungry, and nobody's husband refused to dance. When the night chilled us we built a huge bonfire, and nobody fell into that either. Midnight found me belting out backup harmonies with my cousin Linda to "You Can't Always Get What You Want" by the Rolling Stones. The over-fifty crowd stayed on its feet until two in the morning. You get what you need.

I'd asked for no presents. The stuff-acquisition curve of my life has long since peaked and lately turned into a campaign against accumulation, with everyday skirmishes on the kitchen table. Not just mail and school papers, either, I mean *stuff* on that table. (Shoes, auto parts, live arthropods in small wire cages.) "No presents," I said. "Really." But here in Dixie we will no more show up to a party empty-handed than bare-bottomed, because that's how we were raised. A covered dish is standard, but was unnecessary in this case. To make everyone comfortable we had to suggest an alternative.

Camille made the call, and it was inspired: a plant. The tiniest posy, anything would serve. And truthfully, while we'd put prodigious efforts into our vegetable garden and orchards, our front yard lay sorry and neglected. Anything people might bring to set into that ground would improve it. Thus began the plan for my half-century Birthday Garden: higgledy-piggledy, florescent and spontaneous, like friendship itself.

This is what my friends brought: dug from their own backyards, a division of a fifty-year-old peony, irises, a wisteria vine, spicy sweetshrub, beebalm, hostas, datura, lilies, and a flowering vine whose name none of us knows. My parents brought an Aristocrat pear, a variety bred by an old friend from our hometown. A geographer friend brought Portuguese collards; another indulged my fondness for red-hot chile peppers. Rosemary and sage, blueberry and raspberry, fountain grass, blue sweetgrass, sunshine-colored roses, blue-and-white columbines, scarlet poppies, butterfly bush and "Sunset" echinacea—the color scheme of my garden is "Crayola." Our neighbor, to whom we'd taken the tomato plant, dug some divisions of her prettiest lemon lilies. "Oh, well, goodness," I said as I received each of these botanical gifts. "Well, look at that."

I thanked my parents for having me, thanked the farmers for the food, thanked family and friends for the music, the dancing, the miles traveled, and the stunning good luck of having them all in my life. But I did not say "Thank you" for a plant. My garden lives.

Corn as a Way of Life

Loyal Jones

Parched corn and seed corn that various Indian tribes gave to the Colonists not only saved their lives but also changed their diets, their habits, and their entire culture. Corn became the most important crop in America. It fed families and their livestock and thus established and sustained a new way of life in a new land. According to Nicholas B. Hardeman, in his book *Shucks, Shocks, and Hominy Blocks*, by 1849 the South had eighteen million acres planted in corn as compared to five million in cotton.

Corn's reproductive return is greater than any other crop, with one grain producing anywhere from five hundred to four thousand kernels. Products made from corn syrup and carbohydrates are used in numerous foods that we consume every day. In addition, there are more than five hundred industrial uses of corn. It is in automobile paint, plastics, tires, textiles, library paste, gunpowder, baby powder, sandpaper, soap, surgical dressings, insecticides, shoe polish, embalming fluids, rubbing alcohol, deodorants, mattresses, varnish, brake fluid, adhesive tape, and fireworks.

I grew up on farms in Cherokee and Clay counties in North Carolina, in the mountains that flowed into the Great Smokies and the Blue Ridge. My father and our family were renters. This was a fairly benevolent arrangement for the time and place (about 1935 to 1945), contrasting with sharecropping in parts of the Deep South. Since we had our own workhorses, a wagon, turning and cultivating plows, a disk harrow, and a one-horse corn planter, we paid one-fourth of the corn crop to the owner. We had ample acreage for a garden, sorghum cane patches, pasturage for cows and horses, pens for hogs, chicken houses, and woodland that provided fuel for our stove.

We said we lived so far back that the sun set between our house and the road; that the fields were so steep that we had to shoot the seed corn into the ground from another hill with a shotgun; that we planted our potatoes in rows up and down the mountain so that we could just dig the bottom hill and hold the sacks to catch the whole row; that we planted crook-necked cushaws instead of pumpkins because a pumpkin might roll down the mountain and kill somebody whereas a cushaw would just hang around a cornstalk and stay put.

We plowed the ground with a moldboard turning plow, disked and drag-harrowed it, and then laid off rows with a single-foot of "bull-tongue" plow. We planted corn when the oak leaves were the size of a squirrel's ear or when the dogwood was in bloom. My father gave some attention to the signs of the zodiac and phases of the moon when planting, using *The Farmer's Almanac* or calendars that businesses gave out. In general the below-ground crops, such as potatoes, were planted on the dark of the moon, and the above-ground crops, like corn, were planted when the moon was waxing.

My older brothers had all fled the cornfields for the cotton mills of the Piedmont, although I had two sisters still at home during this time, and they did duty in the cornfields, especially when the corn needed hoeing. They wore stockings on their arms and big straw hats, because suntans marked you as a country person. One of my tasks was to mix pumpkin seeds into the fertilizer so that the planter would distribute them randomly over the field. One year we grew seventeen wagonloads of pumpkins.

In the early days we grew Hickory Cane corn and then later a seed corn simply called "Prolific," meaning it had two or more ears per stalk. After the corn was up a few inches, we began the long task of cultivation. Our two-horse riding cultivator was a wonderful tool, and when I was old enough to operate it, I found that with our well-trained mares, I could read books while cultivating—until my father caught me.

The hoe was the most-used tool in our cornfields. Weeds were virulent and relentless. For us, the most dismal phrase in the English language was "hoe corn," and the most anticipated and joyous was "Time to lay the corn by," meaning it was tall enough to outgrow the weeds and cultivating would do more harm than good.

When the corn had reached maturity and the blades were turning red or brown, we cut tops—that is, cut off the part of the stalks above the ears and bound them into bundles for winter livestock fodder—to supplement the hay crop. After the bundles had dried, we either hauled them to the barn or stacked them in the field around a pole. Sometimes we pulled the blades below the ears and tied them into bundles for fodder. For nearby corn patches, we cut the green but mature corn off just above the ground and made large shocks of it in a way that allowed it to continue drying for both fodder and grain.

When the corn was dry and hard, we pulled it by hand and threw it into the wagon as the horses ambled along, and then we stored it in a crib, with every fourth wagonload going into a separate crib for the farm's owner.

We also planted rows of sweet corn for "roasting ears," and after the corn was up a ways, we'd plant some variety of cornfield beans that would run up the cornstalks, producing bushels of beans. We ate corn and beans every day when they were in season, and my mother and sisters canned large quantities. We pickled both corn and beans by putting them in crocks, adding water and salt, weighing them down with a plate, and allowing them to ferment. Then we canned them. We dried beans and used them during the winter as "leatherbritches" or "shucky beans." When the sweet corn was still young and juicy, we had creamed corn or corn pudding and corn on the cob, and as it got harder we had whole kernel corn cut from the cob and made "gritty bread" from the soft kernels.

We planted several rows of popcorn and popped it in the fireplace and melted butter to pour over it. My mother and sisters also made popcorn balls held together with homemade sorghum. At Christmastime, we threaded popped corn onto strings to make loops to decorate the tree and mantle. We put these strings out for the birds after New Year's.

In the older days the field corn would be piled up in the barnyard, and there would be a corn-shucking, with food, music and dancing, and some whiskey out in the barn. There'd be red ears mixed into the pile, and anybody who shucked one could kiss the person of his or her choice.

We ate cornbread twice a day, with biscuits for breakfast, although some poorer people ate cornbread three times a day. My mother also baked cornbread for the dogs, to supplement table scraps. When my father put fish traps in the river, my mother would bake unleavened cornbread with onions for bait to attract catfish.

When we killed hogs and rendered lard, my mother made crackling bread—cracklings being the fried, brown pieces. It made for a tasty, greasy, calorie-laden bread. Another kind of cornbread was "gritty bread," made from hardening green corn grated off as a soupy meal to which regular meal or flour, soda or baking powder, and bacon fat were added.

At least once a year, my mother made up a batch of hominy. She soaked corn kernels in a solution of Red Devil Lye to take off the hull, washed the unjacketed kernels in clear water, and then cooked them in a pot out in the yard.

We were Bluenose Baptists who never made corn liquor, although my father would obtain a pint of moonshine and mix honey or rock candy into it for cough medicine. It had to be administered with a tablespoon.

Other uses of corn had to do with play. We boys had corncob fights. A dry cob could hurt, but a well-soaked one could raise a knot and addle you. We also made fiddles, cows, horses, and primitive dolls and dollhouse furniture out of cornstalks. Dried cornsilks made wonderful handlebar mustaches glued on your lip with pumpkin sap.

Corn was indeed a way of life because we spent so much time with it: preparing the land, growing the crop, harvesting it, turning it into feed or our own food. It sustained us and all the farm animals that supplied the power for farming, or the eggs, milk, butter, and meat that supplemented corn in our diets. It was mainly a subsistence way of life, with little left over to sell except for a few bushels of corn, a few chickens, eggs, a calf, some pigs—to buy new shoes, dresses, overalls, and the necessities of salt, sugar, and baking soda.

For many it was a hard, discouraging, and defeating existence, but in our case, it was a way of life rich in values: family closeness, hard work, responsibility to one another, reliance on spiritual hope beyond the cornfield, humility and modesty, confidence in making do with what you had, biblical restraint in thought and deed and against avarice and greed.

Recently I was reading Willie Nelson's *Facts of Life and Other Dirty Jokes* and came across what Willie claims were Elvis's last words: "Corn? I don't remember corn." I don't know whether or not these were his last words, but if they were, people ought to quit looking for him, 'cause if he—a Mississippi boy—don't even remember corn, he ain't goin' to be no good to nobody.

Between the Rows with Both Hands

Bean-Picking in Northeast Tennessee

Margaret Carr

"There's a art to it; you have to know how to do it." These are the words of Betsy Stout, who, as a teenager, worked in the bean fields in the Shady Valley and Stoney Creek communities in northeast Tennessee. Betsy, her mother, and her sister are "bean pickers." In the days before the large numbers of migrant workers we know today, local people took to the fields to harvest crops as seasonal workers. Most of them also harvested other crops—greens or tobacco—but they were primarily known as bean pickers.

Betsy began working with her friends picking beans as a teenager in the 1960s. "My friends wanted me to go. We made money to buy school clothes," she says. Her mother, Ruth Garland, used her earnings to supplement the household budget when she began picking several years later at the bidding of grower J. N. Taylor. Betsy's sister, Lisa Putman, eventually joined the pickers for many of the same reasons as her sister—to earn spending money. The Garlands, J. N., and Murray Taylor all lived in the Stoney Creek area of Carter County, but J. N. and Murray had large fields of green beans in Stoney Creek and Shady Valley. These were commercial bean fields, and the harvest required large numbers of workers in order to get the crop gathered and ready for market.

The field owners would monitor the crop and schedule pickers when the beans were at their peak. The beans had to be clean and free from dirt, rocks, and other debris. If they had been picked following a rain, they were washed, although this was not usually among the pickers' responsibilities. Upwards of 150 workers might be in the fields at any one time—men, women, and children. Often entire families would work shoulder to shoulder. "Kids would help pick—three and four and on up," says Betsy. "It was for everybody."

Bean boys carried the filled baskets to a weigh station and deposited them into trucks for transport to market, and water girls walked the fields offering water to the pickers. "You'd holler when you were wanting the bean carrier, 'Bean carrier,'" remembers Betsy. "He'd come put them in the sack, and seemed to me like we had a little old piece of paper with a number and he'd take them and go weigh them and pour them out and bring me my paper back and tell me how much my beans weighed. Then we had a girl that we'd holler at, 'Water,' that'd bring us a drink of water around. She carried the water with her."

The work was hot and back breaking, the day began very early, and the workers picked for hours on end. The pay was calculated by the bushel, not by an hourly rate. Speed was the key to making money. The pay was about fifty cents a bushel in the 1960s, two dollars and a half per bushel in the 1980s. A good day would be about fifteen bushels.

The art of picking beans, as Betsy calls it, was taught to the younger workers by the older and more experienced ones. She learned the art of "making money," picking beans quickly, from a woman who had been a bean picker for a number of years. "Oh, they was there from all ages. The woman I picked with, Viola, was about fifty-some years old, and I picked with her, but she taught me the trade, and she learnt me everything that I knew how to pick."

It was easiest to go down between the rows picking with both hands. The workers generally picked through two rows at a time, setting the bushel baskets in front of them.

"Well, the way I do it, I put my basket up in front of me and I got two rows and then I'd pull the bean vines over on one side and take both hands and just pick them—just like milking a cow—just pick them if they're great big old beans," explains Betsy.

The crews picked half-runners, shellies, and pole beans. Betsy, Lisa, and Ruth agreed that pole beans were easiest to pick. There was no bending over or kneeling involved in their harvest. According to Lisa, "Pole beans is the best beans to pick. It don't take long to fill a basket up with them. You could fly through there picking them."

The pickers enjoyed the camaraderie, but the work was tedious. They had to work through bad weather such as summer thunderstorms and be cautious about finding snakes and bees' nests in the fields. Bean fields were frequently surrounded by pasture land where cattle were kept, and workers had to beware of charging bulls. There were also few amenities. There was no outhouse, for instance, and restroom breaks had to be taken behind barns, trees, or whatever else might be available.

Generally, the day's picking began before dawn and ended prior to dusk. Workers' lunches often consisted of lunch wagon–style burgers and soft drinks. Betsy describes the day:

> Well, I'd get up about five o'clock in the morning. They'd come pick me up about six, then we'd pick beans 'til about eleven or twelve. Then we had this man called Earl Lodter—used to have a restaurant up there at Stoney Creek. He had a little old truck that he'd bring our lunch to us. You'd get a hamburger, pop, and a fried pie for fifty cents. And then we'd eat and then we'd go back and we'd pick 'til four or five o'clock and come home.

While the Garlands' and the bean owners' relationship was that of employee and employer, they were also neighbors, and the Garlands and some of the other workers benefited from the generosity of their bosses. After the beans that were to be taken to market were harvested, workers were permitted to clear out any "leftovers" for their personal use and take them home for canning, drying, freezing, or pickling.

"Mama canned them, she dried them, she froze them," Betsy recalls. "We did everything in the name of God we could with them beans."

Ruth's work resulted in a bounty for the winter, but as Betsy put it, "I hated green beans for a long time."

Even though the work was difficult, the Garlands speak fondly of the experience and reminisce about the friends they made and the good times they had. Playful fights with the produce and flirting with the opposite sex provided diversion from the arduous work. There were also opportunities to socialize, make new friends, and become reacquainted with old ones. "You made a lot of friends and people that you'd get used to," says Betsy. "From one year to the next, you know, you're ready to go back to see if your friends has come from different places that you don't get to see the whole year."

Ruth, who died in her late seventies a few months after my interview, said she always enjoyed picking beans. "Buddy, I liked that work though. I wish I could do it now."

Field Pea Philosophy

Scott Peacock

As a young child, I looked forward to field pea season with enthusiasm—and not just because it signaled the arrival of so many good things to eat. It also provided an escape from the sweltering Alabama heat, as my mother's "shelling bees" were air-conditioned affairs.

Before this summer ritual commenced, the braided Sears-Roebuck rug in our den was rolled up, and the window unit turned to its coldest setting. Grandmothers and great-grandmothers from both sides of the family sat in a circle, their laps cradling roasting pans and Tupperware bowls filled with the harvest brought from our farm in bushel baskets.

Sharing gossip and wisdom to pass the time, they nimbly shelled for hours, tossing the empty hulls into a large galvanized washtub in the center of the room. Not yet in grade school, I apprenticed at their feet, captivated by their stories and chasing the occasional errant pea as it rolled across the floor.

This nostalgic scene, in one version or another, is no doubt familiar to many a Southerner—particularly those of a certain age. But seriously, when was the last time you sat in a shelling circle? My guess is it's been awhile.

Labor intensive to pick and prone to spoil, fresh field peas (and yes, that includes butter beans) are no longer the dinner-plate staple they once were, but an uncommon delicacy. And the job once done by Granny's fingers has largely been taken over by modern shelling machines.

Common varieties like black-eyed peas and lima beans are readily available dried or frozen—which is all well and good if you've a hankering for hoppin' John in January. But they're no substitutes for farm-stand fresh—the kinds that come in a wide array of shapes, sizes, and colors, and go by many different, often idiosyncratic names such as pink eye purple hulls, calico crowders, washday cowpeas, and Mississippi silver hulls. My mother's summer table always held at least one variety and often three or more, sometimes in individual preparations, sometimes cooked together.

For years, the field pea of choice in Geneva County, Alabama, where we are from, was one called "cream 8"—a small green pea similar to a white acre or lady pea. But as fashion goes, a newfangled version, "cream 40," arrived on the scene. Most of the pea-eating public took to it, but there were naysayers who complained that it was less tender and harder to cook right.

While cream 40s prevail today, my mother tells me there's a single old-timer at the edge of the county who still stubbornly grows the old cream 8s. Once they're picked, he takes them to a senior citizens center in the neighboring town, where they are hand-shelled and then sold to those pea aficionados fortunate enough to know the secret number you have to call just to get on a waiting list.

Why would someone go to so much trouble for a simple plate of peas? My father believes that commercial shellers bruise peas and distort their flavor. My mother agrees and is adamant that hand-shelling is supreme. "Machine shellers are rough on the peas," she says. "You get a lot of trash mixed in and, worst of all, there's no snaps."

By "snaps" she means the small, immature pea pods that, too underdeveloped to shell, are "snapped" and added to the shelled peas for cooking. "Now that," my father contends, "makes a pot of peas that tastes good."

Field peas have an affinity for smoked pig; it enhances their natural meatiness while at the same time providing a contrast to their more nuanced flavors. In my view, a pot of freshly shelled peas, slowly simmered with a piece of cured pork, is as iconically Southern as fried chicken or collard greens.

At Watershed, in Decatur, Georgia, we cook them this way every day by the bushel during their season and serve them as part of that great regional tradition, the hot vegetable plate—where their pot likker mingles beautifully with the slow-cooked crookneck squash and thick-sliced sun-ripe tomato, just as I remember them from childhood. Field peas cooked in this manner are as classic as it gets. But you needn't stop there.

Butter beans have always been my favorite, and I love them cooked thoroughly tender, then warmed gently in a little cream with bits of country ham and thinly sliced chives. These same flavors, whirled in a blender, produce a surprisingly silken and satisfying soup.

Folding crowders into a light tomato sauce enhances their particular flavor. Tossing lady peas and pink eyes in a salad and drizzling with garlic mayonnaise brings them into the twenty-first century.

But for me, no matter how you cook them, they all taste like home.

The Season of
Fried Green Tomatoes

Martha Stamps

It all began as a practical matter. In the fall your tomato plants will still make tomatoes, up until the first hard frost. But as the days grow shorter, the tomatoes stop turning red. So what are you going to do with a basket of green tomatoes? In the South, there's only one answer: Fry them. Fried green tomatoes were a standard part of my family's weekend breakfasts, alongside eggs, sausage, bacon, country ham, and biscuits. But only in the fall. Daddy loved his sliced ripe summer tomatoes with homemade mayonnaise too much to let anyone pick one green, so fried green tomatoes had a season, like most things did back then.

I grew up around so much good food, I took fried green tomatoes for granted until one teenage morning when I cooked them myself, far away from home. I was on a campout in the Cumberland Mountains of Tennessee on a brisk October weekend. Breakfast was my job. First I cooked the bacon, sizzling and popping on my tender-skinned hand, over the open flame. My eyes stung from the smoke, but the aroma of bacon fat and burning wood in that clean mountain air smelled like heaven. In the grease, I fried the tomatoes we had "borrowed" from someone's field. I had a hard time keeping the breading intact, and they may not have been evenly cooked, but I was awfully proud and applauded roundly by my fellow campers.

We ate the tomatoes on tin plates—just bacon and tomatoes. It was perfect. Cornmeal breading, tangy green tomato, salty smoked bacon, sitting on a rock by the fire.

Now people want fried green tomatoes every day of the year. Maybe it was the movie that made them mainstream years ago. I'm not sure, but fried green tomatoes are the most requested item at my restaurant, where we make a fried green tomato BLT, and a salad topped with them, too. Of course, we serve them on their own, and on the side of a plate of eggs. I like to think that people are getting a pretty good experience eating fried green tomatoes at Martha's in Nashville. We drizzle them with creamy horseradish, and I always suggest a dash of hot sauce. But I just can't give them what I had that autumn day, when a fried green tomato tasted as fresh as my youth and opened my blue eyes wide.

Fried Green Tomatoes
Serves 8.

4 green tomatoes	Salt
1 quart buttermilk	Black pepper
1 cup cornmeal	Cayenne pepper
1 cup flour	Vegetable oil

Slice the tomatoes about ¼-inch thick. Soak them in buttermilk for at least 30 minutes or overnight. Mix together the cornmeal and flour, seasoned with salt, pepper, and cayenne. Lift the tomatoes from the buttermilk and dredge them well in the breading. Lay the breaded slices flat on a cookie sheet. The breading will stick better if you let the tomatoes sit for awhile in the refrigerator.

Panfry the tomatoes in a skillet with about ½ inch of vegetable oil. Drain on paper towels and serve with creamy horseradish sauce.

Onion Medicine

Anthony Cavender

Of the many foods used as medicines in the South, none was more important than the onion. It ranked near the top of the list of the truly sovereign folk medicines, up there with whiskey, turpentine, and vinegar. The reliance on onions for the treatment of many health problems—especially for colds, pneumonia, earache, yellow fever, typhoid fever, and for cleaning blood—prompts us to think of the onion not as a food used secondarily as medicine but instead as a medicine used secondarily as food.

Onion medicine is old medicine. The origin of much onion therapy extends far back in time to the ancient Greek theory of humors. The Greeks classified the onion as having a hot essence and thus as good for treating health problems caused by too much cold, or phlegm, in the body. The ancestors of those who settled the South were no doubt familiar with early English herbals like John Gerard's *The Herball or Generall Historie of Plantes* (1597) and Nicholas Culpepper's *Complete Herbal and English Physician* (1814), both of which align with the ancient Greek medical tradition in identifying the onion's "hot and dry" essence. Although the folk medicine record in the South, at least from the late 1800s to the present, indicates that residents never regarded humors as causes of illness, the humoral connection is nonetheless apparent in their explanations for why onions were used to treat a cold and pneumonia. Southerners did not talk about using onions to diminish an excess of the cold and wet humor, phlegm; rather, they talked about how onions serve to "burn," "sweat," and even "blister" a cold or coldness out of the body.

Burning or sweating a cold out of the body involved first and foremost the redoubtable onion poultice. There were two types. The one most commonly used was made by first frying sliced onions in a skillet with lard. Once the onions turned translucent, a little cornmeal or flour was added to bind the onions together and retain the heat. Next, the onions were slipped from the skillet into a flannel pouch or wrapped in a piece of cloth, returned to the skillet to heat some more, and then placed on the ailing person's chest. Others favored a more tactile application: slipping the cooked onions directly out of the skillet onto the chest. This often had a blistering effect that was viewed as salutary. The other type of poultice was made by wrapping one or two onions with a cloth into a ball and then beating them with a hammer into a pulpy consistency. The resulting poultice was then placed on the chest. The "hot" essence of the onions, together with the thermal heat of the poultice and the inhalation of the strong fumes, served the intended purpose of breaking up congestion and forcing the cold out of the body.

A more aggressive onion therapy was employed for pneumonia: the "onion jacket." The "jacket" consisted of an onion poultice on the chest and the back of the patient, bound to the body with a cloth wrapped around the abdomen.

Gerard's *Herball* notes that "the juyce of Onions sniffed up into the nose, purgeth the head, and draweth forth raw flegmatic humores." Southerners didn't favor sniffing onion juice up their noses, but they did use onion juice to relieve congestion. The juice was obtained by roasting an onion in a wet paper bag in a fireplace or oven. Once cooked, the juice was squeezed out and ingested or rubbed on the chest and sometimes on the soles of the feet. As with the onion poultice, it was believed that the juice would "pull the cold out of the body." Presumably to make the juice more palatable, before roasting the onion some caregivers cut a core deep into it and filled it with sugar. The result was a soothing "onion syrup" good for congestion, croup, and hoarseness. Another method of manufacturing onion syrup was placing several onion slices in a jar, covering the slices with sugar, and then letting the mixture set for a few days.

Until the World War II era, the most common remedies for an earache were pouring warmed sweet oil (olive oil) or urine into the ear, or blowing smoke into the ear, but some folks resorted to warmed onion juice or placing a hot onion poultice on the back of the ear. As with onion therapy for a cold and pneumonia, these remedies were based on the assumption that the application of thermal heat in combination with the inherently hot essence of the onion cured an earache by diminishing the cold state of the inner ear.

The regular consumption of onions prior to the onset of and during the cold season was a popular cold prevention strategy. Onions were served up creamed, fried, and as a soup; in a glass of sweet milk; as a garnish for soup beans; as a tea; or eaten raw.

Gerard's *Herball* warns readers that eating onions, especially raw, "provoketh overmuch sleep." This negative side-effect of onion eating transformed over time into a positive cure for treating insomnia. Eating raw and cooked onions, drinking onion tea or a glass of sweet milk with a slice of onion, and ingesting a spoonful of onion juice ensured a good night's sleep.

Prior to the emergence of the germ theory of disease, many people, including "regular" doctors and folk healers, believed that some diseases were caused by the inhalation of putrid particles in the air emitted from sources of decaying organic matter such as latrines, dead animals, and swamps. The putrid matter was thought to accumulate in the blood and poison the body, resulting in contagious diseases like typhoid fever, measles, malaria, and yellow fever. The rationale underlying the belief that onions both prevent and treat contagious diseases is explained in Culpepper's *Complete Herbal*: "Mars owns them [onions], and they have gotten this quality, to draw any corruption to them, for if you peel one, and lay it upon a dunghill, you shall find it rotten in half a day, by drawing putrefaction to it; them being bruised and applied to a plague sore, it is very probable it will the like." To prevent yellow fever and typhoid fever, people carried an onion in a pocket, strung onions over windows and doors, and scattered peelings on the floors. Some folks thought the onion absorbed the putrid matter in the air; others thought the onion's strong odor repelled it. To aid those afflicted with a contagious disease, onions were tied to the bedposts and walls in the sick person's room, and plates of sliced onion were slid under the bed. Even after the emergence of germ theory, people continued these practices in the belief that the onion warded off or absorbed germs.

Southerners in the 1800s and early 1900s believed that a sedentary lifestyle and restricted diet during the winter contributed to an accumulation of toxic waste materials in the blood and the bowels, which in turn resulted in various illnesses and a state of feeling "puny." In the spring, therefore, purgatives like castor oil or Epsom salts were taken to clean the blood and bowels, and tonics like sorghum and sulfur and various herbal concoctions were administered to restore vital properties. Onions and, in Southern Appalachia, ramps (*Allium tricoccum*, a close relative of the onion), were also part of the blood-cleaning and blood-building regimen.

Although the old-timers' reasoning about onion therapy was flawed, recent clinical studies indicate they were more right than wrong in terms of its intended outcome. The onion has antiviral properties that aid in cold or flu prevention, and its immune system-boosting effects shorten the duration and severity of these illnesses. The onion also contains a compound, allicin, which functions as a kind of blood cleaner, preventing and regressing atherosclerosis by reducing the production of bad cholesterol and lipids and inducing the excretion of these substances from the blood, thus inhibiting the formation of plaque in the arteries.

Kitchen medicine once played an integral role in lay health care in the South. Cultigens like the potato, cabbage, tomato, carrot, wild and cultivated greens, lettuce, corn, apples, watermelon, pumpkin, cayenne pepper, and beans were widely used as medicines, perhaps even more so than the wild medicinal plants for which the South, especially the Appalachian region, is so well known. Unfortunately, this valuable healing lore was displaced by over-the-counter and prescription drugs; indeed, it was intentionally abandoned by Southerners out of a sense of shame about their folk heritage and a desire to become more modern. Recent scientific research on traditional food medicines like the onion and increasing recognition of the toxic effects of many synthetic drugs suggest that kitchen medicine is worth serious reconsideration.

Coveted, French, and Now in Tennessee

Molly O'Neill

The town of Chuckey is located on the upside of the Nolichucky River valley in an eastern jut of Tennessee about twenty miles from the crest of the Blue Ridge Mountains and the North Carolina line. The East Tennessee and Virginia Railroad used to stop in the town to pick up grain and tobacco, but the red brick station, built in 1906, is long since abandoned. Many of the farms have given way to middle-income housing, and the workers among the town's eight hundred or so residents tend to punch the clock at the Wal-Mart Distribution Center or in factories that make gift wrap, automotive parts, or lawnmowers.

Chuckey is not the sort of place one expects to find the holy grail of the food-loving world. But on the edge of town, perched on a south-facing slope overlooking the birthplace of Davy Crockett, an orchard of 350 hazelnut trees has begun to sprout Périgord truffles, the fragrant black fungi that can send epicures, as well as rooting pigs and dogs, into fits of frenzied greed.

The truffles from Chuckey are not the first American-grown Périgord truffles. They are, however, the first American-grown black truffles to excite some of the country's top chefs, like Daniel Boulud, Thomas Keller, John Fleer, and Jonathan Waxman.

Although unexpected, the Tennessee truffles were not unplanned. Tom Michaels, a plant pathologist, pianist, and Scrabble tournament competitor, sprouted the hazelnut trees from seeds. He inoculated their roots with *Tuber melanosporum*, the Périgord truffle, before setting them in his backyard in 2000.

He resisted dreams of a truffle bonanza as assiduously as he limed his soil and trimmed his trees. Michaels had, after all, grown up on a mushroom farm west of Chicago and had written his thesis on the difficulty of the in-vitro cultivation and growth of *T. melanosporum*.

He knew that millions of dollars have been lost since the 1970s in the attempt to cultivate truffles in the United States. Some of the failures were spectacular. One multimillion-dollar orchard in Hext, Texas, is now being managed as a game preserve.

When he noticed patches of the tawny Tennessee soil bubbling up like blistered asphalt in his orchard, however, Michaels lost his circumspection. "I was jumping around yelling 'Eureka!'" he said. And that was before he saw the size of the bulbs, before he felt them and smelled them and tasted them, before one of his truffles had found its way into the chef Daniel Boulud's kitchen in Manhattan, before the chef had confirmed the grower's suspicion.

"This is it," Boulud said. "The first time in America. This Tennessee truffle is the real thing."

Only then did Michaels realize that up to 150 pounds of world-class truffles could be ripening in the ground behind his modest three-bedroom ranch, and that he had neither dog nor pig to sniff them out before they withered and disappeared.

"Growing truffles is not like growing tomatoes," he said. "You don't just plant them one day and know that a certain number of days later they will fruit."

In fact, to grow truffles is to govern an intricate culture of plant and fungus life, as well as environmental conditions, not all of which are known and most of which are hidden underground.

Tending a truffle orchard is as much of an art as it is a science and it is, most of all, an act of faith—it typically takes six to twelve years for the fungi to form truffles in the earth. Mystery and scarcity are part of the truffle's allure.

According to James M. Trappe, a professor emeritus of mycology at Oregon State University and the coauthor of *Trees, Truffles, and Beasts: How Forests Function*, there are about sixty species of true truffles, the subterranean fungi that attach to a plant's roots and issue long tendrils that gather nutrition for the plant and use the carbohydrates that the plant returns to eventually form the "fruit" we call truffles—but only a dozen are prized in the kitchen.

Most fungi sprout a stem and cap that contain reproductive spores. The truffle does not. The truffle is a "sack of spores," explained Trappe, and while other mushrooms need nothing but a rustling wind to loosen and spread their seed, the subterranean bulb needs to be digested and excreted by an animal. In order to attract rodents and marsupials, the truffle, like a tiny underground perfume factory, produces up to fifty different chemicals that combine to create a scent powerful enough to penetrate up to three feet of earth.

"Some smell like cheese, some like garlic, some like fruit, some like sewer gas," Trappe said. The aroma of *T. melanosporum*, generally a mixture of musk and fruit and forest floor, and the earthy, garlicky *Tuber magnatum*, or Italian white truffle, are the most prized.

The Burgundy truffle, which thrives in a cooler climate and is currently being tested by Johann Brunn at the University of Missouri, and the white Oregon truffle also have pronounced aromas. The summer truffle and the pecan truffle from the American South are milder.

Truffles occur naturally, but the most prized ones have been disappearing since the late nineteenth century. By all accounts, current Périgord truffle production is only about 5 percent of what it was back then. Until recently, they resisted all attempts at controlled cultivation.

French scientists, Trappe said, patented a technique for inoculating the roots of traditional host trees—the hazelnut and three different varieties of oak—with truffle spores. The result was seedlings that could be planted in any hospitable soil. In the late 1970s, orchards were planted in northern California, and in 1980, Franklin Garland, a greenhouse owner from Hillsborough, North Carolina, bought some of the French-inoculated trees and planted them outside his hometown.

Meanwhile, at Oregon State University, Tom Michaels was completing his doctorate, running field trials of truffle cultivation research. Michaels worked in mushroom research for six years before starting his own button mushroom farm. He sold it in 1992 to follow his wife, a physician, to Tennessee, where she had accepted a position. He had intended to be "Mr. Mom," he said, but his plans changed after he drove across the mountains to North Carolina's Piedmont to visit Garland.

"He only had a couple of truffles," Michaels said. "He had significant 'brûlé,'"—the circle of burned vegetation around the base of trees that is the classic signature of the presence of the truffle fungus. "As soon as I saw that, my truffle light went on."

His doctoral research had demonstrated that truffles prefer warm, dry summers; cool, wet winters; and alkaline soil like that of eastern Tennessee. He knew that *T. melanosporum*'s natural enemies are the dozens of other fungi eager to colonize the roots of hazelnut or oak trees. The limestone soil in his backyard, he figured, was similar to the soil of the Périgord region, to which *T. melanosporum*—but not necessarily its competitors—had, over millennia, adapted. After several years of experimenting with different ground covers and fertilizers, he put in his first orchard in 2000. By January of 2007, when his first crop appeared, Michaels had three separate plots of land with about 2,500 trees in cultivation.

Michaels is the first domestic truffle farmer to produce commercial quantities of truffles of a quality that commands top dollar ($50 an ounce, $800 a pound). But he is not the only one panning for black gold. There are, said

Charles K. Lefevre, the owner of New World Truffieres in Eugene, Oregon, about three hundred promising orchards on American soil. "The same sort of people you find growing grapes in California are starting to plant truffle orchards," said Lefevre, whose company supplied about thirteen thousand inoculated trees to about fifty hopeful growers in 2006.

In Hillsborough, Garland's nursery, Garland Truffles, supplies a similar quantity of inoculated trees. With a $235,000 grant from the North Carolina Tobacco Trust Fund, which supports research that may benefit former tobacco farmers, Garland has also supplied forty-five of those farmers with trees. If even a small number of these orchards succeed, truffles will be more plentiful and their prices may begin to drop.

But while the science of truffle cultivation has improved, the secret of coaxing Périgord truffles from the earth remains tucked in an unlikely corner.

"Take a right at the House of Hidden Treasures," Michaels instructs visitors to Chuckey, "then follow that road past some mobile homes. I'm the last driveway on the right."

Living through the Honey

Daniel Wallace

Florida's Highway 22, heading east out of the renowned beachside paradise that is Panama City, is so straight that if your tires are true you can drive the entire stretch without touching the steering wheel. The highway comes to an abrupt end in Wewahitchka. The locals—all eighteen hundred of them—call it "Wewa." It's a place where everybody knows everybody, and their dogs, too. The kind of place where, if you had moved there thirty years ago, you'd still be known as "the new guy" today. It's a sweet little town.

In fact, it's very sweet. This is because, for two weeks every spring down ten miles of the Apalachicola River, the tupelo tree is in bloom. Nowhere else in the entire world are so many tupelo trees blooming white in such profusion. During these two weeks, honeybees journey from flower to flower in search of pollen only their tongues can retrieve; with it they return to their apiaries. In these manmade beehives the tasty "champagne of honey" is made—a honey that's removed and bottled by men and women as industrious as the bees.

Tupelo honey. You've heard of it; you may have seen the movie it inspired, *Ulee's Gold*. And you may have even sung along to the song Van Morrison wrote about it, the one that compares the syrup to the woman he loves. So, you have to figure this stuff is either really good, or the honeybees hired an amazing publicist.

It's really good. But what person in their right mind would try to make a living off a crop produced by insects over a period of fourteen days? Frankly, there isn't one.

Which brings me to Ben Lanier.

Ben has been in the Tupelo honey business around fifty years. And he's *definitely* not in his right mind. Ben is the "son" on the sign at the outskirts of Wewa, which reads, *"Tupelo Honey Since 1898 L. L. Lanier and Son."* He took over the business in 1991 from his father, L. L., who took it over from *his* father, Lavernor Laveon Lanier Sr., half a century before that. Who Ben's become is due both to nature and nurture, with a dash of his own brand of craziness thrown in.

"I do exactly what I want to," he said. "Always have. Never worn a tie, never punched a clock. I've never done anything but bees my entire life." Then apropos of almost nothing, he asked, "Ever had a mullet gizzard? Mullets are the only fish with a gizzard, you know. They're real good."

That's Ben Lanier. He's the kind of man one usually describes as "colorful," but the word doesn't really do him justice. Ben is all the colors in the big box of crayons. A tall man who used to be taller ("I've shrunk a little since I had my back operated on"), he's funny, as easygoing as a dog on a hot day, and proudly self-described as "one-quarter swamp rat, one-quarter beach bum, and one-half redneck."

This must be the perfect combination of traits for a beekeeper.

I met Ben one fall, long after the arduous weeks of late April and May. He wasn't doing a lot with the bees right then. Glynnis, his beautiful wife, was taking care of business: filling orders, talking to customers on the phone, and managing the website from a closed-in back porch at the Lanier home. But Ben was busy. He pointed to his two-year-old son, Heath. "That's my job now," Ben said. "Raising him. He's all I do these days, and all I need to do."

The only child of an only child of an only child, Heath is next in line for the business, all nine hundred hives, roughly 4,500 pounds of bees all told. But there's a question as to whether the bees will be there when he's ready for them. The bees are being assaulted by both nature and man. The Varroa mite is killing them directly, and cheap imports are killing small family businesses.

According to Ben, honeybees pollinate 60 percent of all that we eat. He leaned in close then and almost whispered, "If the terrorists killed all the honeybees, there'd be a famine of biblical proportions. And they'd win. How could you fight on an empty stomach?"

I asked Ben what he would do if the bees were wiped out and the honey they ship came to an end. I expected a somber answer, but Ben just smiled. "I'd fish," he said. "Live off the land. I'm a hunter-gatherer." He doesn't have to go far to gather: The land around his property is full of oranges, grapefruits, okra, peas, and grapes. Although he doesn't drink himself, he makes wine. He also can satisfy the meaty part of his food pyramid, and he has the guns and the antlers to prove it. They're everywhere.

But for now, at least, he doesn't have to don a bearskin and crawl through the forest. The honey is flowing. It begins, of course, with the bee, which makes hundreds of trips from the flower to the hive to make just a teaspoonful of honey. The nectar is deposited in the manmade comb, or plank, and after it's full, it's taken to an extractor, a drum that spins and spins, flinging the honey onto the sides of the tank, draining through a spigot. It is then drained through a cheesecloth, bottled, and that's it: you have Tupelo honey— northwest Florida's unique gift to the world.

Ben might hire two or three people to help bring in the honey, but that's just temporary help. Justin Sizemore, who's in his early twenties, does most of the labeling and bottling; Louisa Bryant has been lending a hand with the odds and ends for almost thirty years; and Glynnis runs the day-to-day business operations. All this happens in a small tin shed in the Lanier backyard. Ben, of course, takes care of the bees.

And the process of making Tupelo honey requires additional expertise. To ensure that the hive is pure, a colony has to be stripped of the honey that was in it before the bloom began. Then the new crop has to be removed before it can be mixed with other honey sources.

Timing is critical. What honey tastes like depends on what the bees are eating. Black tupelo, titi, black gum, and other honey plants bloom prior to the white tupelo tree and help build up the colony, but it is the white tupelo that produces pure Tupelo honey. Nowhere else in the world does the tree exist in such concentrations as in Ben's virtual backyard along the Chipola and Apalachicola rivers and their tributaries.

Tupelo honey is special in another way, too: Because of its high fructose content, around 44 percent, it lasts forever. In fact, it's so special, the high-fructose/low-glucose ratio allows some people with diabetes to enjoy it. Fine, unmixed Tupelo honey is more costly than typical honey because it contains no additives and is not filtered, colored, or heated. All the nutrients, living enzymes, and pollen are still there, intact as nature made the honey. To make that happen, it takes someone with real experience. Say, a hundred years of it, which is what you get when you add up Ben's years in the business and those of his forebears.

Ben and his father L. L. echo each other in the most fundamental ways, their philosophies consonant. In the end, it's not about the bees, or the honey, at all. "It's about people," both of them told me. "Outside of people, there ain't nothing."

The Laniers have friends all around the world. When I was talking to Ben, Frank Buckner and his wife walked in for a surprise visit. They're from Alabama and hadn't seen Ben in six years. I asked him how they met. "Through the honey," he said. Later I asked Glynnis how she met Ben. "Through the honey," she said. And then I asked Ben how Victor Nuñez came to make a movie about their bees. He just smiled at me. He didn't even have to say it.

Capturing Summer in the Ice Cream Churn

Dan Huntley

If one were to capture the breath of summer in the South, it would smell of honeysuckle, delicate as a butterfly kiss in the dewy night. The aroma conjures images of barefoot children catching lightning bugs, of old friends on a screened porch chatting in the dark.

Every child of Dixie knows how to "milk" a honeysuckle blossom. You lightly grasp the end of the flower and slowly pull the filament thread across your tongue for that pinhead of nectar.

It was chef Bill Smith's challenge to capture that essence in a dessert. Or to be more indelicate: The prolific vine was growing like a weed beside Crook's Corner restaurant in Chapel Hill, North Carolina, and Smith's boss, Gene Hamer, said "Can't you make some food out of that thing?"

Smith, who grew up in New Bern, North Carolina, was intrigued but doubtful. Most sweet-smelling flowers—azaleas and magnolias—taste bitter. Smith started researching old cookbooks. He came across sorbets for watermelon, cantaloupe, mint, and most every kind of berry. But nothing on honeysuckle.

He did stumble across a Sicilian dish made by Arabs—flower ices. He found a recipe but was still skeptical. He made a tiny amount with honeysuckle, not expecting it to perform to his discriminating taste buds.

"The first bite tends to silence people, particularly if they grew up in the South," said Smith. "You instantly recognize it as the taste of summer. It's like walking around at night with your mouth open."

Smith gathers the honeysuckle on his way home from the restaurant on his bicycle. He picks the blossoms at night when they are most fragrant. He distills the blossoms in cool water overnight. He then combines the blossom water with dissolved sugar and makes the sorbet in a standard ice cream churner.

He serves the sorbet straight up—two frozen scoops garnished with a single golden-throated blossom. Think of homemade ice cream without the milky sweetness, just airish crystals of frozen nectar.

Customers start calling in early May, asking when the honeysuckle sorbet will be on the menu. "We have customers who get angry when we run out. It's like they're entitled to it. But that's the beauty of serving food fresh during its season. It's like soft-shelled crabs—when they're gone, that's it. You can't hold 'fresh' in the freezer."

Honeysuckle Sorbet

Serves 6.

4 cups of honeysuckle flowers (stems and leaves removed), tightly packed but not smashed	1⅓ cups water
	2 cups sugar
	Few drops of freshly squeezed lemon juice
5⅓ cups cool water	Speck of cinnamon

Place the flowers in a nonreactive container (glass or stainless steel) and cover with the cool water. Weigh down with a plate. Let them stand on the counter overnight.

In a small saucepan, make a syrup of the sugar and water by boiling until all the sugar is dissolved and the liquid begins to look lustrous and slightly thick, 3–5 minutes. Add a few drops of lemon juice to prevent the sugar from recrystalizing. Cool the syrup completely.

Strain the honeysuckle infusion, gently pressing the blossoms so as not to waste any of your precious efforts. Combine the two liquids and add the merest dusting of cinnamon. Churn in an ice cream maker.

Adapted from Seasoned in the South: Recipes from Crook's Corner and from Home, *by Bill Smith.*

Sweet Potato Pie

Marilyn Kallet

Cobalt blue it landed,
loaded with aspic and whipped cream.
"Blue potatoes," the waiter
explained. We tucked in, sampled
the soft wall: potato mortar,
coconut bricks.

Picture the Aztec farmer
who pulled the first blue potato
like a musical note from the earth. His kids
mocked him—"Dad's a dreamer!
Who's going to swallow this?" His wife,
a weaver, fell in love
with the blue spud. "Potatoes
bore me," she said. "At
least this one offers
night sky, filling romance,
flavor for the eye."

"At least this one
makes me laugh
a little when I
crave more than
mashed potato nights,
laugh a little
when I cry."

Coops, Pens, and Pits

Ode to Chicken

Kevin Young

You are everything
to me. Frog legs,
rattlesnake, almost any
thing I put my mouth to
reminds me of you.
Folks always try
getting you to act
like you someone else—
nuggets, or tenders, fingers
you don't have—but even
your unmanicured feet
taste sweet. Too loud
in the yard, segregated
dark & light, you are
like a day self-contained—
your sunset skin puckers
like a kiss. Let others
put on airs—pigs graduate
to pork, bread
becomes toast, even beef
was once just bull
before it got them degrees—
but, even dead,
you keep your name
& head. You can make
anything of yourself,

you know—but prefer
to wake me early
in the cold, fix me breakfast
& dinner too, leave me
to fly for you.

Mulling over Mull
A North Georgia Foodways Localism

Charles C. Doyle

As known in the vicinity of Athens-Clarke County, in northeast Georgia, mull is a sort of thick soup, the base of which is milk and pulverized cracker crumbs, flavored with minced onions, salt, and black pepper, simmered together with finely chopped chicken or game meat. Residents of Clarke County—both black and white—and of the close-by, more rural counties are widely familiar with chicken mull, which is available at restaurants, prepared in quantity as the main dish for church suppers and festivals, sold at fund-raising events of civic and religious organizations, served at hunting lodges or camps, and featured at large family gatherings. However, the familiarity diminishes sharply beyond a short radius of twenty-five miles from downtown Athens.

Most Athenians remain oblivious to the fact that the dish they call *mull* is unknown in other parts of the state or the region at large. Perhaps the distinctiveness of North Georgia mull has been partly obscured by the existence of some very different preparations called *mull* in other areas of the Southeast; those are stews made with chunks of seafood and vegetables, without the milk and crackers, the smooth, semiliquid texture, or the whitish appearance.

Especially since the term *mull* has various senses in different subdialects of the American South, a philological folklorist will naturally wish to examine the word itself, its possible (as well as fancifully supposed) etymologies and its developing uses.

Often in such investigations, it is illuminating—though, obviously, not conclusive—to ask the people who prepare, serve, and consume the food what they suppose to be the origin of its name. In the case of mull, the question sometimes elicits the speculation, or wild guess, that maybe *mulligan stew* has some connection with the term *mull*. That suggestion can be rejected out-of-hand, not only for lack of any lexicographical evidence but also because mulligan stew is a wholly different concoction—in color, texture, taste, and ingredients. The same can be said of *mulligatawny*, an East Indian soup strongly flavored with curry, which shows up in a few cookbooks of Southern cuisine. Likewise to be rejected, almost certainly, is the occasionally elicited analogy of *mulled wine*, in which phrase the participle *mulled* seems in fact to signify "heated with spices or other flavorings."

More plausible is a suggestion proffered by a number of educated connoisseurs of mull, in our sense of the term: That it derives from the verb *mull* meaning to "grind finely" or the corresponding noun *mull* in the sense of "something reduced to small particles" (*Oxford English Dictionary*)—cognate with *meal* and (more distantly) with *mill*. The reference would presumably be to the chopping of the chicken or perhaps the pulverizing of the crackers.

The only dictionary to record *mull* in a culinary sense is the *Dictionary of American Regional English*, or *DARE*. The extensive questionnaire used in the preparation of that dictionary included the following item, for which informants were asked to supply local or regional terms: "Dishes made with meat, fish, or poultry that everybody around here would know but the people in other places might not." Asking native informants about that category would not have been highly productive, since most North Georgians are not aware that *mull*—both the dish and the name of that particular dish—remains such a narrowly focused regionalism, unknown in "other places." Nonetheless, that item on the questionnaire elicited a handful of *mull* responses, three from Georgia informants (all in the late 1960s, when the interviews based on the questionnaire were made), and one, marked simply "Southern," from Roy Wilder's book *You All Spoken Here*, which describes one of the other preparations called *mull*. Apparently on the basis of that ratio, and I suspect wrongly, *DARE* marks *mull*, defined simply as "a stew," as "esp[ecially] G[eorgi]a."

DARE gives, as the probable etymology, the noun *mull* in the sense of "a mixture, muddle, mess," a usage that the *OED* marks as "colloq[uial] or slang," and which, in turn, it indicates to be "of obscure origin," possibly from the verb *mull* in the sense of "pulverize, crumble."

As far as I am aware, no one has made the connection between the term *mull*, as an Americanism designating certain kinds of thickened soup or stew, and a Scotticism entered in the *OED* under the spelling *mool*. The verb *mool* (derived from the noun *mool*, a dialectal variant of *mould*, "loose soil, earth") meant, from the late sixteenth through the early nineteenth centuries, "to crumble (bread) into a bowl in order to soak it in liquid." One of the *OED*'s illustrative quotations for *mull* in the sense of "pulverize, crumble" seems better to illustrate the Scotticism, with a slightly later date than the illustrations of *mool*; it comes from John Trotter Brockett's 1829 *A Glossary of North Country Words*: "oaten bread broken into crumbs, is called *mulled* bread."

One other connection is tempting to ponder (this is my own hypothesis, and I'm sure it's wrong!): The middle syllable of the word *emulsion*. An emulsion is a liquid in which another substance is suspended but not dissolved. The root word of *emulsion* is a Latin verb meaning "to milk." Mull is a milky suspension of minced chicken, cracker crumbs, and onions: an emulsion!

Apparently separate from the etymology of *mull* as the name for more than one kind of soup or stew—that is, *mull* in the sense of "a mixture, muddle, mess"—*DARE*'s entry for *mull* gives a cross-reference to the noun *muddle*. In senses other than the culinary, the *OED* likewise cites *muddle* as synonymous with *mull*—as signifying both "a mixture of things" and "a state of confusion." No one has suggested, however, that *mull* may actually represent a dialect contraction of *muddle*.

The food items called *muddle* share a few defining properties with our *mull*: both are soupy preparations made from various ingredients simmered together. *DARE* marks the word *muddle* as "esp[ecially] e[astern] N[orth] C[arolina]," where, according to an 1833 description, it designates a soup or stew made from chunks of fish and pork boiled in water with red pepper, the mixture finally thickened with pieces of cornbread. Other North Carolina descriptions call for coon meat or various combinations of vegetables: onions, potatoes, tomatoes, butter beans, carrots, celery. One Carolina source specifies the addition of hard-boiled eggs. Another source dubiously defines *coon muddle* simply as "Brunswick stew." No record indicates the use of milk instead of water as the liquid base of any so-called muddle.

The *Century Dictionary* in 1890 defined *muddle* within its entry for *pottle*, "a dish made by Connecticut fishermen" of fish pieces boiled in water with fried pork. The dictionary notes, "*Muddle*, made by Cape Ann fishermen, is the same dish with the addition of crackers." That reference is interesting for a couple of reasons. First, it locates the dish called *muddle* much farther north (Cape Ann is in extreme northeastern Massachusetts) than any other reference, nearly all the others coming from various parts of North Carolina. Second, the Massachusetts reference specifies the thickening of the preparation with crackers, like North Georgia mull. Curiously, the *OED*, citing the *Century Dictionary* entry, defines the Americanism *muddle* as "a kind of chowder; a pottle made with crackers"; yet the *OED* does not enter *pottle* in the quoted sense at all.

Which brings us back to *mull*. The various quotations in *DARE* refer not only to *chicken mull* but also to *turtle mull*, *rabbit mull*, and *squirrel mull*. One Georgia informant tersely defines rabbit mull as "rabbit stew made with milk."

The only non-Georgia record is the one marked general Southern, from the 1984 book *You All Spoken Here*: "Muddle, mull: A stew, usually with fish or squirrel as the main ingredient, as in rockfish muddle or squirrel muddle," the erroneous implication being that *mull* and *muddle* are synonyms.

Even with this small sampling of records from *DARE*, we begin to discern two principal defining properties of mull, in the North Georgia sense of the term: the milk base and the thickening with cracker crumbs—although, in the unique 1890 reference, Massachusetts muddle was also thickened with crackers. Some of *DARE*'s entries for *mull*, we must assume, refer to a different Southern dish, the chunky stew, often made of seafood. In fact, the 1981 cookbook *Recipes and Reminiscence*, produced by the Oconee Center for Senior Citizens of Watkinsville, just six miles down the road from Athens, contains a recipe for turtle mull that is actually mull in that *other* sense—the one not common in North Georgia. That version of turtle mull contains one to five pounds of turtle meat along with one big hen, ten pounds of beef, three pounds of pork, three pounds of onions, and a half gallon of catsup—no milk and no cracker crumbs. We might say, in pondering those proportions, that it's a turtle mull recipe for those who don't appreciate turtle meat. The case was very different with one of my informants, Marie, a sixty-nine-year-old African American woman from Madison County, one county to the north and east of Clarke County. Following a detailed description of how to fix chicken mull (the normal North Georgia form), she remarked, on her own initiative, "You know, you can make it with turtle meat, too." After explaining how to prepare the turtle, dipping it in boiling water and peeling back the lower shell, Marie commenced a rhapsody on "the most beautiful white meat you have ever *seen*!"

Cookbooks from southern Georgia, coastal Georgia, and other parts of the South give recipes for shrimp mull, a few of which call for thickening with cracker crumbs but never with a milk base. A cookbook from St. Simons Island, Georgia, *Frederica Fare* (1977), and one from Albany, Georgia, *Quail Country* (1983), direct that the stew is to be served over rice, whereas North Georgia mull would always be served alone, in a bowl or cup.

As far as I am aware, North Georgia mull can be made of chicken or turtle or various game animals but never fish or shrimp. James Villas, in his 1997 cookbook *Stews, Bogs, and Burgoos*, describes, without any geographical specification, a dish called "turkey, corn, and lima bean mull," which contains neither milk nor cracker crumbs. In fact, all of those "other" mulls seem to be variants of the dish elsewhere called *muddle*. Many of them contain a prominent portion of tomatoes or tomato sauce or catsup, whereas North Georgia mull never does—although it may be treated with a small dollop of catsup or Tabasco sauce, mainly for the coloring; as one informant put it, "so the stuff won't look so damn *white*."

As for North Georgia mull, not only is it a distinctive dish, but no very similar preparations appear currently to exist elsewhere with other names. An amusing incident from one of my own accidental collecting forays suggests itself here. Connie is a Filipino in her late sixties, the widow of a career U. S. Army sergeant from Athens, where she has lived since her husband's death. By coincidence, when I was beginning this investigation, she brought me a container of delicious chicken mull. Naturally curious, I began questioning her:

Charlie: Did you learn to make this in Athens?
Connie: Yeah, I ate it, and I talked to some people and figured out how to make it.
Charlie: So, y'all don't have anything like this in the Philippines?
Connie: Oh, yes, we do!
Charlie: [Heart sinking; foodways hypothesis shot] Well, what was it called in the Philippines?
Connie: Arróz caldo.
Charlie: Hmm, doesn't that mean "rice soup"?
Connie: Well, yes, but you *could* make it with cracker crumbs instead.

In a profound fashion, Connie was constructing cross-cultural connections, identifying a food item of her new home—structurally, so to speak—with an analogous (though by no means synonymous) item from her native culture. In her own shrewd taxonomy, she was relating two varieties of soup made of chopped-up chicken and thickened with a starchy substance.

The history or ancestry of North Georgia mull is as obscure as the etymology of the term. Some of my own informants, as well as other commentators, have recalled the dish from as early as the 1940s but not earlier—which in no way implies that it did *not* exist prior to that. *Could* the dish have been hiding under another name? *The Warm Springs Receipt-Book*, published in 1897 in Richmond, Virginia, gives a recipe for "puree of chicken," the ingredients of which are finely chopped chicken, chicken stock, cream, and cracker crumbs soaked in milk—plus "the yolks of three hard-boiled eggs," which are to be rubbed into the chopped chicken prior to the mixing of the ingredients. I don't know what effect the rubbed egg yolks would have on the texture or the flavor of the dish, but "structurally" this so-called puree of chicken does resemble our chicken mull. And a good many Virginians migrated to North Georgia during the nineteenth century.

In Georgia, mull was probably originally prepared for meals within individual families. More often, in recent years at least, it is regarded as food for special occasions. In a June 17, 1998, story in the *Athens Daily News*, a longtime resident of the city tells how, in the early 1970s, she would entertain groups of visiting naval officers from foreign countries (Athens is the site of a U. S. Naval Supply Corps School): "I made a chicken mull every time, because it's a regional dish, and everybody can eat chicken."

In recent years, chicken mull is almost always prepared in quantity. Some reports say it is commonly brought from home in large kettles and served at hunting lodges or camps—less often, apparently, cooked on the site by the hunters themselves, the preparation being a rather long and tedious process. Very often mull is the featured dish (or the *only* dish) at church suppers or other sizable gatherings of friends and acquaintances. Most frequently, nowadays, it is sold by churches or civic groups—on a "to go" basis—as a fund-raising enterprise. As is the case with other foods prepared in quantity, the communal preparation itself can be a festive "folk" event.

A colleague, Elissa R. Henken, and I observed one mass mull-making at length in December 2000, on the grounds of a small Disciples of Christ church in Oconee County. The well-advertised fund-raising event has been held every year for the past twenty-five or thirty years, according to participants. The men of the church, ranging in age from the midteens upward into their eighties, dominated the process. They gathered in the predawn hours to build some thirty hardwood fires in oil drums cut in half, crosswise, into which would fit large, footed iron kettles, like the ones used to boil laundry in earlier times. Around daylight, when the stewing of whole chickens in the pots was almost finished, the men fixed an open-air breakfast for themselves. Then the serious, technical part of the mull preparation began. The women of the church commenced their limited role as pullers of boiled chicken meat from the bones. Some of the men remarked that the more delicate feminine hands were better suited for the thorough performance of that task, which is also the messiest part of the entire operation. Meanwhile, the men were pulverizing carton-loads of saltine crackers ("soda crackers," in the vernacular of the region; Nabisco brand was deemed the only suitable kind) with a meat grinder, in which the chicken meat was subsequently ground as well. The chicken meat was then returned to the pots of stock to be simmered and "reduced." In the last hour, the milk and pulverized crackers, along with chopped onions, powdered black pepper and red pepper, and salt, were added.

Finally, in the midafternoon, the finished mull was ladled into one-pint plastic containers for sale to drive-up customers. A lesser quantity was dispensed to diners-in, seated at long tables in the church basement, where a bowl of mull could be complemented with ice tea, whole crackers, coleslaw, and dessert of pie, cake, or cookies brought from home by the church women. The whole preparation process spanned some thirteen hours.

Despite its narrow distribution geographically, mull does not discriminate on the basis of race or social class. Even though the churches that raise funds by selling mull tend not to be those where the social "elite" worship, customers come from all strata and sectors of society. The same observation holds for the serving of chicken mull at commercial eateries: It is not the upscale, uptown restaurants that offer mull on their menus; however, the persons who come to the modestly appointed establishments to partake of mull belong to all classes—aristocrats and tycoons, professors and day laborers. No difference is discernable along racial lines either. The "sociology" of mull resembles that of barbecue: Members of all groups relish the food equally, and they are willing to cross the normal boundaries of race and class to enjoy it. Symbolically, however, mull is more interesting. In its very composition, in its structure, it represents a mixing, a blending so total that all distinctions among individual ingredients disappear—just as, in the preparation and consumption of mull, Georgia crackers become just another element in the melting pot of society.

Chicken Mull

Most chicken mull recipes feed large numbers of people. This one is adapted for the home kitchen.

Serves 10 to 12.

One 5-pound hen (or two 2½-pound fryers)
1 large onion (or 2 medium), finely chopped
1 teaspoon salt or to taste
2 teaspoons ground black pepper or to taste
1 stick butter

1 quart whole milk
¼ pound saltine crackers ("soda crackers")—that's one "sleeve" of crackers as they are usually packaged—finely crushed with a rolling pin or by hand-squeezing the crackers in the plastic sleeve wrapper

Cover chicken with water and boil—3 hours for a hen (2 hours for a pair of fryers). Cool chicken and remove the meat from the bones. Grind or very finely chop the chicken. Return the ground chicken to the pot of stock. Add the chopped onion, along with the salt, pepper, and butter. Bring to a boil, then simmer for 10 minutes. Add the milk, and, while stirring, bring the mixture just barely to the boiling point. Immediately remove from the heat and stir in the crushed crackers. It might be wise to hold back a portion of the crackers, to see how thick the mixture will become (and it may continue to thicken a little as it cools). Mull should be served hot as a thick soup, to be eaten from a bowl, with a spoon. At the table, red pepper sauce, other seasonings or condiments, or additional crumbled crackers may be stirred into the bowl.

Some Like It Extra Hot

David Ramsey

My friend, on his first visit to Nashville, is trying to make his way through a breast of our fair city's strange specialty, hot chicken. On my suggestion, he ordered the Hot, and I am feeling guilty. He is crying. Sweating heavily. His face has turned the color of watermelon fruit and the hue is growing redder and spreading down the neck. His eyes are bloodshot and his lips are puffed out to about twice their size.

"Don't try to talk," I say.

And he dives back in, droplets of his own sweat and tears landing on each bite of chicken before it reaches his mouth. The thought that he might pass out crosses my mind, but slowly, gruntingly, he manages to finish off the breast.

To my surprise, around midnight, he insists that we make a return visit to Prince's Hot Chicken Shack, and there is no talking him out of it. He is smiling, but his tone is firm and serious. "I gotta get some more of that chicken."

Though Hot Chicken is not peculiar to Nashville, the city is uniquely obsessed with the dish (which gets its own category in the weekly paper's dining listings). Prince's is Nashville's oldest hot chicken joint still in business, and the best. Despite the moniker, it's not actually a shack; the small restaurant is located alongside several hair and nail salons in a small shopping center just off Dickerson Pike in north Nashville, near a stretch infamous as an active pickup spot for the city's prostitutes.

Prince's serves its bird piping hot, fresh out of enormous cast-iron skillets, over slices of white bread: crispy-fried breast, leg, or wings, thoroughly marinated in the most savage combination of spices I've ever encountered (recipes are closely guarded, of course, but there's no doubt that copious doses of cayenne are involved). The result is a truculent rethinking of the very possibilities of fried chicken.

Prince's chicken is offered in degrees of heat, and you can tell them apart by the color of the crust. The Mild is orange and plenty spicy, what most restaurants would label "hot." The Medium is dark red and even more sizzling, what most folks would label "unreasonable." Ordering anything above that will earn you a stern warning from the staff if you're a newcomer: The Hot is a deep, peppery maroon, hotter than the spiciest Indian or Thai food. Cayenne, much of which has caked into little bunches, has been applied so generously that the entire outer layer, though moist, is also dusty in texture.

The first bite is like taking a punch, the muscles stiffening and the heart beating fast. You feel like every organ in your body is saying, "What the hell was *that*?" It's otherworldly, so fierce you're ready to make up brand new cuss words because no existing exclamation is sufficient.

And that's the easy part—thereafter, the heat steadily amplifies. The tingle on the lips and the tongue slowly turns to outright pain. Sinuses explode open and everything from the neck up swelters.

Among those eating at the restaurant's five tables (still with the original benches from sixty-odd years ago), there's never much talking. This isn't a meal, but rather an experience, and getting through it takes a healthy measure of sheer will, endurance, and guts. Once finished, folks wear a different brand of satisfaction on their faces: Not simple fullness or the light afterglow of a pleasant meal, but a sense of *accomplishment*. Wiping the orange-red coating off their lips, eyes wide and watery, sighing and smiling and sighing again. They look like mountain climbers who have just planted the flag.

Maybe to eat at Prince's you have to be a little crazy. To order the Hot certainly requires a basic neglect for personal safety. But for true culinary psychopaths, there is one other option, a fearful choice that sits off to the side on the menu, beckoning the loony.

Extra Hot.

I have a pretty high tolerance for hot food (I have won bets by putting away substantial lumps of wasabi in one swallow). But this is something altogether different. I already order my chicken Hot and the very notion of a meaner, nastier cousin is almost unfathomable.

But, if you eat chicken at Prince's long enough, if you work your way up to the Hot and start to get used to it (and hooked), the temptation to take that final step becomes overwhelming. For more than a year, in fact, I have pondered taking the plunge. And now, I have decided, the time has come to try the Extra Hot. I pray that I am ready.

I am taking on this mission against the wisdom of anyone with sense. My mother briefly concerns herself with the possibility of an ulcer. Customers in the store guffaw at the very idea. "Make sure you bring plenty of toilet paper," one counsels me. "There's no polite way to put it."

And then there are the dire warnings from those who've tried before me.

About a year ago, I was in a parking lot in downtown Nashville, about to hit the honky-tonks and eating some Hot chicken I'd picked up from Prince's. A homeless guy wandered up to me. "I knew it," he said. "I could see by the look on your face that you just came from Prince's." I shared a few bites with him and we agreed that Prince's served up some life-changing poultry.

"You know," I told him, "I've been thinking about trying the Extra Hot."

The man stopped eating, took a step back, and looked at me like I was a ghost.

"Well, I've been eating the Hot for a while," I said. "I think I'm ready to take the next step."

He just shook his head. "Hot is all right," he said. "I love Hot. But Extra Hot." His eyes squinted. "I tried it once. I want you to look at me. Now you can see that I can't afford to be wasting no food. Well, I tried that Extra Hot, took two or three bites, and had to throw away a whole bird. That there was *too much*."

Andre Prince Jeffries has been running Prince's for thirty years. The business opened in 1945 as the Bar-B-Que Chicken Shack, and Jeffries changed it to the family name when she took over in 1980.

The restaurant's founder was Thornton Prince, Jeffries's great uncle. According to legend, it was a girlfriend of Thornton Prince who got this whole thing started. Prince was a notorious womanizer, and on one occasion when he stayed out all night long, his girlfriend—an adroit cook—decided to get back at him. If the way to a man's heart is through his stomach, she must have figured, it's not a bad pathway for revenge. She spiked his fried chicken with a vicious bevy of hot peppers. She wasn't trying to kill him, exactly, but it wouldn't be too far off to say that she meant to poison the man.

She served it to him, and the strangest thing happened: He loved it. Couldn't get enough. And so, the story goes, hot chicken was born.

"She was mad, but her madness turned into something good," explains Jeffries. She smiles, adding, "She did it for punishment, but he liked it."

And that remains just about the perfect way to describe eating chicken at Prince's—like you're being punished, but you like it.

"You hear all kinds of things," says Jeffries. "One man said it took the hair right off his chest, another one said it put the hair *on* his chest."

"We'll have pregnant women come in. I advise against it, of course. But they want it. Some of them come when they're overdue. They eat this chicken and the baby pops right out."

If customers don't call in the order ahead of time, a wait of an hour or even more is not unusual, even in the wee hours (Prince's is open until four in the morning on Friday and Saturday nights). "This is definitely not fast food," says Jeffries. "We're known as the mature chicken. This is adult chicken."

The long wait doesn't slow down the demand a bit; customers aren't just devoted regulars, they're addicts. "I don't know what it is," says Jeffries. "It has something to do with the chemistry of the body. It ignites something—have mercy!"

Jeffries is right; it does have something to do with chemistry. The chemical in question is capsaicin, the active component of chili peppers. While such spices as pepper, cinnamon, ginger, cloves, and turmeric have been popular in Europe, Africa, and the East for thousands of years, food as diabolically hot as Prince's was exclusive to the Americas until Columbus's landing.

The ante for Old World spice was considerably upped with what Columbus found: scalding New World peppers like cayenne, habanero, and jalapeño. "*Mejor que pimienta nuestra*," he wrote—better than our own peppers. Just as it's hard to imagine Italians without tomatoes or Russians without potatoes to make vodka, it's hard to imagine, say, Thai cuisine without chilies. But all of that came after sixteenth-century fusion using New World crops.

Capsaicin is what gives these peppers their kick. The chemical is fat-soluble rather than water-soluble, which is why fatty foods or milk ease the residue's burn and water doesn't. It's also the active ingredient in pepper spray (if you eat at Prince's, wash your hands before wiping your eyes!). It would take a whole lot of chili peppers, but a capsaicin overdose is theoretically possible. If you could manage to drink, say, a gallon of Tabasco sauce, you would probably turn from red to blue, pass out, and die from respiratory paralysis.

Capsaicin has also been used as an animal and insect deterrent (birds are not affected, so it's a good way to keep squirrels away from feeders). Indeed, biologists theorize that the very reason that plants came to produce it in the first place is to keep away mammalian predators. Human beings are the only mammals nutty enough to actually *enjoy* the painful reaction.

No one knows exactly why this is. One popular theory is that sufficient quantities of capsaicin release endorphins. Endorphins are natural painkillers produced by the pituitary gland. They act like morphine (the name itself is a shortening of "endogenous morphine"). In addition to an analgesic effect, they produce a feeling of elation and euphoria. "Runners' high" is thought to come from endorphin-release, and riding on a roller coaster is another way to get a dose. Or, if you can handle them, chili peppers. A need for the endorphin buzz might help explain why so many Nashvillians can't go long without a fix of Prince's.

There's another addictive effect of capsaicin, which may or may not be separate from endorphins: It reconfigures the experience of flavor. "*Sin chile, no creen que están comiendo!*" remarked Bartolome de las Casas, a sixteenth-century Spanish explorer, of the Native Americans. ("Without chili, they don't think they are eating!")

When I'm recommending Prince's, I usually say, "It will change the way you think about chicken." Imagine someone whose only exposure to dairy had been skim milk suddenly trying a pungent cheese. That's the kind of new possibility represented by hot chicken. It is flavor mutated, and fresh nuances emerge. (Some folks, of course, think this is a bunch of hooey—and argue that severe heat represents the negation of flavor. This argument is usually expressed thusly, often by a wimp: "It's so hot I can't taste a thing!")

Finally, there's the simple thrill of grappling with the extremity, the rush of powering ahead despite the danger signals screaming inside the body. "There is no more lively sensation than that of pain," wrote the Marquis de Sade, on a slightly different subject. "[I]ts impressions are certain and dependable, they never deceive."

The most intense varieties of pleasure and pain might feel close to the same. It's not that big of a jump, in other words, from "this is so good it hurts" to "this hurts so good." A little bit of torture, within reason, can be a lot of fun. Of course, the idea of what's reasonable varies dramatically from person to person, which is why Prince's offers different degrees of heat.

Maybe it's the endorphins or maybe it's just damn good. Either way, hot chicken takes me somewhere I'd like to go.

With this kind of heat, strategy becomes important. Ordering with fries is a must, and one must be careful to conserve them, as well as the two slices of bread and four slices of pickle. The pickle is a surprising coolant and the carbohydrates are your lifeline.

Though sodas are offered, they're a bad idea; the carbonation prickles too harshly on the way down. I always go with lemonade. Technically, nothing water based can provide relief, but I find that holding the drink and swishing it around is a comfort, however fleeting.

The other key is to not pause in the eating for too long. The scorching inside the mouth only gets worse. Like a drug, when eating hot chicken, the only cure for the pain is more of that which causes the pain.

Then there are more creative approaches. "We have one man who always gets the Extra Hot to go," says Jeffries. "He takes it home, runs a tub full of cold water, and eats his chicken in the bath."

Once consumed, hot chicken affects different people different ways.

"There's a prostitute who picks up men at the truckstop and brings them here every Saturday night," Jeffries tells me. "She makes them buy her this chicken before they get involved. She always gets the Hot. It turns her on. One time she just couldn't wait. She got out there and did the final act right on the hood of the car. That chicken—it does something to her."

New Jersey indie rockers Yo La Tengo came upon Prince's while recording in Nashville and were so smitten that they have named several songs in honor of the restaurant. Former Nashville mayor Bill Purcell, a longtime regular, had Prince's officially designated as the best restaurant in the state of Tennessee in 1996, when he was the majority leader in the state House of Representatives. "It was my last act, using all the powers of the office, which were unlimited— at least that's what I decided on that day," says the mayor, who always has the Hot and conducts business meetings at Prince's with anyone willing. "Hot chicken is Nashville's one unique food. It's unlike anything you've had before. It's an immediate connection. I find myself renewed for all purposes. Eating it immediately reinforces whatever is best about you."

Jeffries herself has never gone past Mild. She's a solid and sensible woman, one gathers, who just happens to be in the business of feeding maniacs.

When I tell her I'm planning to give the Extra Hot a go she pulls back and sighs. She looks half like she wants to scold me and half like she wants to give me a hug. "Just make sure you get an Alka-Seltzer," she says, patting my arm. "And don't travel any long distances."

It's a good twenty-five-minute drive from Prince's to my house, which I decide I'd better keep to myself.

"When you get done, lay down a little while, rest yourself," she says. "Get comfortable. This is what I call twenty-four-hour chicken. Be near a restroom. This is a cleansing. This is a filter. Allow it to just filter on through."

My day of reckoning comes on Friday, January 28. The whole day is spent on prep work. In the morning I do some stretches, some jumping jacks to get loose. For lunch: two toasted bagels. This seems solid. I mix some aloe vera juice with my orange juice. I try to visualize success. I have read about basketball players picturing the ball leaving their hand and falling through the net before a game; I try to imagine picking up the final bite with a corner of bread and wiping my mouth upon completion, but other, more disturbing images come to mind: the collapse of several internal organs, taste buds swollen beyond function, a breast of chicken personified as a fanged, marinated devil.

I arrive at Prince's around seven o'clock in the evening. Though I called ahead, my order's not quite ready. I pace around the restaurant, trying without much success to appear calm and collected. I rub my belly.

Someone finally calls my name and casually repeats my order: Extra Hot breast, fries, and a lemonade. At the mention of "extra," a couple of heads turn. "Oh boy," says one guy, and his friend just stands there trying not to laugh. The chicken is several shades darker than blood. It's almost brown; almost black, in fact.

A customer has just left, so I'm lucky enough to have a table to myself. The bread beneath the chicken has been entirely soaked through with red. I break off a small piece and use it to pick up some chicken. I take it in. The crust crunches softly under the bread. There's the jolt, but at first it's more or less the same as the Hot. Okay, I think, I can do this. Then comes the afterburn: It's as if a chute of lava enters at my throat and runs down the length of my body and right back up. I can feel the prickling all the way to my fingertips. I try to calm things down with a french fry, but it's no use. I have to keep going. With each bite, the crust singes every nerve in my mouth. Only the tender white meat inside briefly eases the burn.

About halfway through, sweaty and a bit dizzy, I start to wonder whether I'll be able to finish. Every breath hurts. I feel a bit faint. My vision seems to be going.

An ambulance happens to pull up. For a moment, I honestly think that it has come for me. I am fairly certain that I might be dying.

I stop and breathe slowly. I eat a small piece, and another. Then it happens: The fire starts to feel good. I feel the surge of what distance runners call a second wind. I may be a little woozy, but I am in the home stretch. I'm a cartoon character with steam coming out my ears; I can't wait to take another agonizing chomp. I can no longer feel my lips. It no longer matters.

"How was it?" someone asks me as I scoop up the final morsels of fiery skin with my remaining dabs of bread. "Are you all right?"

But I can't answer him. I can't even speak. I am gone, on some other planet, loving it, burning away.

Victory or Supper
The Easter Egg Fights of Peters Hollow

Kara Carden

People in Peters Hollow, Tennessee, are quite particular about their eggs, because they don't just eat them—they fight with them.

The annual Peters Hollow Egg Fight is a tradition begun in the mountains of northeast Tennessee over 185 years ago, when farmers from adjoining "hollers" used to sit around a general store chatting. Somehow, the men hit upon the question of whose hens produced the strongest eggs. Since nobody was willing to defer to his neighbor, the men staged an egg fight. No one claims to remember who won that first event, but hundreds of residents still fight it out every Easter Sunday.

It works like this: Each competitor starts with a set number of hard-boiled eggs, then picks one and taps it end-to-end against an opponent's egg. When a crack appears, the egg is turned and tapped on the other end until both ends are cracked. The twice-cracked egg is replaced by an unbroken egg, and the process is repeated until only one egg remains crack-free (or half-cracked, perhaps). Its owner then competes with other winners of the first round. The last person to possess an unbroken egg is declared the champion and takes home the egg trophy bought with participant donations.

Everyone brings his own eggs—two to six dozen per competitor—to compete in one of three age divisions: infant through six, six to twelve, and twelve and up.

Whatever the outcome, egg fights are a can't-lose game if you have Norman Peters's attitude. His motto: "This egg's going to take me to victory or supper."

Although most fighters belong to one of a half dozen families in the Stoney Creek community—such as Norman's, whose forefathers settled the area—curious newcomers also are welcome to observe or participate.

The proceedings, which take place on the lawn of an area home in this community of seventy-five families, are monitored by mockingly serious judges who suspect some fighters will take questionable measures to win the coveted title.

Ruth Peters Jones, who won her tenth trophy at age ninety, is quick to separate herself from that crowd. "I've never cheated and used a guinea egg," she states proudly. "Just chicken eggs."

Guinea eggs are tougher than permitted chicken eggs, but illegal. Chicken eggs can be strengthened, insist many participants—and for some it's a year-round scientific experiment.

Norman's wife, Patsy, feeds her chickens calcium tablets. Another woman claims boiling eggs weeks in advance yields an impervious shell. Still others swear that adding red onion skins or coffee grinds to the pot is the path to victory. Because the focus is on strength—and not aesthetics—the eggs rarely are decorated.

Many competitors buy their eggs, but Jerry Peters still raises his own hens. He feeds them a secret diet that includes lots of oyster shells, for calcium. Three months before the event, he and his wife begin saving their harvest in a second refrigerator reserved for that purpose. Before fight day, they stage their own mini-competition to eliminate the weakest eggs from the arsenal. This has resulted in dozens of championships between themselves, their children, and grandchildren.

Despite the elaborate preparation, most participants insist the event's real attraction is fellowship. "It's a way of socializing, and you go to church together," Jerry says.

Families and friends share meals and catch up on each others' lives. They also discuss what to do with some two thousand eggs in the next few days.

Through it all, most fighters maintain a good-natured rivalry. When Norman found himself losing to C. W. Rambo, who has been fighting eggs for sixty of his seventy-two years, he joked, "I'm just getting rid of these soft eggs. Now I'm going to get down into these tough ones."

But his eggs weren't as tough as his talk. As C. W. claimed the victory, Norman accused with a sly grin, "Those were duck eggs fished out of the pond, I just know it."

But it's all in good fun, and everyone agrees the tradition is everything it's cracked up to be.

There's a Word for It—the Origins of "Barbecue"

John Shelton Reed

What could be more Southern than barbecue? Even when entrepreneurs have taken the dish to other parts of the world, the names of their establishments pay tribute to the origins of their product, either explicitly (Memphis Championship Barbecue in Las Vegas, Memphis Minnie's in San Francisco, the Carolina Country Kitchen in Brooklyn, the Arkansas Café in London) or at least by implication (Jake and Earl's in Cambridge, Massachusetts, Daisy May's in Manhattan, Dixie's in Bellevue, Washington). Rivaled only by grits as the national dish of the South, barbecue would appear to be as Southern, as indigenous, as it comes.

But this symbol of the South, like kudzu, is an import. The technique of cooking over hardwood coals or a low fire, or with smoke and indirect heat from hardwood, at a low temperature (about the boiling point of water) exists in a great many different cultures, and has from time immemorial: Europeans and Africans were both familiar with it before they arrived in the New World and found the native Indians doing it. The hogs and cattle that are the usual subjects of the enterprise were brought from Europe, as was the vinegar that goes into most sauces. The peppers that usually go in as well are a West Indian contribution. And tomatoes—well, that's a long story, but let's just say that they weren't grown and eaten in colonial North America.

Even the word *barbecue* seems to have been imported, although it underwent some changes after it was naturalized in Great Britain's southern colonies. The word came into English only some five hundred years ago. In the first decades of the 1500s Spanish explorers in the Caribbean found the locals using frameworks of sticks to support meat over fires. They did this either to slow-cook it or to cure and preserve it—as we do with country hams and jerky today—which one depends on the heat of the fire and the height of the framework. Both on the island of Hispaniola (modern-day Haiti and the Dominican Republic) and on the northern coast of South America this apparatus was called something that the Spanish heard as *barbacòa*, which soon became a Spanish word—one that is making its way into the South these days, via Mexico. A French expedition to Florida in the 1560s included an artist, Jacques Le Moyne, one of whose sketches of Timucua Indian life shows a mixed grill of alligators, snakes, and some kind of wildcat on just such a frame. The native Floridians also had a word like *barbacòa* for this rig, and indeed for all sorts of wooden structures, including watchtowers and raised sleeping platforms.

Some twenty years later, in 1585, Sir Walter Raleigh sent some folks to look things over on the coast of what would later be North Carolina. One member of that party was John White, "Gentleman of London," who later became governor of the ill-fated Roanoke Island colony (and grandfather of Virginia Dare, who was, as every North Carolina schoolchild once knew, the first English child born in North America). White made sketches of what he saw, including Croatan Indians "broyling their fishe over the flame—they took great heed that they bee not burntt." Unfortunately, he didn't say what the indigenous Tar Heels called their cooker, but whatever they called it, it's obviously a *barbacòa*, too.

William Dampier, naturalist and sometime pirate, wrote in 1697 about a visit to some West Indians when he and his companions "lay there all night, upon our Borbecu's, or frames of Sticks, raised about 3 foot from the Ground." Yankees and Australians who talk about putting meat "on the barbecue" can appeal to Dampier for precedent, but in colonial North America and England, as in the South today, the word usually referred to a process of cooking or to what was cooked, rather than to the frame on which it was done.

The earliest use of the English word that I've encountered comes from 1661, when Edmund Hickeringill's *Jamaica Viewed* reported that animals "are slain, And their flesh forthwith Barbacu'd and eat," but by 1689 in a play called *THE Widow Ranter OR, the HISTORY of Bacon in Virginia*, "the rabble" fixing to lynch one Colonel Wellman cry, "Let's barbicu this fat rogue." That the word could be used casually on the stage shows that by then it must have been familiar to London audiences. (The play was written by the remarkable Aphra Behn, the first Englishwoman to be a professional writer, and "Bacon" in the title refers to the leader of Bacon's Rebellion of 1676, not to side meat.) About the same time, the Boston Puritan Cotton Mather used the word in the same gruesome sense when he reported that several hundred Narragansetts slaughtered by New England troops in 1675 (among them women, children, and elders burned in their lodges) had been "terribly Barbikew'd."

A few years later John Lawson, surveyor-general of North Carolina, also used the word without explanation. In his *New Voyage to Carolina* (1709) Lawson encountered "barbakued"—that is, smoked and dried—venison, fish, and even peaches. Some Santee Indians served him "fat barbacu'd Venison" that sounds like a sort of jerky: "the Woman of the Cabin took [it] and tore in Pieces with her Teeth"—pulled, not sliced—'so put it into a Mortar, beating it into Rags," then boiled it. But he was also served "roasted or barbakued Turkey, eaten with Bears Fat." Not long after that, the physician and naturalist John Brickell gave a very similar account (so similar in fact that it may have been plagiarized) in his *Natural History of North Carolina* (1737).

The one suggestion I've found that the English word was *not* taken from the Spanish version of a Caribbean Indian word comes from Robert Beverly's *History and Present State of Virginia* (1705). Beverly reported that the Indians of the Carolinas and Virginia had "two ways of Broyling viz. one by laying the Meat itself upon the Coals, the other by laying it upon Sticks rais'd upon Forks at some distance above the live Coals, which heats more gently, and drys up the Gravy"; this latter, he added, "they, and we also from them, call Barbacueing." (Whether they had the same word as their Caribbean cousins or not, they plainly got the grilling versus barbecuing thing.)

The English may have copied the Indians' vocabulary, but they didn't feel constrained to copy their stone-age gear. Anglo-Saxons and Celts had been roasting meat for a few thousand years themselves and had made a few improvements in the matter of cooking frames. In 1732 Richard Bradley, in *The Country Housewife*, gave directions for "an Hog barbecued": "Take a large Grid-iron, with two or three Ribs in it, and set it upon a stand of iron, about three Foot and a half high, and upon that, lay your Hog, . . . Belly-side downwards." And a 1744 advertisement in the Boston *News-Letter* offered for sale "A Lusty Negro Man, works well at the Smith's Trade; likewise a Grate for to burn Coal; a large Gridiron, fit for a large Kitchen, or a Barbeque." It also offers the earliest example I've found of the *-que* spelling, although spelling was so random at the time that it hardly signifies.

Still, the process of cooking or smoking meat on some sort of frame remained identified with the Indians. When Colonel George Washington, trying to get provisions for his troops during the French and Indian War, wrote his superior officer in 1758, "We have not an ounce of salt provision of any kind here; and it is impossible to preserve the fresh (especially as we have no Salt) by any other means than barbecuing it in the indian manner," he was evidently writing about smoking meat to cure it, not to cook it. Later, however, the future Father of His Country often wrote about going to "barbecues" where cooking was the object: for example, "Went in to Alexandria to a Barbecue and stayed all Night" (1769), "Went to a Barbicue of my own giving at Accotinck" (1773), "Went to the Barbacue at Accatinck" (1774). (Notice that his spelling was as independent as his subsequent politics.)

Washington's use of *barbecue* to refer to a social event was not unusual: That use of the word dates from at least 1733, although it was apparently an Americanism. When a young Virginian wrote to a London friend in 1784 that he was "continually at Balls & Barbecues," he added, "the latter I don't suppose you know what I mean" and went on to explain: "it's a shoat & sometimes a Lamb or Mutton & indeed sometimes a Beef splitt into & stuck on spitts, & then they have a large Hole dugg in the ground where they have a number of Coals made of the Bark of Trees, put in this Hole. & then they lay the Meat over that within about six inches of the Coals, & then they Keep basting it with Butter & Salt & Water & turning it every now and then, until it is done, we then dine under a large shady tree or an harbour made of green bushes, under which we have benches & seats to sit on when we dine sumptuously."

This was the kind of thing the itinerant Anglican parson Charles Woodmason probably smelled, roaming the South Carolina backcountry in 1768, when he wrote in his journal: "I had last Week Experience of the Velocity and force of the Air—By smelling a Barbicu dressing in the Woods upwards of six Miles," and it sounds pretty nice, if you get to sit under the "harbour." Less so, of course, if you're a slave on the digging and basting crew.

Even though the word had been naturalized in the thirteen colonies, the British continued to see it as West Indian. Also, most references at this time were to whole hogs (or whole other animals) being cooked—the practice in the Caribbean and, now as then, in eastern North Carolina. When the poet Alexander Pope wrote in 1733 that a man named Oldfield, who was famous for his appetite, "Cries, 'Send me, Gods! a whole Hog barbecu'd!'" he added a note for his English readers explaining that "a whole hog barbecu'd" was "a *West-Indian* Term of Gluttony, a Hog roasted whole, stu'd with Spice, and basted with *Madera* Wine."

Just so, Samuel Johnson's famous *Dictionary* (1755) defined the verb *to barbecue* as "a term used in the West Indies for dressing a hog whole; which, being split to the backbone, is laid flat upon a large gridiron, raised about two feet above a charcoal fire, with which it is surrounded" and *barbecue*, the noun, as "a hog drest whole in the West Indian manner." Virtually identical definitions, probably cribbed from Johnson, can be found in many, many subsequent dictionaries. In 1828 Noah Webster's *Dictionary of the American Language* also defined the word as, "in the West Indies, a hog roasted whole," but expanded the definition: "It is, with us [i.e., Americans], used for an ox or perhaps any other animal dressed in like manner."

Webster was from Connecticut, but an 1816 *Vocabulary, or, Collection of words and phrases, which have been supposed to be peculiar to the United States of America* [etc.] had given the first indication that barbecue was becoming a Southern thing. Quoting an English source from 1798, it said that barbecue was "a porket . . . stuffed with spices and other rich ingredients, and basted with Madeira wine," then added, "*Used in the* Southern *states*" (although "not peculiar to the *United States*; it is used in the *West Indies* also").

Notice that these dictionaries show the emergence of yet another use of this versatile word: a *barbecue* could mean the critter being barbecued—and not just a hog. In 1796 Hugh Henry Brackenridge wrote a humorous reply to a challenge to duel, which read in part, "I do not see any good it would do me to put a bullet through any part of your body. . . . You might make a good barbecue, it is true, being of the nature of a raccoon or an opossum; but people are not in the habit of barbecuing anything human now."

So by the mid-1700s we had *barbecue* as a kind of equipment for a style of cooking called *barbecuing*, and we had *barbecue* as an event of the sort that George Washington and his contemporaries went to, and we had *barbecue* as a word for the subject of the undertaking—pig, ox, shad, whatever (although this last use seems to have disappeared). But we apparently did not yet have *barbecue* as the point of all this: the dish prepared on a barbecue-device and served at a barbecue-event, what a barbecue-creature becomes after it is barbecue-processed. When did barbecued pork become *barbecue*?

Someone may come up with an earlier example, but the earliest I've found comes from 1808. Oddly enough, it comes from a Yankee—although he was disparaging Southern folkways at the time. In a speech on the floor of Congress, Representative Josiah Quincy of Boston denounced the kind of partisan stump speech commonly delivered "in this quarter of the country . . . while the gin circulated, while barbecue was roasting." (It was a Southern thing. He didn't understand.)

By the middle of the nineteenth century this use of the word was increasingly common in print, especially in Southern newspapers, usually in the context of political rallies. In 1859, for instance, the *Weekly Standard* of Raleigh wrote that one politician's "constituents had been bought up by whiskey and barbecue." The next year, the same paper wrote of a gathering in Shelby, "The barbecue was excellent. Not a Douglas man was found upon the ground." In 1868 the *Petersburg Index* reported that the three thousand Democrats at a rally in Nash County, North Carolina, "marched to the grove, near by, where a bountiful supply of barbecue, vegetables, etc., etc., refreshed the 'inner man,' and to which ample justice was done."

True, as late as 1894, when the Statesville (North Carolina) *Landmark* wrote of an occasion where "several hundred ladies were present, and the contents of their baskets, supplemented by 'barbecue' from the committee, composed the repast," the paper put the noun in quotation marks, suggesting that the usage remained colloquial. Still, by then everyone seems to have known that it meant something you could put on a plate or a sandwich.

Only after that was understood was the way open to argue about what barbecue *is*. But that's another long story.

A Jewish Yankee's Quest for the Last Great Country Hams of Western Kentucky

How a City Boy Fell Madly for Country Ham and Wound Up Eating It Raw

Alan Deutschman

"Country ham or city ham?" asked the waitress at the Waffle House.

I stared at her. I had never heard of "country ham" during my thirty-eight years living in the Northeast and on the West Coast. I had just moved from San Francisco to Roanoke, Virginia, and this was my first cultural shock: I felt like that character in Moliere's play, *Le Bourgeois Gentilhomme*, who is disconcerted to learn that there are two ways of speaking French—prose and verse—and his whole life he's only been using one of them.

So I tried the country ham. Even the Waffle House version, which I assumed to be a cheap knockoff of the real thing, had much more flavor than normal ham. It was saltier and chewier, and it didn't look as though it came out of a can.

Intrigued, I went to the farmers' market and bought a package of raw country ham slices. Back home I consulted Southern cookbooks about what to do with it. They said to sauté a thin piece and make "red-eye gravy" from the drippings by deglazing the pan with strong coffee.

It was a revelation: very salty, sweet, somewhat bitter, and intensely flavorful with smoky aromas that infused the air for the rest of the morning.

My friends in San Francisco and New York City thought they knew all about food, but here was something wonderful that none of us had ever experienced.

What exactly was country ham?

From the settlement of Jamestown, Virginia, in the 1600s until the machine age of the 1920s, all ham in America was "country ham." Farmers killed their hogs in early winter. They didn't have refrigeration, but the cold weather kept the meat from spoiling. Farmers cut off the hind legs of the hogs and rubbed them with salt (as a preservative) and sometimes also sugar (as a tenderizer) and black pepper (an insect repellent as well as a seasoning). Then they hung these pig haunches from the rafters of a tightly sealed, windowless shack. For several weeks they left a pile of hickory shavings smoldering below.

Through the cool climate of springtime, the salt and sugar settled more evenly through the interior of the legs. Then the hams sweated in the heat of summer, dripping off liquid and losing 25 to 30 percent of their original weight, shrinking down to about fifteen to twenty-five pounds each. By autumn the hams were ready to eat: salty and sweet from the dry rub and smoky from the hickory. The flavors were greatly concentrated and intensified by drying and aging. Just as with the best wines and cheeses, aging meant that country hams from different producers were unpredictable and unique, their flavors richly complex. Country ham was a product of peasant genius and simplicity—a natural product that evolved through long tradition and required considerable labor and patience.

Country ham's sad decline began in the 1920s with the introduction of mass-produced hams by Hormel. Instead of the traditional dry cure, the new hams had a wet cure, meaning that the manufacturers injected the meat with brine. The salt penetrated rapidly through the meat. The water diluted its natural flavors, so the manufacturers relied on chemical additives as flavor enhancers and preservatives. The new hams were made in a day, not a year. They were canned and sent directly to market. Traditionalists derided them as "city hams." But like other inexpensive convenience foods, the inferior product eventually became the standard, forming a new conception of ham in the American mind. Still, many Southern seniors remember the glorious country hams from their childhood, before city ham became ascendant.

Country ham with red-eye gravy became my favorite breakfast. But when I opened the plastic package, felt the silky texture of the raw meat, and enjoyed its delicious aroma, I wanted to eat it raw. It came with a government warning label about undercooked pork. But I couldn't see how country ham was different from prosciutto, which was dry-cured with a salt rub and long-aged, then sliced thin and served raw. If anything, country ham was more "cooked" because it was smoked over hickory for several weeks, while prosciutto wasn't smoked at all. And the other great hams of Europe—Spain's Serrano, France's Bayonne, and Germany's Westphalia—were all made with dry rubs and long aging. Connoisseurs consumed them all raw, too. Why, then, did every piece of raw country ham come with a dire warning label about undercooking and cross-contamination? Why did the two dozen Southern cookbooks on my shelf all say to cook it? Why did *The Country Ham Book* not talk at all about eating it raw?

The Internet provided contradictory answers. The About.com website explained that the trichina parasite, the terror of American hog lovers, has never been found in Europe or Southeast Asia, where people have eaten raw pork safely for centuries: "Some country-cured hams are being advertised as American prosciutto with the claim they can be eaten raw like the Italian original. Not true." And the Food Network website said trichina is eliminated only at an internal meat temperature of at least 137 degrees Fahrenheit, so country hams "must be cooked before serving." However, a merchant's website, HouseofHams.com, claimed all the salt in country ham kills trichina by drying out the moisture it needs to survive. Besides, the site said, trichina is nearly eradicated in the United States.

I needed definitive answers. I wanted to eat country ham raw. And I yearned to find the South's most delicious hams. I wanted country ham in its purest and most aboriginal form as a handmade farmstead product. I wanted a connection to the eras when small farmers fed their own families by raising and killing their own hogs and curing hams. I wanted to meet farmers who had deep instinctual knowledge about country ham that came from making it for decades.

These people were still out there, but their hams were nearly illegal. Since the federal government didn't inspect all aspects of hog raising, slaughtering, and curing, the small-timers weren't permitted to sell hams to restaurants or ship them across state lines. To buy the purest country hams, you had to seek out these farmers and trek to their acreages. I consulted John Egerton's 1987 book *Southern Food*. He wrote that one of the best places to find farmstead hams was his native Trigg County, Kentucky, which held a judged competition every October at its Country Ham Festival. I had to go there.

Cadiz, Kentucky, is pronounced KAAAAY-deez. It's in the western end of the state, just north of the Tennessee line, around eighty miles from Nashville. Cadiz is too small to have a Wal-Mart. The outlying drag of Main Street looks much as it must have in the 1950s, while the inner reaches—a classic small-town stretch of Victorian houses and ornate brick-facade storefronts—looks as though it has had few alterations since World War I.

On the first morning of the Country Ham Festival, I can't find any authentic country ham to eat or buy or even to look at. The festival doubles as the county fair. It looks like a Fried Festival rather than a Ham Festival. I see fried green tomatoes, fried bologna, fried pickles, and an array of fried brands: fried Ding-Dongs, fried Twinkies, fried Snickers Bars, and fried Oreos.

When I page through the festival guide, I find an ad with a picture of the rafters of a smokehouse: "81 Years Curing Experience. A Vanishing Art of True

Smokehouse Cure." The ad is for Colonel Newsom's Old Mill Store twenty miles away in Princeton.

At Newsom's, fresh produce rests on haystacks on the sidewalk in front of a century-old brick warehouse. Inside, country hams in white cotton bags hang from the ceiling.

"Looking to buy a ham?" asks Jesse, the African American counterman.

I quiz him about the store's process. Yes, they cure the hams themselves. Do they raise the pigs, too? No. Then do they deal directly with the farmers to make sure the animals are being fed and raised so that they'll make the best hams?

"We got to get the hogs from the government now, not the farmers," he says. "Can't do anything anymore without the government seal of approval on it. I used to raise my own hogs and kill them when they got to 200 to 300 pounds. Now the government won't even let you do that. So I raise chickens now."

"How long has this been going on?" I ask.

"It's been that way about ten years now."

A dozen cooked hams are visible behind glass. Alluringly pink and marbled, they remind me of prosciuttos on conspicuous display at pricy gourmet stores in San Francisco. Jesse asks whether I'd like samples. He cuts me some pieces of country ham that's already been boiled.

"What about eating it raw?" I ask. "Like prosciutto."

"Prosciutto? You mean sliced real thin?"

He leaves for a minute, then returns with paper-thin slices that look and smell indistinguishable from the finest prosciutto. I overcome my fear of trichinosis and eat, and it's as good as anything from Parma. This is an overlooked treasure of American food.

I wonder: What's the cost compared to the famed Italian stuff? Jesse sells me one of the Colonel's fifteen-pound raw country hams for forty dollars, one-fifth the price of an import.

I drive back to Cadiz, hoping by now the ham makers have arrived. At the information tent near the town square, I ask one of the organizers: "Are there any farmers here selling country hams?"

"Doug Freeman usually sets up a table in front of the Bank of Cadiz."

I find the bank but no ham. But at least I have a lead. The program lists Douglas Freeman as the first-place winner in the previous year's country ham competition. Back in my motel room I find his phone number in the white pages. His wife answers and gives me directions to their farm, six miles from town.

I find Doug Freeman inside the back-porch door. He's seventy-six, tall but stooped, with straight white hair visible beneath a baseball cap.

I ask him why he isn't at the ham festival today.

"The bank used to let us set up a booth for free in front of their building on Main Street," he says. "Then they made us rent the booth. But now it's ninety dollars."

He takes me behind the home to his smokehouse, a small, red, windowless wooden shack. Two dozen fully aged hams hang from the rafters.

"I do around two hundred hams a year," he says. "I used to do five hundred with shipping, but the government complained so much, I quit shipping across state lines. They said, 'We've got to have a government man there whenever you put down the hogs. We've got to be there.' Two years ago I said, 'I'm going to put them down this week,' and they said, 'We can't get a man out there.' So I say, 'Just forget about it.' They got to see everything you do. That's just the way they are."

Now Doug buys hogs from the government-supervised slaughterhouse.

"They deliver them here in the truck. I take them and put them in the salt and sugar mixture here"—he points to big long troughs on the floor—"for three or four weeks. Then I retrim them, cut the bones off, put them in here in the smokeroom."

He takes me through a narrow door into a dark room with some two hundred hams hanging from the rafters. "Roll it around in hickory and sassafras wood an inch, half-inch down." He lets the wood smolder for about five weeks.

He points out that the floor is covered with grease stains from fat that dripped down in the summer sweat.

"I started these last Christmas," he says, showing me the burgundy-colored hams that have aged for nearly a year and are ready to sell. Then he gestures toward hams he put up two Christmases earlier. They're cocoa-powder brown.

"I've been putting up my hams ever since I remember," he says. "My daddy and granddaddy did it." His father bartered hams for groceries at the local store. In his earlier days Doug traded hams for fertilizer.

I pick out a ham to buy. He puts it on an ancient kitchen scale. Fifteen pounds. At two dollars and a half a pound, that's only thirty-seven dollars for an amount of meat my wife Susan and I might take the entire winter to consume.

As he's leaving he points at my ham, which is still on the scale.

"It ain't getting a bit heavier," he says with mock regret.

Even for Doug Freeman, who has won first place in the Cadiz ham festival three times, country ham is something of a sideline. "I raise cattle and a little tobacco. Just got 110 acres here. Paying taxes on 118, but I think I've got 110."

The next morning I arrive at the town square in Cadiz at seven-thirty, when farmers are supposed to start bringing their hams to enter in the judging. In front of the courthouse, I meet Beth, who, along with her husband, is the owner of Broadbent Foods, a commercial producer of country hams that sells about seven thousand a year. She's lining up three folding card tables to display the hams and an old creaky scale to weigh them. She puts down a bunch of papers with the official rules and regulations. They say that the hams must weigh fourteen to forty pounds each. The contest is open only to Trigg County residents, who must cure and age the hams by themselves. The first-place winner receives a brass tray and fifty dollars.

Doug Freeman is the fourth entrant to arrive carrying his ham. He's followed by Jimmy Adams.

"I need to pay the entry fee," Jimmy tells one of Beth's workers.

"Ain't no entry fee!"

An old man wearing a baseball cap inscribed with "Heavy Duty Grandpa" arrives to enter his ham, which gets tagged as entry number eleven. His ham is much more heavily smoked than Doug's and is chocolate in color. He looks like all the other farmers with his blue plaid shirt, but he's set apart by his suspenders, eyeglasses, and cigarette. His name is Pink "Tiny" Guier, and he's a past champion. Like Doug, his forearms show that he's been a farmer for several decades. They're reddened and leathery like the skin of country hams.

Tiny is the last contestant to arrive with his ham, just before the deadline. Ten minutes later Neal Waldington, a black man in his late forties or early fifties, shows up carrying two hams—one from his father, Charlie Bell Waldington, and one he cured himself. Then he returns with a ham produced by his brother.

Beth doesn't hesitate to allow the entries.

The judge, Nicky Baker, finally arrives. He sports a downward-sloping handlebar mustache and wears a straw hat, blue button-up shirt, jeans, and New Balance running shoes. His main qualifications: He is from outside Trigg County (as the rules specify), and he has cured country hams himself, though his real business is selling alfalfa for animal feed.

The Waldingtons' hams are much darker than Doug's, Nicky shows me. "Appearance is personal preference," he says. "That's why some people like blondes and some people like brunettes."

He plunges a metal probe near the bone in the thickest part of the ham.

"Why there?" I ask.

"That's the trickiest place," he says. "It's where the problems might be if it's not smoked through."

He removes the probe and lets me smell it. The aroma is delirious. Then he wipes the probe with a paper towel and pokes elsewhere. Later he lets me sniff again. This time the odor is surprisingly foul.

"Nothing stinks worse than a bad country ham," he says.

As he continues his work, I ask about how long ham should be aged.

"The old folks—now I'm a throwback—you didn't eat the ham until the second summer. If you're new to country ham, you have to work up to the taste of a year-and-a-half ham. Growing up on a farm, we ate four or five hams a year. And we killed our own hogs. Now the government is ruining everything. And even if you make great hams, it doesn't matter if people don't know about it. Instead of country hams, a lot of people are eating chemical hams these days."

"What about eating it raw?"

"Like prosciutto?" he asks. He pauses to gauge my reaction. "Bet you didn't think I knew what prosciutto is." He smiles. "You heard about Newsom's in Princeton? Nancy Newsom told me when she got into mail order, the people who like prosciutto began ordering country ham instead. I haven't eaten prosciutto myself. But I reckon it's just raw ham on a cracker, sliced real thin."

I turn away from the hams and notice the three Waldington men standing together. Charlie Bell Waldington, the patriarch, is neatly turned out in a monogrammed yellow polo shirt. Neal stands with his hands on his hips, looking on as though he's trying to make sure the judging is honest.

By noon the fourteen hams are visibly sweating in the day's heat. A radio announcer proclaims the winners. First place goes to Tiny Guier, second to Charlie Bell Waldington, and third to Neal Waldington. Their hams look extraordinarily similar. All are darkly colored, ranging from deep red to purple and brown in places. All three have patches of exterior fat that nearly glistens.

Doug's ham places fifth, and he seems disgruntled.

"He picked the darker color ones, didn't he?" he says to Tiny.

I'm not sure whether Doug means the darker hams or darker contestants.

Later that afternoon I drive a dozen miles north to visit Charlie on his farm and buy hams that look very much like this year's runner-up. Charlie walks me back toward the smokehouse.

"How long have you been putting up hams?"

"I've been doing it ever since 1944. My parents did it before that, and my grandparents."

The ceiling of the smokehouse is low, and I have to bend down so the hams don't hit me in the head. They're encrusted with a layer of mold.

"My grandma used to say that country ham wasn't any good if it didn't have mold on it," Charlie tells me.

He takes me into a second smokehouse, where the hams aren't as old. I notice the blackened coloring on their skin.

"That ain't nothing but pepper to keep the bugs off."

I start asking questions about his process, trying to find out whether Doug Freeman is right about Charlie doing it all, hog to ham. He confirms that he still raises his own pigs. "I feed them fresh corn and try to move them around pretty good." But the government doesn't allow him to slaughter them himself anymore.

He pauses and stares at me as I write down his words on my notepad. Even though I had said I'm a writer, he seems to suspect other motives.

"Why are you asking so many questions? Are you interested in going into business yourself?"

He guards his secrets. And I buy one of his year-old hams.

Susan is appalled to see the four large pig's legs lined up on the floor of our kitchen in Virginia. She begins plotting to give them away as Christmas presents. She is skeptical about my desire to eat the pork raw.

"Doug Freeman says it's safe," I say.

The next morning I hoist Doug's fifteen-pound ham onto the kitchen counter. From reading about hog anatomy in Southern cookbooks, I know I'm supposed to start by chopping off the hock to make a flat surface for slicing the largest and most desirable "center cuts." Even with my largest kitchen knife, it's difficult to penetrate the skin, which is dry and impossibly hard from the aging. I try stabbing with the knife point, as though I'm trying to wound the pig rather than carve it. Then, slowly, I manage to work the rest of the long blade down into the ham. But the bone is too hard.

I go out and buy a handsaw. Back home I wrestle with the pig and saw it open. Never have I felt so manly in the kitchen. I feel like one of the barbaric boys in *Lord of the Flies*.

I put away the saw and try carving the center with my sharpened knife. But the interior meat is too soft, and I can't make razor-sharp slices. I wind up with a few small pieces that are thin but not really thin enough. Mushy clumps of meat stick to the blade.

It's easier to eat country ham sliced thin to look like prosciutto. It's scarier to eat raw ham that looks like sushi.

I realize what I need is one of those oversized commercial deli-meat slicers so that I can eat Cadiz ham like Parma ham.

But then I grasp why the Kentucky folks prefer to cook their farmstead hams. I keep staring at the outer layer of protective fat. It's an inch or thicker in places. The fat is simply beautiful. I cut most of it away before I sauté ham slices and make red-eye gravy. But rather than throwing away the trimmings, I want to keep sautéing the white fat and inhaling its transfixing smoky aroma. I cut chunks right off the carcass and render it so I can use it for my other culinary experiments.

After a long allegiance to olive oil, I've been seduced by glorious pig fat.

From Southern Waters

Ode to a Catfish House

Katherine Whitworth

The Lassis Inn hunkers alongside the Interstate in a small, royal-blue building. It is the architectural equivalent of minding your own business, and it's hard to notice unless you're looking for it. But if you're traveling east on I-30 toward downtown Little Rock—from the airport, say—it might catch the corner of your eye.

What goes on there is excellent catfish. Fried catfish, to my mind, is best rated by its lack of negative qualities, at least one of which is usually found in any random sample: soggy crust, oily fish, watery fish, overcooked crust, flavorless fish, too-thick crust, and sharply tapered fillets (which leave behind those curled nubbins of fishless, overfried cornmeal). None of these descriptions apply to the fish at the Lassis.

When Elihue Washington Jr. took over the Lassis in 1989, it was eighty-four years old and he was thirty-nine. Though he had been eating there since the early 1970s and knew the owner's family pretty well, he never dreamed he'd one day be running the place. The restaurant had been closed for months after the owner died, and the grocery chain where Washington worked for nineteen and a half years had been sold, so when he was invited to reopen the Lassis, he took a chance and invested his savings in the business.

He was nervous at first. The popularity of the Lassis was well established: I-30 had been designed in 1957 to run straight into the restaurant, and the owners, rather than rebuild elsewhere, had merely picked up the Lassis and moved it fourteen feet to the left.

Washington got rid of the ancient gas stove, with its giant cast-iron pots—too cumbersome for his cooking style, which is a methodical dance of second-to-second calibrations—and replaced them with stainless-steel deep-fat fryers.

This was the first of several good ideas: within a few months, Washington's weekly raw-fish order increased from fifty to six hundred pounds.

With one exception, every time I've taken a group of first-timers to the Lassis, at least one person has felt compelled to talk about his grandmother. And there is something grandfatherly about Washington, who insists that every fillet be trimmed of fat and fries every batch to order. He watches the darkening fish carefully and lets each basket drain for longer than most fish fryers would have the patience to.

Along with catfish, the Lassis serves fried ribs of buffalo fish (another, larger, bottom-skulking mud-eater that, unsurprisingly, tastes like catfish—but more so), hamburgers, cheeseburgers, "lassie" dogs (which unfortunate pun must refer to a hot dog), and beer. There is always some kind of cake under a glass dome on the counter. And there are never hushpuppies. Fish dinners come with coleslaw, french fries, and sliced white bread nailed to a Styrofoam plate with a toothpick. While you're eating, make a mental list of all the people you know who have no idea how good a piece of catfish can be when it's cradled in a slice of Wonder Bread with mustard and a generous shake of hot sauce.

The interior of the Lassis—with a dozen narrow, pewlike booths, built by the original owner in the 1940s—is overwhelmingly blue, from the walls and the furniture to the tablecloths and curtains. Blue is Washington's favorite color, and, he says, "It kind of goes along with fish."

The jukebox is stocked with r&b, blues, and soul—Curtis Mayfield, Aretha Franklin, R. Kelly, Johnnie Taylor. It's music that demands movement, in one way or another. But above the jukebox is a small yet forceful blue-lettered sign that reads "No Dancing." It is an impossible order, and customers rock in their seats or shuffle discreetly in front of the electric box.

"Look," says Washington in explaining that rule, "if you're dining out, and this guy is all over your table, pulling on you, 'Come on, dance, baby, come on'—the dancing and the beer, I just couldn't get it to go together."

When he leans across the table and tells me, like a child with a secret, that the Lassis used to be a hideout, I feel like I'm supposed to know exactly what he means.

Soft-Shell Science

Carroll Leggett

A few miles east of Bath, North Carolina, on Highway 92, you come to a cross-roads and the Cartwright store is on the right. It's been years since the last Nabs and Pepsi colas were sold there, and its sign is faded and weathered. But the grounds around it are neatly kept and vandals have spared it. The clapboard building with a shelter where farm folks and watermen once lingered and talked about life and death, droughts, floods, fishing, crabbing—and maybe even the good local plum and scuppernong wine—is a landmark, and it helped me find my way to the Crab Ranch, owned and operated by Debbie Cutler.

When my friend Gregg Jamback and I reached the Cartwright store and jogged right down Kelly Road, I kept looking back over my left shoulder. In my mind was the country store—much like this one—that my Uncle George Leggett operated during the 1930s and '40s on Highway 17 in Bertie County near where the road runs into the cypress swamp and then takes you over the Roanoke River into Williamston by way of the Trooper G. T. Davis, Jr. Memorial Bridge. "You know," I said to Gregg, "I think I could be content now running the Cartwright store, selling hoop cheese, soda crackers, and soft drinks and holding court out front."

When Kelly Road dead-ended into North Creek, our car filled with film equipment took a right on a dirt road and in a hundred yards or so we were at the Crab Ranch. It was my second visit. Not a soul was in sight among the various trailers, shelters, refrigeration equipment, and docks that comprise the operation, but hunting dogs penned at the edge of the woods announced us, and turkeys wandering about gobbled their welcome. I remembered that old Toms sometimes are easily offended, so I glanced about to make sure I would not be subjected to the indignity of fleeing a ruffled turkey. But soon

Debbie emerged, cell phone to her ear, walking briskly while trying to make sure she had a buyer for the day's catch.

My friend Molly Urquhart of Raleigh had introduced me to the Crab Ranch. She invited me down for a weekend at her place on the Pungo River between Bath and Belhaven. "Pungo Palace" is a gracious, gussied up farmhouse facing expansive waters that can be calm as a millpond one moment and full of whitecaps the next. It was a bridge weekend for Molly, husband Bill Mears, and friends Angela and Dave Bradfield. Consequently, Molly had made a list of divertissements for me that included the Crab Ranch, a few miles back toward Bath. I had to pass the turnoff at Cartwright's store on my way to her place, so I stopped to check it out. That was my first visit.

It was the right time or the wrong time, depending upon how you view it. Crabbers were bringing their catches in, and every hand was busy dumping crabs, culling, grading, and packing them for shipment. Debbie is a no-nonsense woman, and she had to have things ready when the truck arrived to take the crabs to Maryland. Curtis Wilkins, a veteran crabber and rare character with something of a "hoigh toider" accent, deftly picked up a protesting jumbo crab and announced with irony in his voice, "Now tomorrow this big boy from the Albemarle Sound will become one of those famous Chesapeake Bay blue crabs." In fact, there are those who believe that crabs from eastern North Carolina waters are tastier than those from the Chesapeake.

I took a few photos but knew to stay from under foot. I retreated from the hard crab processing area to the peeler shed where crabs were being babied through the molting process until they became soft-shells, destined for upscale restaurants in places north. In the shed I discovered Larry Pinland, "the Crab Whisperer." He has been shedding crabs for more than twenty years, and his intriguing descriptions of the process as he walked from tank to tank prompted my return visit with Gregg, owner of Swiftwater Media, a film company with a history of producing quality documentaries. My enthusiasm had sparked his adventurous spirit, and we decided to capture the story of how soft-shell crabs make their way from Down East creeks, rivers, and sounds to white-tablecloth restaurants.

Crabs outgrow their shells and molt many times during their lives, Larry explained. Their shells crack across the back, and they take in water until the shell separates and they back out, the tips of their claws being the last to exit. As a crab attempts to shed, other crabs often sense difficulty and come to help, giving gentle pushes to get the old shell to release. The shedding process drains a crab's energy, Larry said, holding a crab in his hand that was totally limp. Without sharp pincers, they are vulnerable to natural predators and even to aggressive Jimmies (mature male crabs) when they first molt. In fact, they are so depleted that they can be packed alive by the dozen, refrigerated, and shipped out to restaurants and seafood dealers without ever breaking rank.

If soft-shells remain in the water after shedding, their shells will begin to harden again within a couple of hours, so there is a small window in which they can be harvested. Consequently, crab-shedding at the Crab Ranch is a twenty-four-hour-a-day business during the six-month crabbing season. Every two hours Larry "fishes" the tanks, removing discarded shells and the soft crabs which will be shipped live to market. They are sold in grades ranging from the smallest, *cocktail*, to *hotel, prime, jumbo,* and *whale.*

Curtis explained that when the crabs emerge from the mud in the spring, the males are the first to molt, and they do so en masse. During this period, crabbers drop empty "peeler pots" into the water. Seeking a safe place to molt, the crabs go into the pots and from there to the Crab Ranch. Crabs just starting to molt may spend several days in the tanks under the watchful eye of Larry, who pulls long shifts and grabs cat naps. Diners consider soft-shells to be in season at this time in the spring, and they are available in most restaurants. In fact they are available, but not in such large numbers, until cold weather, although the price may increase with scarcity.

In late summer and fall when mature females shed and prepare to mate, the peeler pots are baited with live Jimmy crabs, to which the female peelers (Sooks) are strongly attracted.

During the hot summer months, crabbers bring in peelers caught along with hard-shell blue crabs. Getting them to the Crab Ranch is something of a process, which we learned from Josh Hopkins, a former Belhaven policeman who crabs in the Albemarle Sound. He and Captain Hughes Foster, a lifelong waterman, work his pots several days a week. Josh took Gregg and his camera with him, leaving at five-thirty in the morning on his boat, Mayor's Money, from the Bethel Fishing Center between Edenton and Elizabeth City.

Crabbing is a family affair for Josh. His father and brother crab, and his mother has a small shedding operation. He will turn to oystering in the fall.

When Josh pulls in his pots, he separates peelers from the hard blue crabs, identifying them by the color of the second section of the back fin—white (about two weeks to shed) to yellow to orange to pink and red. Red is described as a "hot" crab due to shed in two or three days. The peelers are the crabbers' gravy and bring a dollar apiece at the Crab Ranch.

I prefer soft crabs dusted lightly with a seafood breading mix and then cooked only a couple of minutes on each side in 350-degree oil. Larry said soaking them in milk for several hours makes them softer and sweeter. Folks who want to be a bit more uptown sauté them in butter and serve them with toasted, slivered almonds.

Lord only knows when our dream of a short film on soft-shell crabs will come to fruition, but we have met some colorful, hard-working folks Down East whose stories we are eager to tell.

Humble Paddlefish Fulfills Southerners' Caviar Dreams

Jeffrey Gettleman

While caviar might go with canapés, it does not usually go with y'all. But tell that to Lewis Shuckman.

A plucky, compact vendor of fish, Shuckman spent years peddling Southern paddlefish roe from his seafood shop in Louisville, Kentucky, knocking on doors of fancy restaurants and country clubs, asking anyone who would listen, "Y'all want some caviar?"

Noses were turned up, he says, and chef after chef dismissed his product as a far cry from "the gray pearls" of the Caspian Sea and just the eggs of some toothless, goofy-looking creature that swam the Mississippi.

But then things changed. Markedly. Pollution, overfishing, and corruption ravaged the once bountiful stocks of Caspian Sea sturgeon, mothers of famed sevruga, osetra, and beluga caviar, a salty jam sometimes costing as much as one hundred dollars a spoonful. A recent Iranian report said 140 million prized sturgeon had disappeared.

Now Shuckman and his paddlefish eggs are the toast of homegrown caviar aficionados, an industry growing as fast as a well-fed fingerling. Ten years ago, domestic caviar accounted for a sliver of American consumption. Today, some seafood experts say, the cheaper (though mushier) roe feeds 60 percent of the market.

Chef Wolfgang Puck calls the paddlefish eggs "the Chevrolet of caviar."

In the briny holds of Shuckman's Fish Company, Shuckman played host to a delegation of Ukrainian fish farmers.

"Goot, Lewis, goot," said Igor Misevra, as he stuffed into his mouth a cracker slathered with Kentucky Spoonfish Caviar, Shuckman's trademarked product.

Antonina Slobodchuk, another visitor who had come to America to learn the ins and outs of the fish business, said, "It tastes like Russian caviar, but the way he presents it, with all that excitement, it's so, so, American."

Shuckman tipped back a bottle of vodka with his new Ukrainian friends and beamed.

It is hard to measure the domestic caviar boom, because unlike that for catfish, cod, tuna, or salmon, the caviar trade is small and not extensively tracked.

But over the past several years, dozens of fishermen and seafood sellers in Missouri, Arkansas, Kentucky, Georgia, and Tennessee have jumped into the market for the slimy, precious treat that nearly everyone has heard of but few people buy. Conservationists now worry that the paddlefish, a dinosaur-age filter feeder with a head shaped like a giant Popsicle stick, may need to be protected like the sturgeon.

Tom Cassidy, president of the American Seafood Company, a major distributor in Memphis, said paddlefish roe had taken off as a low-cost alternative to Caspian caviar. It usually sells for ten to twenty dollars an ounce, compared with fifty dollars an ounce for the least expensive imports.

"I'd say 60 percent of the market is now American," Cassidy said. "Take your classy wedding. Folks will get a pound of paddlefish caviar for the spread and maybe four ounces of beluga for the bride and groom."

John Fiorillo, editor of "The Wave," a seafood industry newsletter, said the roe from paddlefish (also called spoonfish) was one of the fastest growing sectors of the seafood market.

"Five years ago, if you said spoonfish caviar, people would say, 'What the hell was that?'" Fiorillo said. "Now, I'm seeing it all over the place."

Puck sprinkles paddlefish roe on his smoked salmon pizza. "It's not the same as what comes from the Caspian, but it's good," he said.

Right now, great fortunes are being built on paddlefish eggs. As Mike Kelley stood on the banks of the Tennessee River, near his home in rural Savannah, Tennessee, he recalled all the things he has pulled out of the water: a Lincoln Navigator, an addition to his home, a custom-built summer cabin.

"That bend up there has been good to me," Kelley said, pointing to a curve of the river where he has netted thousands of paddlefish. He and his wife, Vickie, sell the roe out of the back of their house. After the *Wall Street Journal* called Kelley's Katch Caviar the "new egg in town," so many people placed orders, the Kelleys enlisted neighbors to fill out FedEx forms.

Most people around here still think fish eggs belong on hooks.

"When I first brought caviar to a church luncheon on deviled eggs, people said, 'Eewww, what's that?'" Vickie Kelley said.

Paddlefish converts say the taste is similar to more expensive Russian caviar, but the eggs are half the size of some, about two millimeters around compared with the buckshot-size, four-millimeter beluga.

And, strictly speaking, for purists the term "caviar" is like "Champagne." It should be used only to refer to roe from sturgeon, not other fish. There are a few sturgeon farms in California, where fish farmers are producing true caviar. Armen Petrossian, president of the International Caviar Importers Association in Paris, said paddlefish eggs had a muddy aftertaste.

"He is taking the earth with all the rest he eats," Petrossian said of the paddlefish, "giving the eggs a little taste of the earth."

But even caviar snobs are easily fooled. Five importers were arrested in 2003 and accused of passing off American roe as Russian caviar. Then there were Franklin and Carolyn Hale, a Tennessee couple sentenced to prison the next month for various charges, including catching paddlefish out of season. They said they had gotten the fish from a fish farm, but federal agents spotted net marks.

The biggest caviar arrest at the time of this writing was in October 1998, when United States customs agents seized one thousand pounds of tuxedo grade beluga at Kennedy Airport. The shipment had a street value of over one million dollars. The ring was led by Andrzej Lepkowski, then deputy chief of police of Warsaw, and included Polish airline employees.

Environmental groups are alarmed about decreasing sturgeon stocks, though some caviar dealers say the numbers are not so clear. In a 2000 report, Iranian officials estimated that the Caspian Sea's sturgeon population plummeted from two hundred million in 1990 to sixty million five years later. Caviar Emptor, a sturgeon advocacy organization, said beluga sturgeon numbers had decreased by 90 percent in the past twenty years.

Many people blame increased pollution and the collapse of the Soviet Union, which once tightly regulated caviar production. In 1998, strict international controls were put on sturgeon exports, which led to a spiral of higher caviar prices, more smuggling, more controls, even higher prices, even more smuggling, and so on. The United States Fish and Wildlife Service is considering listing beluga sturgeon, one of the largest fish that can live in fresh water, as an endangered species. That could lead to an outright ban on the gray pearls.

These days, the focus has shifted to paddlefish, a distant cousin of the sturgeon. Drawing data from state fish reports, law enforcement, and conversations with fishermen, the wildlife group Traffic has concluded that American paddlefish, which have survived for 150 million years, are now in trouble.

"There's no question that the declining catch in the Caspian Sea has increased pressure on North American species to fill the caviar void," said Craig

Hoover, a Traffic official. "They are not on the brink of extinction, but they are threatened."

Limits on paddlefish roe could end the gravy days at seafood businesses like Shuckman's.

Lewis Shuckman first tasted the little gray eggs in 1994, when a catfish supplier introduced him to them. Now, he is selling eight hundred pounds a year, at fifteen dollars an ounce.

He is careful not to pack the tins himself, he said, "because I got all these crackers and capers around, and it gets dangerous. I say, 'One for the customer, one for me, one for the customer, one for me.'"

His sixteen Ukrainian guests polished off a five-pound bowl (and three bottles of vodka). When asked, Shuckman did not care to calculate the cost of his hospitality.

Bayou Coquille

Garland Strother

No longer working for pay, a pride of old men
fish canals under shade along Lafitte Highway
or trawl without nets the duckweed waters
of Bayou Coquille green with the lure of trout
big enough to keep. Casting their lines
from canvas chairs, they load hooks with bait
from soil feeding a forest of gum trees
and palmettos, the random cypress spared
the cutter's tool, the knees a plaintive sign
from the past. Keeping watch in rows, tall
blue herons stand regal as royalty on a bank
of shadows, whistling the dark to sleep.
With a full catch and clear weather to come,
the brokers of the canebrake will share
their bounty on fires of kindling wood, bark
and stump gathered again for currency deep
inside a delta of marsh and ridge, the only
place they've ever known how to call home.

Lamentations

USDA Approved
The Mark of Discrimination in Twentieth-Century Farm Policy

Pete Daniel

My first recollection of U.S. Department of Agriculture (USDA) farm policy goes back to the early 1950s, when the Franklin County, North Carolina, ASCS office—that's the Agricultural Stabilization and Conservation Service—sent my grandfather his annual tobacco allotment. It set Calvin Hunt off. He damned the committee for making it impossible for him to survive on a continually shrinking tobacco allotment and, drawing on his Populist heritage, allowed that the committee rewarded family and friends at the expense of small farmers. I witnessed this scene in the Hunt homeplace kitchen, that very same kitchen where my grandmother, Annie Sykes Hunt, presided over a majestic woodstove as she served up three meals a day until her daughters forced her to go electric when she was in her eighties. I am reminded of a woman, interviewed by Lu Ann Jones, who also had an electric stove forced on her, but she only cooked biscuits on it one time. She complained that she could taste the electricity in the biscuits.

After tossing the letter from the ASCS onto the kitchen table, my grandfather drove the two miles to Avery Stallings's store at Seven Paths and purchased himself a Cocola (as Coca-Cola was often pronounced) and a BC headache powder. I can still see him take out that BC, crease the paper just right to channel the powder, hold it above his mouth at an angle, and funnel the powder into his mouth, followed by the Cocola chaser. Some people argued that a Cocola and a BC gave a high. I wouldn't know. Calvin Hunt neither smoked (though he raised tobacco) nor drank, and my grandmother tolerated no alcohol in her house except on Christmas Day. The men were forced to "go riding" for their nip. I always thought that during Jimmy Carter's dry years in the White House the prohibition on liquor might have led guests to ride around the District of Columbia.

Despite the ASCS allotment cuts giving my grandfather a headache, it never occurred to me as a youngster that his situation was not uncommon throughout the South. Calvin Hunt was a small farmer with something under ten acres of tobacco allotment, enough to fill his barns and keep the two mules, Buck and Roady, busy.

Early in my graduate education, the energy of Franklin D. Roosevelt's New Deal and Henry A. Wallace's AAA farm programs had great appeal, especially compared with drab Republicans such as President Dwight D. Eisenhower's Secretary of Agriculture Ezra Taft Benson, who scorned not only alcohol and tobacco but also playing cards, and who, like more recent Republican leaders, had an unfortunate way with words. Apparently, Benson's only contact with life below the Potomac materialized as an outraged Jamie Whitten protesting acreage cuts in cotton. There is no indication that Benson had even a passing knowledge of African Americans. He was a zealous anticommunist. When Nikita Khrushchev visited the Beltsville agricultural research complex near Washington, he ended up in a car with Ezra Taft Benson's son Reed, who spent the ride back to Washington attempting to convert the Soviet leader to the Church of Latter Day Saints. One of my favorite Benson photos shows him drinking milk even as the USDA and its Agricultural Research Service were covering up the fact that the country's entire milk supply was tainted with pesticides.

Over the years my view of the USDA has soured. When writing *Breaking the Land*, I found that such USDA intrusion appeared as part of its blueprint for rural America—the rural South in particular. After spending a year doing research in agricultural records at the National Archives and then working as a Senate aide for two years, I miraculously ended up at the Woodrow Wilson International Center for Scholars in 1981. By then my research had aged, and, like good bourbon, aging had done it good.

Now as I work on the USDA's efforts to erase African American farmers, I often look across the Mall and envision there not the USDA headquarters building but a National Museum of Agriculture that would tell the incredible story of rural life in this country, including, of course, the history of food.

For those not instructed in USDA legerdemain, the department's power derives from its ability to please everyone with political power, no matter how much this results in contradictory programs. The USDA is a large feeding trough for a mixed brood of greedy hogs. Not that there is anything bad about hogs.

USDA programs are unfathomable and shrouded in obscure rules and practices that have a high boredom quotient. The genius of these programs is that they are not only incomprehensible but also theoretically democratic. As an example, let's look at ASCS elections. Imagine the election of the county committee from the perspective of Calvin Hunt. First, he receives a letter from the ASCS office in Louisburg, North Carolina, announcing election of community representatives who will then meet to elect the committee. The people standing for office are the usual suspects, and although small farmers can nominate others, they seldom do. He mails in his ballot, the community representatives meet, and the ASCS committee is formed. The committee divides up the county allotment and mails farmers their share.

The U.S. Commission on Civil Rights investigated USDA programs, interviewed farmers as well as county, state, and federal bureaucrats, and issued a report in 1965 that among other revelations showed that as of 1965 no African American had ever been elected to a county ASCS committee or any other USDA committee. Studies have shown that the best educated and wealthy farmers were reelected continually. While most served with honesty, some handed out favors to family members or friends, and most discriminated against African Americans. Despite vows from Secretary of Agriculture Orville Freeman and each successive secretary since the Civil Rights Act of 1964, few blacks ever were elected to ASCS committees. Blacks remained outside the magic circle of power, as did poor whites.

After the 1954 *Brown v. Board of Education* decision, local committees, the land-grant schools, and the USDA headquarters agreed (and conspired) to use federal programs to punish African Americans who sent their children to white schools, registered to vote, or belonged to the NAACP. In addition to landlords evicting tenants and sharecroppers, blacks could be denied credit by the Farmers Home Administration, have their acreage cut by the ASCS committee, or be denied credit by local merchants and bankers. Paradoxically, in the very years when civil rights law promised justice to African American farmers, they were not allowed to enjoy it.

The decline of black farmers during these years contrasted dismally with their gains in the half century after Emancipation, when, demonstrating tremendous energy and sagacity, they negotiated a maze of racist laws and customs; during these harshest years of segregation, peonage, and violence, they gained land and standing in Southern communities. By 1910 African Americans held title to some sixteen million acres of farmland; by 1920, there were 925,000 black farms in the country, accounting for fully 14 percent of all U.S. farmers. In the teens and twenties, however, the graph of rising ownership faltered and then plunged downward. Depression, mechanization, and discriminatory federal programs devoured black farmers.

The results were devastating. Robert S. Browne's study of African American farmers revealed that between 1950 and 1969 acreage owned by black farmers dropped from 12 to 5.5 million acres, a 50 percent decline.[1] Ten years ago the census recorded fewer than twenty thousand African American farmers, who in all owned some two million acres.

Statistics relating to black farmers sound bad, but it is instructive to look at individual lives. Lu Ann Jones interviewed Howard Taft Bailey in Lexington, Mississippi, on October 16, 1987, as he was nearing his seventy-ninth birthday. He traced his family back to his grandmother, Phoebe, who was born a slave in Virginia, "where," Bailey explained, "they bred and reared slaves. They didn't do no farming there." She arrived in Mississippi in a wagon, never learning the fate of her sixteen siblings. Bailey described his grandmother as "kind of vicious" and described her reaction to her master when he asked her to work in bad weather: "I ain't going out. Just kill me." In fair weather, grandmother Phoebe pulled her end of a cross-cut saw, picked as much cotton as the men, knitted and spun, used herbs to dye clothes, and traded with neighboring poor whites. She passed in 1924 at the age of 117.

Bailey explained that his father, Washington S. Bailey, studied with missionaries from Northern colleges during Reconstruction. Washington Bailey saved his money, got married, and bought 160 acres of land in Holmes County. He sent his children to school, and Howard Taft Bailey boarded in Lexington with an aunt.

After Howard Taft Bailey's brothers and sisters moved away and his mother passed in 1939, he bought a hundred acres from his father in 1945 "and just kept adding on" until it reached 360 acres. Rural life changed, he observed. "Mechanism and herbicides just knocked out the sharecropping. You don't find nobody sharecropping now." In the mid-1950s, planters who worked forty mules bought two or three tractors and dismissed the sharecroppers, who often moved to nearby Lexington, Tchula, or Durant. A few day laborers remained, Bailey observed: "Just the tractor drivers and the fella who knows how to mix the herbicides and pesticides." Bailey grew cotton until 1972 and then turned to soybeans. When Lu Ann Jones interviewed him, he was still growing "a few beans and corn." African American farmers who needed credit applied to the Farmers Home Administration, but, Bailey recalled, "they'd give just enough to barely make a crop and the white, shoot, they'd let him have money to hire labor and just do everything." In 1957 he built a "modern home" with "running water and gas and everything."

---

1 See Robert S. Browne, ed., *Only Six Million Acres: The Decline of Black Owned Land in the Rural South* (New York: Black Economic Research Center, 1973), 3; see also Jess Gilbert, Gwen Sharp, and M. Sindy Felin, "The Loss and Persistence of Black-Owner Farms and Farmland: A Review of the Research Literature and Its Implications," *Southern Rural Sociology* 18, no. 2 (2002): 7.

Bailey joined the NAACP in 1929. During the 1960s, he would some-times put up a dozen civil rights workers. When involved in the Civil Rights Movement in the 1960s, he sometimes received threats from the Ku Klux Klan, and he let it be known that "I was going to kill them if they come up there." That was his nature. "I guess it come from my grandmother and all like that," he explained.

During the Civil Rights Movement, the bank cut off Bailey's credit because he hauled people to Lexington to register to vote. With children in college, he needed credit, but the banker told him, "You been fooling around with that old controversial mess and you've got a bad credit." Bailey replied, "I thought what give a fella a bad credit was didn't have the collateral and didn't pay his notes on time." When the banker countered that Bailey might get killed, he replied that he had a policy with New York Life, and his family would be bet-ter off if he did get killed. Bailey turned down the banker's offer to lend him half of what he needed. He went to Greenwood and borrowed from a white man who used to hunt his land.

One son, Stephen, taught vocational agriculture in Woodville, Mississippi, and is now superintendent of schools in Holmes County. He lives in the old home place, but all of his siblings moved off to New York, Michigan, and California.

Bailey's life spanned decades of major change in the South. Born in 1909 in the heyday of segregation and discrimination, he played a role in their de-mise. He worked with Fannie Lou Hamer, Aaron Henry, Bob Moses, Stokely Carmichael, and other civil rights leaders. Farming with mules as a young man, he ultimately turned to machines and chemicals. He watched black farmers leave the land.

While Howard Taft Bailey resolutely fought the white power structure, Henry Woodard was less successful. He explained to Lu Ann Jones on October 5, 1987, that his family had owned land in Tate County, Mississippi, since slavery ended, and in 1937 his father had bought forty acres of land in Tunica County. Henry Woodard moved to Tunica County and got married in 1948. He established credit and did well until he participated in the Civil Rights Movement, and then his creditors refused to lend him money. "When the civil rights push got to its peak," he recalled, "that's when they went tearing the houses down and moving us off the farm."

During the Nixon administration in the 1970s, Henry Woodard heard a voice telling him to grow rice, which was then gaining favor in the Delta. When he asked the county agent for help, he was dismissed with abusive language. Then the grain elevator owner told him, "Naw, I ain't got no room for your rice." A year later he went to the FHA office, and the bureaucrat told him, "You don't know nothing about no rice and I wouldn't even furnish you on it." Woodard stubbornly went ahead and planted rice, but the harvest was a disaster as the custom combine operator maliciously used soybean settings, throwing out the rice. When Woodard hired a crop duster, the pilot flew high and, according to an informant, sprayed water instead of herbicides.

As he stood in his rice field with Lu Ann Jones and photographer Laurie Minor Penland, Woodard explained that he was hoping he could find enough money to harvest the grain. He observed that the few black farmers left in Tunica County found it difficult—and in some cases impossible—to get production loans, and even the smaller white farmers were having difficulty. During these years, there were congressional hearings about the FHA denying black farmers loans and about other USDA abuses, but black farmers in Tunica County and throughout the South found no relief.

In the post-*Brown* era, many whites feared that African Americans would become equal competitors for education, jobs, and largesse from USDA programs. Instead of working with their African American brothers and sisters to bring justice to the region, many whites reacted with hate, manipulation, and sometimes violence.

In many ways the resignation of Secretary of Agriculture Earl Butz for telling a racist joke in October 1976 epitomized the USDA's blatant and self-satisfied racism. When Ronald Reagan took office in 1981, all civil rights activity at the USDA came to a halt under Secretary John R. Block. By 1983 the USDA had dismantled its civil rights office and no longer even investigated complaints by black farmers. Congressional hearings and U.S. Commission on Civil Rights investigations had no effect on the USDA's racism.

In January 1999 the USDA agreed to settle the important class-action suit, *Pigford v. Glickman*, but it did not admit that it had discriminated against black farmers. Black farmers could take $50,000 tax-free and have their debts to the USDA forgiven, or those with larger claims and documentation could negotiate for higher settlements. Even after the favorable decision, black farmers complained that the USDA offices were still racist. The *Pigford* case continues, now joined by women, American Indians, and Hispanics. The scope of USDA discrimination is vast, and it all is stamped: USDA Approved.

My grandfather Calvin Hunt raised a token row of cotton until his death at age ninety-four. None of his eleven children farmed.

So Long, White Lily

Jack Neely

Knoxville, Tennessee, is no longer home to White Lily Flour, which had been milled at its original location at Central Street and Depot Avenue for well over a century. For reasons that must make sense to somebody with a calculator, Smucker's has moved the production to a couple of different mills in the Midwest.

The old factory along the north side of the Old City has been expanded a lot over the last 125 years, resulting in an interesting conglomeration of mixed architecture and machinery, with its seven tall metal silos and loading docks fronting the freight yards. But the original four- and five-story biscuit-colored brick building on Central—the one you can see in a famous bird's-eye portrait of Knoxville in 1886—is still there.

As I walked by at lunchtime one day before the plant closed, a thin, middle-aged man stepped out of that old building into the sunshine, took off his hairnet, and exhaled. I asked him if he was moving to Ohio. "No, they're just shutting us down," he said. "I need to look for another job."

It's not just another local industry biting the dust. White Lily is one of Knoxville's handiest claims to fame. People who don't know the University of Tennessee has a football team know White Lily as one of America's finest flours. Some chefs and cookbooks specify White Lily, especially for certain delicate desserts. Though it's always been distributed primarily in the Southeast, upscale chains like Williams-Sonoma have carried it. In 1992, *New York* magazine ran an excited item heralding the fact that White Lily was finally available in New York, at Dean & DeLuca: "Any Southerner who knows his pie crust knows that White Lily is the only flour worth stocking."

When the plant closure was announced, the *New York Times* ran a story, illustrated by a photograph of the historic factory, that raised the question of whether the White Lily magic would survive the move from Knoxville north.

Writer Shaila Dewan interviewed several baking experts, including Shirley Corriher, a well-known Atlanta cookbook author, who was quoted as saying, "There's an incredible difference" between White Lily and other all-purpose flours. "It's much, much finer, much whiter, and much silkier." Corriher is said to be "skeptical that a process perfected over more than a century of milling and subjected to Knoxville's intensive quality control could be easily replicated."

That's not a phrase I hear every day—"Knoxville's intensive quality control"—but I like the ring of it. White Lily's nonpareil reputation was one of our city's few positive superlatives. I always thought Knoxville should have made something of the association. Sponsor an annual international biscuit-baking championship, for example. Or maybe a giant Capture the Flag battle using only pure White Lily Flour in the grenades.

Only in recent years has Knoxville tried to capitalize on its association with White Lily: When the tourist center reopened at Gay Street and Summit Hill, they sold, along with T-shirts and tour books, souvenir bags of White Lily Flour, produced just three blocks away. Recently there's been talk of a biscuit festival: Believe it or not, there apparently isn't any such thing elsewhere, and Knoxville's connection to White Lily gave the city its most credible purchase on the idea; boosters were looking to launch it in 2009. There's been random discussion of encouraging pedestrian traffic through that undervisited part of downtown, and some were reportedly enthusiastic about the possibility of a museum or bake shop in the White Lily factory. They were great ideas, but none ever happened.

White Lily has a history and, up until now, all of it was based in downtown Knoxville. Georgia-born James Allen Smith came to the war-shaken town as a young man, around 1873, and founded a grain business on Gay Street, followed by a small mill on Broad. The Knoxville City Mills, of which he was a cofounder, was reorganized as the J. Allen Smith Company. The building alongside Central was built in 1885. English industrial manufacturer W. J. Savage fitted it out with machinery, including a big roller mill, new technology at the time. It was a full-service flour factory, making not only flour but also the elm-stave barrels to pack it in. For a long time, it was pretty easy to find. Its 175-foot smokestack was one of the tallest structures in East Tennessee. The smokestack was torn down in 1943, after the plant went electric.

The company made several brands, various grades of flours for different purposes, some of them with odd names. One, a "special baker's cake flour," was called Evidence. Another, for pastries, was called Jasco. A cookie flour was Clover Leaf. By 1904, J. Allen Smith was making Roller King, New

South, Majestic, Knoxville Leader, Mayflower, Orange Blossom, Alpine Snow, Standard Fancy, and Piedmont flours.

Somewhere along the way, Smith created a new flour that he reputedly was inspired to name for his wife, Lillie. There's another story, too: An early partner of Smith's was one Jasper Lily. Regardless of the etymology, White Lily and its sister flours made Smith's factory one of the biggest flour mills in the South, and made J. Allen Smith himself a rich man. He used his money to benefit the community. He was a big backer of the major Appalachian Exposition of 1910, the Knoxville Welfare Association, the University of Tennessee's agricultural experiment station, and the Red Cross during World War I. He established a public clinic on Clinch Avenue.

As an old man, he built an unusually gorgeous hacienda on Lyons View Pike, designed by the then-young firm of Barber & McMurry. Smith died there in 1920, at age seventy. Cherokee Country Club's controversial acquisition and destruction of the J. Allen Smith House a few years ago was a great aesthetic loss, but the real historic building, thirty years older, is still intact, and that's the White Lily factory. I hope we can find a worthy use for what remains of it. A building isn't the same as a tradition, but it's all we've got left.

What Happened to Poor Man's Pâté?

Chuck Shuford

> Everything in a pig is good. What ingratitude has permitted his name to become a term of opprobrium?
> *Grimod de la Reynière (1758–1838)*

Livermush. There, I've said it. As repugnant an appellation as that is, it's about as accurate a description as can be packed into one word to describe this geographically challenged working-class food. Unless you've lived in North Carolina, it's unlikely you've ever heard of it, much less tasted it. The livermush story begins in the mid-1700s when available land in the upper colonies grew scarce and German farmers, including my ancestors, hit the Great Wagon Road down Virginia's Shenandoah Valley and into the western Piedmont of North Carolina. They brought with them scrapple, a type of pork mush made from hog scraps that is still found in the mid-Atlantic states. Scrapple is a mixture of leftover meat parts and flour (frequently buckwheat flour) cooked in a meat stock until it thickens. It is then allowed to set and is made into a loaf. I grew up eating the unappetizingly named descendant of that food.

Livermush is populist fare. Don't expect to find recipes in Junior League cookbooks. Early settlers made it in cast-iron pots and stirred with wooden paddles, incorporating whatever bits of the hog that were not used previously. A regional food born of necessity and hard times, it grew in popularity during the Civil War when anything edible was valued. Now electric agitators and stainless-steel steam kettles are used, but the primary markets are still the mill towns and small rural communities of North Carolina.

When I was a child, mom-and-pop groceries in the mountains and in the western Piedmont made their own livermush, but most have disappeared. An exception is Walsh's Grocery in Connelly Springs, where they've been making livermush since 1934.

The store sits on U.S. Highway 70 in the foothills of the Blue Ridge Mountains. While the storefront is nondescript, the interior is anything but: bottles of carp bait, some flavored like egg custard and sweet potato; North Carolina's own Cheerwine, sweetened with cane sugar, not corn syrup; a bargain bin with an unopened 2002 Elvis calendar; and stacks of cooking pamphlets with titles like "High Protein Meals for Children," featuring a picture of a skillet of ground beef topped with fried eggs.

Mr. Walsh places a high priority on taking care of his customers, and that includes conversation. He stands ready to tell you about how his grandfather and father built the business and developed a high-quality product. He oversees the making of around three hundred pounds of livermush a week, all sold in the store. Walsh says a major supermarket chain wants fifteen thousand pounds a week, but he refuses: "I already work seven days a week."

The primary component of livermush is hog liver—at least 30 percent by law. As for other hog parts, it varies from company to company but don't expect anything below the head. And that includes the snout. One operator told me they use only "the liver and the skin." After cooking to a proper mush, the mixture is placed in a pan, cooled until firm, and then sliced into one-pound loaves. Livermush is generally flavored with sage, salt, pepper, and cornmeal.

A product very similar to livermush is liver pudding, and the confusion between the two is not unlike the confusion between sweet potatoes and yams. In fact, one livermush producer told me there is more variance in taste among the different livermushes produced by the five existing commercial producers than between livermush and liver pudding. Generally, liver pudding is devoid of cornmeal, with rice or other cereals used as binders instead. There is also a geographical distinction. Draw a line north to south through North Carolina roughly following the path of the Yadkin River. Anything east of that line is called liver pudding; anything west is livermush.

Even though livermush is cooked before it hits the stores, it still should be fried in order to get a crispy outer crust. It's primarily eaten as a breakfast food, served with grits and eggs or slathered with mustard and placed between halves of a steaming biscuit. A restaurant in Charlotte, North Carolina, offers a livermush and feta omelet.

North Carolina chef and food writer Sheri Castle grew up eating livermush in the North Carolina mountains and admires the taste but stopped eating it, she says, "because I learned to read." Livermush is high in vitamin A and iron, but a two-ounce slice contains ninety calories, forty of them from fat. That slice provides 17 percent of the daily cholesterol requirement.

On the other hand, Ted Alexander, mayor of Shelby, North Carolina, touts livermush as the "world's most perfect food." His opinion is likely influenced by the fact that two livermush producers are located in Shelby, and for almost twenty years the city hosted a Livermush Expo that drew thousands of visitors.

I have yet to meet anyone from outside North Carolina who relishes livermush. The closest I came to hearing an out-of-stater say something polite about it was a statement from John Shelton Reed, a native of East Tennessee. An esteemed sociologist, student of all things Southern, and coauthor of a book on North Carolina barbecue, John clearly has a fondness for pig. His take on livermush? "I've only eaten it once. It was okay. It was fried nice and crisp. I like liver, anyway. But I haven't sought it out since."

Fortunately people have a sense of humor about this mongrel meat. The First Church of God in Drexel, North Carolina, sponsors a Livermush Festival, and it owes its existence to Pastor Tony, an Arizona native who was offered livermush by his adoring parishioners shortly after his arrival. Unfortunately, Pastor Tony couldn't make it slide down his gullet. One day he made a joke about it from the pulpit. Out of that joke came the festival, which draws 800 to 1,000 people with its theme "Everything But the Squeal." The most successful product? Livermush on a stick—livermush rolled in batter, skewered, and fried. Pastor Tony says, "We can't make enough of it. Maybe livermush slushies are next."

As far as I can tell, there are only five commercial livermush producers on the planet. They are all located in North Carolina, and all remain family owned and operated. Two of these (Mack's and Jenkins) are located in Shelby, in the southwestern part of the state, and a third (Hunter's) is forty-five miles north in the mountain community of Marion. In the Piedmont city of Greensboro is Neese's, a company also known for its sausage, and in tiny China Grove, it's Corriher's.

Phyllis Hunter Harmon, whose father started Hunter's in 1955, says the company serves five rural counties and has ten employees, seven of whom are family. At one time, Hunter's produced thirty thousand or more pounds of livermush per week. But that quantity started to decline as the state's demographics began changing. Between 1990 and 1998, North Carolina had a net gain of over 500,000 domestic migrants, with a large portion coming from upstate New York. When I told an old buddy from North Carolina that, he said, "Well, hell, that can't be good for livermush."

Hunter's used to sell 650 pounds a week to a catering service that sent trucks out to the nearby mills and factories, but now there are few factories and the catering service has vanished. There is a Waffle House half a mile from the Hunter's plant, and customers have requested that livermush be added to the menu, but Harmon says it's a national chain and menus must be consistent at each restaurant. Her ten-year-old is already talking about joining the family business, but Harmon wonders if it will be around that long.

But perhaps this story from my son offers hope for this strange food that has nourished millworkers and farmhands. "The restaurant was semi high-dollar with a bistro atmosphere, and I ordered a pâté appetizer. When it came out, it was served cold over a bed of greens and drizzled with a roasted pepper aioli. I took a bite and it was a really familiar taste. When I inspected the dish, I noticed that the pâté wedges were triangular as though cut off a rectangular loaf and then halved diagonally. And the pâté had the telltale livermush bumps on the outside. I knew the chef, and when he came out I asked him if he sold much of his pâté. He said it was a new addition to the menu, but it was catching on fast. I then recommended that he take away the bed of greens and aioli and serve it with a dinner roll and some French's mustard because it reminded me a lot of the cold livermush sandwiches my granny used to eat. He gave me a quick, nervous look and then went over to talk to the manager. Our dinner was paid for by the restaurant, and the chef made sure to send over a nice bottle of wine to go with the rest of the meal. Nothing more was said."

Friends and Fancy Food

Rheta Grimsley Johnson

We are sitting at a fancy-pants restaurant in New Orleans's French Quarter, guests of a generous friend and gourmet whose main hobby it is to ferret out such pink and pleasurable places. There is the clanking of crystal, a stable of obsequious waiters, fresh flowers, and cloth napkins.

Uptown businessmen sniff at corks, and women in Chanel suits toss their coifs. People settle in for some fine dining.

I hate to admit it. But I am more of a Low Church epicurean. In New Orleans, Acme Oyster Bar or Central Grocery suits me fine.

Not friend John. If he reads about a new chef or a popular new restaurant, he does the research. When the place is hot, he's all over it. He likes his plates with pedigrees.

Don't get me wrong. I often benefit from John's bon vivant personality. He is an expert and rarely fooled when it comes to quality.

I worry, however, that he wastes his talents on the likes of me. The problem with haute cuisine for us plebeian eaters is portion size. I do like generous helpings.

No matter how delicious the fare, if I get only a taste on a bed of lettuce, I feel cheated. Comes from being raised up in South Georgia, peanut-farming country, where quality was important but quantity the rest of the equation.

We might not have had much, but food we had in abundance. You can look at us and tell.

So I never can truly appreciate a fancy meal for feeling the ghost of Grandma Lucille. She is looking down right now at my thirty-five-dollar peanut butter and pepper jelly with duck sandwich and thinking, "What a gastronomical gimmick. That's all you're getting?"

My grandmother never served a Sunday meal with less than three meats, at least not in my experience. And if you wanted to hurt her feelings—which wasn't hard to do—mince at a meal. Sturdy country folks needed nourishment, and she intended to provide.

She was a great cook, too, with flourishes worthy of New Orleans. She put Panacea, Florida, oysters in her cornbread dressing and snowy lard in the fry pan. She didn't cut corners when it came to real butter, salt pork, or other fatty seasonings. If her farm table had been magically transported to the French Quarter and covered with a linen cloth, and if her generous servings were subdivided several times, she would have been the toast of this town, its collective sensitive palate notwithstanding.

I can remember eating quail for breakfast, and it wasn't one bird on a pile of rice, but all-you-could-eat fowl. Her ambrosia for dessert would have impressed royalty, and a smorgasbord of fruitcakes and homemade candies for the holidays was typical.

I'm a tough audience when it comes to delicious fare. I want my cake, and seconds, too. You can't fool me with dainty-sized portions of this and that, cleverly named dishes that appeal to food snobs.

I think it must be why country people are, shall we say, often more robust than their city cousins. Poor folks. You'd go broke getting enough good food to eat in the city, at least at the places written up in *Gourmet* magazine.

Eating My Heart Out
The Good and Bad of the Meal of a Lifetime

Beth Ann Fennelly

One night late in the summer of 2005, an old pal of mine—a writer who travels around, enjoying the good life—visited Oxford, Mississippi, where I live, and he wanted to eat at our town's finest restaurant. Happy to comply, I invited a mutual friend, who invited two friends also visiting Oxford. I made a reservation for five.

Although a big storm had been predicted and the atmosphere had been charged all day—the sky oddly ochre and free of bird chatter—it was merely drizzling when we arrived at the restaurant. While we were seated, the rain got down to business. Snug in our booth, we only felt cozier. As Mark Doty says in a poem, "Doesn't rain make a memory more intimate?" I was there with a treasured old friend, a treasured newer friend, and two folks I'd just met. The group was mixed racially and socially. Three of us were married, but our spouses weren't with us, the table a kind of *tabula rasa*, composed of individuals, not teams of two, and thus on more equal footing. The conversation was fluid, leaping over the votive. This is my favorite kind of talking, whether around a table or lazing in a bed—intimate, sometimes veering off, intelligent but not self-consciously intellectual, at times flirty and silly.

My companions, lovely all, seemed to grow lovelier as the candle melted, its erratic flame highlighting a cheekbone, a jaw, a languid finger tracing the mouth of a wineglass as the rain pounded harder on the roof and the wind rattled the windows. Once or twice the lights flickered, sending a surprised pause among the few occupied tables—not many diners had braved the storm—then the music of murmur resumed. Eventually the evening drawled out its end, the last sip of brandy supped. We left reluctantly, having to shoulder open the door into the wind. As I drove home, I had to swerve around fallen branches, and I realized the storm was worse than I'd thought. In fact, my street, when I turned onto it, was dark—a power outage. That night, due to the excess of food and drink and the whipcrack of wind, I slept poorly. I woke to learn that New Orleans had flooded, that magnificent city destroyed. No one knew how many people were dead.

In the months since, when people talk about Katrina, I picture myself stuffing another crab cake down my throat, and I feel a little sick. But then I wonder why. Why do I feel guilty? The fact that I was eating a four-hour dinner while those people suffered was merely a coincidence. Surely I'm not so vain as to believe I caused their misery? No, of course not. But my anxiety about the confluence of that dinner and Katrina's devastation asks me to understand its sources.

I've said a lot about that meal already, but I haven't mentioned what we ate. Because the five writers were connected to the chef either personally or professionally (one wrote for food magazines, and another was a restaurant critic), he sent out a plate of appetizers before we even looked at the menu. Word came from the kitchen that he'd like to select our meal. We were delighted, and the carnival began.

Because it appeared that the food was on the house, my tablemates decided to order fabulous wine. Now, I enjoy wine, but I'm a poet, so I'm pretty much broke all the time. My companions, however, strayed almost immediately from the top of the wine list. Their fingers slipped down, down, down below the menu's waistband, and kept going. Then they were off the page. *Do you have a 1972 something-something*? one asked, grinning at his own audacity. Though I couldn't imagine how I'd pay for my share, I decided to roll with it. I knew the meal of my life was underway.

All this time the food was arriving relentlessly. I ate wasabi-pea-encrusted tuna, quail with figs and chanterelles, duck with port glaze, and truffled potatoes. Although I normally have a Rain Man–like recall for delicious meals, that one is a Thanksgiving plate so heaped that all the sauces slosh and blend. The lobster mac and cheese had not yet given up the ghost when the cornmeal-dusted Apalachicola oysters with tasso elbowed their way onto the table. Then the crabmeat wontons. There was almost something aggressive about the quantity and pace. It went beyond eating for pleasure. I left joy behind me with my redfish skeleton. I persevered until my stomach squeezed my lungs into two little pita pockets up under my clavicles. Who needs to breathe? And then they brought out the filet mignon. I dug deep. Like a mother lifting a car that's crushing a child, I raised my fork, and I ate the hell out of that steak.

Then the veal chop arrived.

I suppose that's a big part of my shame and guilt concerning that August 29. Not just that I was dining while others suffered and died, but that the dinner was excessive, approaching grotesquery. This type of meal isn't entirely uncommon in some circles, mine included. Many of us label ourselves as hedonists; in fact, the last decades have seen a burgeoning food craze. Now, furry-browed Emeril is seen as a rock star, and your average Joe, whose idea of cooking is making toast, thinks he needs a $10,000 Lynx grill.

But this same indulgence in hedonism has improved the American palate and cuisine. Because there is enough food in America to feed the world five times over, we can move beyond subsistence and create art. And God knows our world needs art. Eating well is one of the primary joys of being human, and eating well—I believe this deeply—makes people happier. According to David Kamp's recent book, *The United States of Arugula*, this belief identifies me as a good soldier in our "Great American Food Revolution." Kamp traces how, due to a "quantum leap forward in ingredient availability and culinary sophistication," we became a "gourmet nation," eschewing iceberg for mesclun, Shake 'n Bake for spice rubs, ketchup for salsa.

But only the prosperous seem to be living in that "gourmet nation." Occupying parallel territory are the residents of a garbage nation, eating more heavily processed and more fattening food. They are eating one-fifth of their meals in the car, according to Michael Pollan, author of *The Omnivore's Dilemma*. They are the third of Americans who feed their children fast food every day.

And they are growing fatter by the minute. While starvation used to be linked to poverty, obesity is poverty's running mate now. The low-income residents of Mississippi and Louisiana seen on TV in the aftermath of Hurricane Katrina strengthened this link in many viewers' eyes. Dan Baum's August 21, 2006, *New Yorker* piece on Katrina recorded America's shock (here I think he primarily means the East Coast's shock) at the evacuees' "obesity and missing teeth, the raggedness and strange English." Not just the African American refugees from the ninth ward but the evacuees from the poor white neighborhoods made concrete for many viewers what's been termed "the obesity epidemic."

This link between obesity and poverty has quite complex roots in the South. Part of the problem derives from the eating habits of a culture divorced from the land. For the urban poor in New Orleans, as for urban poor everywhere, such a divorce is somewhat understandable. But in the South, even the rural poor are now divorced from the land. Especially for African Americans, farming and gardening are reminiscent of oppression. Weeding and hoeing seem a little too similar to picking cotton for descendants of sharecroppers. Dorothy Grady, one of the founders of Growing a Greener Mississippi, which teaches low-income children in the Mississippi Delta how to grow their own organic produce, is the child of sharecroppers herself. She recalls being visited by a concerned preacher who told her, "Teach them computers, not agriculture."

The rural poor are encouraged to rely on the processed foods offered by the supermarket chains, which can sell canned tomatoes for less money than it would take to grow them—if only because the environmental and social costs are not borne by the consumer.

Many rural poor children have a grandparent who remembers the tomato—the real tomato—sun-warm and so juicy you had to scoot your feet back to avoid being splattered. But that generation is dying out, and the middle generation is raising children who naturally won't be interested in paying the higher prices of real food. Why grow blueberries (or buy them organically) when one can buy Cap'n Crunch with Smurfberries?

If it's true, as scientists are learning, that our tastes are formed while we're still in the womb and in our infancy, America's poor children, rural and urban alike, will never have the same relationship to food that the children of the wealthy will have. Instead, poor children will be shaped by (and shape) the fast-food industry. They may adopt as their own the eating philosophies put forth by TV advertising, such as the recent Taco Bell commercial that features a happy diner announcing, "I'm full!"—as if the desirable end of every meal is having to unzip one's pants and wait for the swelling to go down. A current Taco Bell ad recommends some fake Tex-Mex monstrosity as "good to go," presumably easier than a taco to eat while driving. America's poor people are not looking to food as an art form because they can't afford to enjoy food as an art form, and therefore don't have a taste for it. But although Mississippi is the fattest and poorest state in the nation, Oxford is also home to the Southern Foodways Alliance, the epicenter of smart thinking about smart eating in the region. Every fall, the alliance hosts a symposium about food, attended by chefs, restaurateurs, food writers, historians, and culture vultures of every stripe interested in using food as a lens to view the South. Since moving here, I've been greatly enlightened about the foodways of the South. I now give more thought to what I eat than I did before. I prefer local produce, chickens that once pecked insects out of the grass, salmon that are salmon colored because they eat shrimp, not because they've been engineered to eat corn and then dyed. I've learned to ask, "Where's the beef . . . *from*?" At the 2002 barbecue-themed symposium, we were invited to sample pork from three pigs. One had been fattened with traditional feed, which is laced with antibiotics and growth promotant, the second with processed corn. The third pig had been fed high-quality grain. It was easy to identify this pig; it tasted so much richer, more complete, more . . . *piglicious*.

Through my immersion in foodie culture, I've learned that eating has a moral dimension, and I've learned to make responsible choices. It's a happy task: I eat well and contribute to a sustainable environment. But it occurs to me that I've indulged in a certain smugness when I've filled my stomach with high-priced luxury items. I pay out the nose for beef from Niman Ranch, where cows, according to the website, "are treated with dignity and respect." But respect don't come cheap. Are the table morals a luxury reserved for the educated and well-to-do? Exactly what environment am I sustaining? What does it mean to make an equation between goodness and eating with value, and then accept that poor folks must have a different relation to value?

My role as a good citizen of our "gourmet nation" is to examine food-table connectivity. I'm encouraged to think about how my meal affects the food chain and the cost to the world's energy sources, and I'm encouraged to take pride in making wise decisions. But now I'm beginning to notice other kinds of connectivity, some of which are less gratifying. I'm haunted by a simple coincidence—a lavish meal and a natural disaster. And haunted by the fact that perhaps it's less of a coincidence than I'd like to believe. There's always been a dollar price attached to a meal, whether I paid it or found someone else to. But now I'm realizing that there's a karmic price, too. In my guilt, and in my discomfort, I fear I'm beginning to pay.

Funeral Food

Kathleen Purvis

Just call me the Angel of Death.

About seven years ago, after shoveling in the trenches of daily journalism for a few decades (so long that I remember when gruff editors would bark at you if you said "journalism"—"it's newspapering," they'd growl), I decided to try my hand at a book.

I needed the experience, and I wanted the luxury of stretching out with a topic. And the thought of a little extra income didn't hurt. So of course I chose the most controversial subject I could imagine.

I decided to write a book about funeral food.

I'll save the story of my agony: I loved the subject, but publishers didn't. They shot my proposal down so fast, you'd think it was skeet-shooting day in Manhattan.

I can kind of see their point. Funerals and death do make people squeamish. For reasons I'll leave to an analyst, those subjects just don't bother me.

Quite the opposite. I loved the time I spent researching. I loved the connections I made between traditions, and the experiences I had with different cultures. I loved learning that while people in Western cultures take food to the bereaved, people in Asian cultures do the opposite. They feed their friends to show how much they honor their lost family member. I loved having an excuse to ask people about something so intimate. The conversations and memories I collected were—are—priceless to me.

There was the old man I met at a history symposium in Murfreesboro, North Carolina, in 2001. Since Murfreesboro isn't packed with restaurants, the ladies from a local church put on a potluck dinner for the visiting scholars and writers.

While the ladies labored in the kitchen to get everything ready, this sweet old man was given the job of manning the iced-tea cart. But what he really did was watch while the ladies brought out foil-covered hot casseroles and loaded the long tables.

He stood beside us while we waited, handicapping the choices. He could spot what was in a dish just by the color of the bowl. Mrs. So and So's tomato pudding, Mary Ruth Whosit's hot chicken salad.

He pointed at one and told us confidently that it was a particular woman's carrot casserole. "Is that your favorite?" I asked him. "Lord no," he said. "I hate the stuff. But she takes it everywhere. Why, when I die, she'll probably bring it to my funeral."

There's life in a small town for you: When you know what they'll serve when you're gone—even if you don't like it.

The thing that makes me saddest about my failed subject (besides that money thing) is all the history I'm now holding. There have been books on funeral history and funeral rituals, and whole shelves are written about grief. But there really hasn't been a thoroughly researched book on funeral foods that stitches it all together.

When I first started on the subject, everyone thought it was going to be a Southern book. We Southerners think we're legendary for our funeral feeds. Listen to Kate Campbell's song "Funeral Food," with its upbeat refrain: "We sure eat good when someone dies."

But it isn't a Southern thing. It predates the South, it predates America. It even predates most of European civilization. If you think Southerners put on a feed, look at what they do in Mexico, or China, or Greece.

But since this is a Southern publication, we'll skip all that. If you want to understand funeral food in the South, you have to start in the British Isles in the Middle Ages, where so many Southern rituals started.

Early funeral feasts were a way to commune with the dead and spread peace among the living. The passing of a feudal lord meant honoring his memory with a feast, but also sharing his bounty with the mourners and starting a relationship with his successor.

It was called an "arvil" or an "averil," a word that traces to at least the ninth century and probably came to England from Scandinavia. It comes from the phrase "heir ale," a toast to the new heir as well as a farewell tribute to his predecessor. Although it may have started as a simple toast, it became a full-fledged feed, with the family's honor resting on the quality and quantity of the food.

Like all rituals, what started with the upper classes worked its way down. Funeral feasts spread and became significant burdens on the middle class. In 1367, the Council of York forbade "those guilty games and follies and all those perverse customs which transformed a house of tears into a house of laughing and excess."

Those early European settlers of America, the Pilgrims, were just as stern in their funeral observances as they were in their religious beliefs. Puritan funerals sometimes didn't even involve the church, for fear of appearing "papist." However, the Dutch settlers in New Amsterdam had no such qualms. Early New York and Philadelphia, and much of Pennsylvania, gained reputations for elaborate funerals, a tradition that worked its way south.

Rural isolation shaped much of Southern culture. Our legendary hospitality stemmed from the sheer necessity of sheltering travelers who might be days between towns, and from being able to depend on that same welcome if you traveled yourself.

Notice the order of importance in this description of public gatherings in Phillip Alexander Bruce's book *Social Life in Virginia in the Seventeenth Century*: "The horse race, the funeral, the wedding, the meeting at church on Sunday, the general muster and county court day."

In *Women's Life and Work in the Southern Colonies*, Julia Cherry Spruill explained why funerals were more important than weddings: "Funerals, though often sad occasions, furnished opportunities for reunions of friends and relatives and for much feasting and drinking. Invitations were issued as for weddings, and guests came from far and near. The family of the deceased, feeling a solemn obligation to entertain liberally those who had come to pay him their last respects, provided quantities of food and drink, the cost of which was sometimes greatly disproportionate to the value of his estate."

That cost was so great that the food expended at funerals was sometimes accounted for in the estate inventory, giving us rare records of what was served. My friend James Jordan, a historian and museum curator, found this in the 1779 estate of Timothy Clear, a merchant in New Bern, North Carolina: "No. 3, case with 10 bottles of them full of wine—expended at his funeral. . . . No. 6, one iron-bound case, key found, contains 11 bottles, 6 full wine . . . used at his funeral . . . One half keg used—ditto."

For the funeral of John Griggs of York County, Virginia, in 1675, the value of the food at the funeral equaled the value of sixteen hundred pounds of tobacco and included turkeys, geese, and other poultry; a pig, several bushels of flour, twenty pounds of butter, sugar and spices, and twelve gallons of different kinds of spirits.

Funerals were entertainment in a remote wilderness where a chance to gather was almost as precious as the life being observed. This was not overlooked by the living in making arrangements for their own passing. The 1650 will of Thomas Wall of Surry County, Virginia, gave instructions for firing over his grave "three volleys of shot for the entertainment of those who came."

The combination of firing over graves and heavy drinking apparently led to predictable consequences. In 1668, the court in Lower Norfolk, Virginia, banned shooting over graves unless there was someone on hand to regulate it.

Southerners do everything to excess, and drinking at funerals was no exception. The problem of funeral drunkenness became so grave that it was targeted in temperance campaigns. The Presbyterian Synod, meeting in Fayetteville, North Carolina, in 1815, recommended that "the use of ardent spirits at funerals be entirely abolished."

Slaves were also likely to imitate, as closely as possible, the observances of their owners. In *Antebellum North Carolina*, Guion Griffis Johnson writes, "In the early antebellum period, it was customary with the black population, as well as the white, to have a feast at the time of the funeral."

The Reverend James Jenkins, a Methodist circuit rider in the Carolinas, apparently thought these feasts were carried past the point of decency: "They would have a great supper, and after this what they called a play for the dead, which was nothing but a frolic, which lasted to the dawn of the day, when they went to the grave of the deceased, making great lamentation over it, and broke a bottle of spirits on the head board, or if this [spirits] could not be had, meal and water were substituted."

After reading that, imagine my interest when I met a reader in Hickory, North Carolina, whose parents came from Africa. She told me her family's tradition always included pouring liquor into the ground at a funeral. If it wasn't allowed at the cemetery, she said, they would dig a small hole in the backyard and do it there.

In black society after slavery, funerals took on even greater social significance. The cost gave rise to burial societies, which predate Emancipation but took off in the late nineteenth century. The Brown Fellowship Club in Charleston was one, founded in 1790.

Typically, members paid a small amount weekly, as little as ten cents, and the society provided funeral, casket, hearse, and tombstone. Many of these groups had strict rules, treasurers, and fines if you didn't attend another member's funeral. The societies also organized women and provided them with aprons, so they could serve the funeral feast.

Today, we hand over so much of our funeral feasts to caterers or take-out. The home-fried chicken has given way to buckets of KFC. We think we just don't have time to get anything ready.

Our grandmothers didn't let time and the suddenness of death stop them. So many elderly women have told me about always keeping something on hand for a bereavement call. My friend Alicia Ross, a food writer in Raleigh, once told me about her grandmother's "death shelf." In her grandmother's deep freezer, there was a shelf set aside for food. If she made a pound cake, she'd cut it in half and freeze part of it, or she'd divide casseroles into two portions and freeze one. When someone died, all she had to do was grab and go.

Alicia and her cousins laughed at this. But when her grandmother died, they suddenly realized they had no cakes or casseroles. The wisdom of the "death shelf" is obvious.

Funeral food is not just about feeding masses of mourners. The rituals of it serve many purposes. Just as the old English arvil was considered important to the honor of a man's family, you can tell a man's standing in the community by the number of dishes his widow has to return after his funeral.

It doesn't matter, really, whether it's a carrot casserole or a take-out bucket of chicken. Funeral food has never been about feeding the body.

It's about feeding the soul.

Sad Streaks and Weepy Meringues

Sarah Anne Loudin Thomas

Illness, death, disease and even divorce
bring out the mixing bowls, the spoons,
the flour, the sugar and the speckled brown eggs.
Good women converge in kitchens on far
sides of town, all for the expression
of love and sorrow, sadness and hope.
They consult stained cookbooks, faded cards
and memories sharpened with use to concoct
something that will stave off the hunger for
knowing what comes next—what comes
after we get through this . . .

And when the pound cake isn't quite done,
with a soft, moist middle that invites us
to sink down and find an almost peace—
When the sugar in the meringue doesn't
quite melt, and caramel drops bloom like
smoky topaz tears—That's when love
and sadness meet the perfect measure,
filling our sorrowing hearts,
if only for a mouthful.

Malabsorption Syndrome

Marianne Worthington

In the end, she starved to death;
the food she had savored and craved
her long life stopped nourishing her.

*If only I had me a green dollar for every garden
I've worked and raised,* she would say.
All those truck patches teeming
with greens and beans,
potatoes, beets and okra, cabbage,
tomatoes, squash, peppers, peas
and cukes, carrots, pumpkins and melons,
leafy lettuce and little spring onions.

Beyond the vegetable earth she knew
orchards and trees dripping fruit,
her applesauce and canned peaches were legend.
She relished cooking every part of a pig,
could kill a chicken fast and neat,
have it plucked, cleaned and fried
in time for weekday dinner.
Her favorite supper of corn dodgers
and sweet milk was all she could eat
at the last, though none of us could fry
the hoecakes to suit her. Even coffee turned
on her, the daily drink she took strong
and black with one saccharine tablet fished

from her jeweled pillbox, dropping
in the tiny white pellet to sweeten the heat.

From her nursing home bed
hollow-cheeked and hungry for death
she dreams of her lilac sunbonnet
and racing her brothers to the garden,
the flat-bottomed harvest basket swinging
empty from her stocky arm.

African American Foodways
Food, Fear, Race, Art, and the Future

Ari Weinzweig

I'm sorry it's taken me so long to write this. Fear is a powerful thing, and I let it get in my way for far too long. For me, fear comes in two forms, both of which work their way into my mind on a regular basis. First, and easiest to own up to, there's the sort of fear that's well founded and of obvious value in living in a safe and healthy way. Stuff like "I'm afraid to stick my hand in a fire." Being fearless with something like that, it's safe to say, would be stupid. Then there's the other, less desirable, form of fear that regularly rises up inside my brain and my body. While on the surface this one feels a lot like the first type, it's actually on the opposite end of the emotional spectrum; these are fears that limit, fears that lead to feelings that often hold me back from doing what I need to do.

There are a thousand things that fall into this second category. Progress comes for me from facing them in manageable "bites," usually one or two at a time. This is why I decided to get down to it and actually put fingers to fret board and write something about African American cooking. The truth of the matter—let me get it over with—is that I have a pretty deep hesitation in tackling the subject. I'm not an African American. And, because it's not my heritage, I have this fear of showing disrespect for African American culture, a feeling that I should never presume to know what I haven't lived—a fear that's kept me away from doing the right thing, from doing the writing I know that I need to do.

Fear, though, is only the negative part of the picture. I also want to build communication and positive connections among different groups of people. I want to bring people together over stuff that they often avoid, and I want to do it in ways that might, in some small fashion or another, make a positive difference in our larger community. Ultimately, I hope that, through my work at Zingerman's in Ann Arbor, Michigan, I can help close gaps by providing opportunities for people to connect in caring conversations over coffee, cornmeal, and cake.

As I pondered all this, I realized I'd had similar, if less loaded, sorts of hesitations when it came to writing about Italian, Spanish, or French foods for the first time. I'm not from any of those places, and yet I've gotten over that fear, now writing and teaching at length about all those cultures. I'd also successfully taken on this challenge by writing about foods that were completely alien to my upbringing. Having kept kosher, my family certainly wasn't allowed access to oysters or country ham when I was a child, but I've now written and taught about them and served them regularly for many years. I even have a whole book coming out on bacon.

Studying, learning, cooking, and teaching are actually the highest forms of honor I can pay to anyone's beliefs, culture, or, in this case, cooking. Learning, for me at least, begets liveliness, which in turn creates more education, better food, and stronger connections to the people from whom I learn.

In 2004 I attended the Southern Foodways Symposium in Oxford, Mississippi. The theme was "Southern Food in Black and White." The symposium took up the rarely discussed but very important relationship between race and food in the South. I have very vivid memories of that conference. Bernard Lafayette, a cofounder of the Student Nonviolent Coordinating Committee (SNCC) and a leader in the Civil Rights Movement, talked about food he ate while he was jailed in Mississippi. His strongest memory was of ice cream, brought by a friendly white guard whom Lafayette later helped by assisting with the man's daughter's college application.

Jazz musician Olu Dara, another Mississippi native who now lives in New York City, was back in his home state for the first time in decades. To my taste he left more wisdom on the table in half an hour of sharing thoughts than I'd heard in one place in a long time. "Racism doesn't scare me," he said. "It's harmful to the person who has it, not so much to the person at whom it's directed."

Writer Marcie Ferris shared a story she'd learned from filmmaker Steve Channing, who produced a documentary about the lunch counter sit-in at the Woolworth's in Greensboro, North Carolina. After the film had come out, the Greensboro Four spoke with contemporary high school students throughout North Carolina. At the end of one session they asked if any of the students had any questions. For an awkward minute or two, no one said anything. Finally one student raised his hand and asked, "If they'd let you order, what would you have ordered?" The answer: "A piece of pie. I just wanted a piece of pie." The story still makes me cry rereading my notes now.

While I didn't grow up with oysters, ham, or bacon, I did grow up with books. I loved them as a kid, and I love them even more now as an adult. Whenever I start to write on pretty much any subject, I go to my ever-larger stacks and see what comes up that might be relevant. Because I never quite seem to make time to shelve them in any organized way, I don't ever really know what I'll find, but I always find something interesting.

First on my stack when I went to work on this essay—literally right on top of one of the ten or twelve piles close at hand at that time—was a short book called *Art and Fear*, by David Bayles and Ted Orland. I'd gotten it as a gift, but I'd put off reading it for six months. Given the internal struggle I was having, rustling up the courage to write on African American foodways, I couldn't really resist reading it for the title alone. According to the authors, "these fears obviously have less to do with art than they do with the artist." What separates artists from ex-artists, the authors explained, "is that those who challenge their fears, continue; those who don't, quit." If I'd needed any reinforcement in my belief that fighting through my fear was the right thing to do, Bayles and Orland were offering it up to me. "Your job," they conclude, "is to develop an imagination of the possible."

Nearby in the stack, coincidentally, was my copy of Malinda Russell's *A Domestic Cookbook*. Published in 1866, it was the first cookbook written by an African American in the United States. Russell was a fascinating figure. Struggling to make ends meet and wanting to escape the struggles of the post–Civil War South, she moved to Michigan, which she refers to as "the Garden of the West." Her slim but very significant volume says a lot about how much African American cooking of that era had already incorporated popular American recipes: She includes dishes like Irish potato custard, Indian pudding, and charlotte russe, which hardly had roots in Africa.

From there the search through the stacks got even more intriguing. Five down from Russell's book, in a pile of small pamphlets, I came upon something called *The Southern Cook Book of Fine Old Dixie Recipes*. Written by three women I know nothing about, it came out in 1935, nearly seventy years after Russell's work. The light brown paper cover looked innocent enough—a nice line drawing of a pretty white woman in high-heeled boots and flowing skirts, carrying what looks like a roasted turkey, on what I assume is a silver platter.

Without anything other than normal curiosity, I started casually flipping through the book. Many of the recipes are pretty much what one would expect: Corn cakes, Savannah stewed prunes, and angel food cake weren't much more than a mental shrug of the shoulders. But then my attention was piqued by a recipe for Pickanniny Doughnuts. Discomfort started to set in. From there the strange feelings only got stranger—aside from the recipes, on most of the pages there were caricatures of black people. Often the drawings were accompanied by "Poems and Spirituals," many of which were loaded up, in what were clearly not considered controversial ways, with words like "niggers" and "darkies" and assorted other racist images and stereotypes.

I guess I shouldn't have been surprised. Racism is hardly a secret. But this material was showing up in a cookbook published in 1935, five years after my parents were born and seventy years after the end of the Civil War. Seeing it here hit me in a weird way, one that every African American—cook or otherwise—has, I'm sure, experienced many times. As I flipped through the book, I realized I wasn't breathing right. Cookbook or not, to me this was scary. Political manifestos are one thing; you can find antagonistic material written in support of almost every crazy cause you can imagine. But when racism and stereotypes are so "normal" that they show up in an innocent-looking collection of recipes, that tells a whole lot more about a culture. Maybe it tells more than one would, in the moment, even want to know.

Having been studying it for most of my adult life, I've learned that every culture and cuisine—American, African American, Jewish, and otherwise—has been formed by some melting pot of positive and painful experiences, of historical turbulence and upheaval, of local ingredients blended with tastes that arrived from far away. But for me, the most interesting belated glimpse of the obvious in studying the origins of African American cooking came in connection with the dehumanization that was necessary to get people to regard slavery as "okay." Less well known is the dehumanization that took place around literacy. The Slave Code of 1740 prohibited South Carolinians from teaching slaves how to write; by 1814 they weren't allowed to teach reading, either. Books back then might have been telling tales, but South Carolina blacks were banned from learning them. People went to jail (and worse) for breaking the code.

TURNING THE TIDE

But the point of this piece is to get past the fear and make connections, to stop allowing the sinister parts of our past to stay in the closet, culinary or otherwise. Our focus on the food at Zingerman's, where I work, almost always starts in the past, learning about and preparing traditional foods. But our organizational efforts are, more often than not, fixed on the future, working to agree upon, and then build, a vision of the future that we desire and can believe in. Blending ideas and insights from the books I'd read with the opportunity to put traditional foods—and their stories—in front of our customers, I fixed on the idea that the antidote to past dehumanization has to be a future of *rehumanization*—that is, to take things out of stereotypes, out of generalizations, out of black and white and into the grayness that is the reality of life, filled with feelings and stories and real people with real pleasures and life's everyday problems.

Although it wasn't in my stack when I started this essay, *The Historical Cookbook of the American Negro* is a work of great import in the study of African American foodways. First published in 1958 by the National Council of Negro Women (NCNW), it is all about the positive dimensions of people and the foods they prepare and enjoy. I don't have an original copy, but fortunately a very nice reprint came out in 2000. Like *The Southern Cook Book of Fine Old Dixie Recipes*, the cover is rather unremarkable: a pleasant, soft yellow with dark red script and a drawing of a classically frosted cake on a platter. The two books are about the same height and width, and if I were organizing them by size, they could logically be shelved side by side. Given the strange workings of my brain, I start wondering if that's good or bad. Is integration of cookbooks a positive thing? Would the spirit of *The Historical Cookbook* be diminished if it had to sit in close proximity to the racist recipe writing in *The Southern Cook Book*? Or would it be appropriate punishment, so to speak, for the writers of *The Southern Cook Book* if one were to put their work on an integrated shelf, sitting day after day right up against one of the first cookbooks fueled by an overt statement of pride in the black culinary heritage?

The Historical Cookbook is a fascinating work. Sue Bailey Thurman, chair of the NCNW, wrote in the introduction of "what we consider a new, unique and 'palatable' approach to history." While *The Southern Cook Book* contributes mightily in its original setting to radical racism, *The Historical Cookbook* is all about rehumanization.

Although the sizes and covers seem somewhat similar, the subtitle of *The Historical Cookbook* makes it clear that these are two very different volumes: "The classic year-round celebration of black heritage, from Emancipation Proclamation Breakfast Cake to Wandering Pilgrim's Stew." The book is actually not all that dissimilar in structure to *The Southern Cook Book*. It has recipes, of course, but also bits of background, illustrations, and some photos. But where the earlier book features Confederate Coffeecake, the first recipe in *The Historical Cookbook* is Emancipation Proclamation Breakfast Cake, and the recipe appears next to photographs of Abraham Lincoln and Sojourner Truth.

As with Malinda Russell's book, many recipes are simple dishes that Americans of any origin might have eaten, such as "Red, White and Blue Fruit Cocktail," with honeydew melon, frozen raspberries, blueberries, and sugar. There are recipes from Howard University sororities for cookies and punch. There are also foods of old and new African American roots woven into the book—a South Carolina Lowcountry pilau; Hopping (interestingly not "*Hoppin'*") John; and peanut dishes that date to Booker T. Washington's time.

"Cornbread Harriet Tubman; Our 'Aunt Harriet's' Favorite Dish" isn't particularly noteworthy in itself—it's cornbread made with salt pork, soured milk, and a bit of brown sugar. But the headnote, written by Vivian Carter Mason, who grew up knowing Harriet Tubman, is fascinating. It's all about fear and food. "We shivered," she wrote, "as we heard the sound of horses' hoofs, fearing the men searching the woods and highways for black Harriet and her runaways. That they never caught up with her was always the triumphant ending of a fearful and frightening recital of days full of danger and suffering. Then mother would call us to dinner, and as the lamps cast a bright light on the huge kitchen, with the teaming bowls of rich soup and the crisp cornbread piled high, it was not hard to imagine that in the darkness outside someone was still searching for Harriet and would take us too." Fear, food, race, art, and the future—all there in one paragraph about people and a plate of cornbread from the past.

My hope is that by writing and teaching, by cooking and caring, we will successfully bring more light, more openness to the African American experience of cooking and foodways. In creating a vision of a better tomorrow, that "imagination of the possible" that Bayles and Orland wrote about, I come back to a few sentences that Sue Bailey Thurman put down in her introduction to *The Historical Cookbook of the American Negro*. Referring to the book and the people mentioned in it—both those who were famous, and those who were known to barely anyone other than their families and friends—Thurman writes, "Those included were selected as symbols of the past who sought only to preserve the life of the future, knowing that the future must be guaranteed in the present. We are their future."

Celebrations

Juneteenth Jamboree

Robb Walsh

Mama Sugar was wearing a straw cowboy hat and a bright red and yellow apron over her cotton dress when I found her on the kitchen porch. She was stirring a soup pot full of okra and tomatoes on a two-burner propane stove, which had been set up under the eaves to keep it out of the rain. Every burner on the stove inside the house was already occupied. Mama Sugar and her daughters had been cooking all week.

"These are my own homegrown tomatoes," she bragged with a big smile, holding up a spoonful by way of a greeting. Her mood hadn't been so cheerful when I called her earlier in the day. A huge thunderstorm had moved across East Texas that morning of Juneteenth. The television news showed cars stalling out in deep puddles on the highways.

The unpaved road that leads to Mama Sugar's 5 Bar S Ranch, a sixty-seven acre horse farm on the outskirts of Houston, would turn to mud if it kept raining. And it would really be hard to reach if there was any more flooding. The big Juneteenth parade in Galveston, forty-five miles away, had already been canceled because of rising water.

But by the time I arrived in the early afternoon, the rain had tapered off. Now the only showers came when a gust of wind shook the cottonwood and pecan trees shading the yard. The afternoon turned cloudy and cool, which is as good as it gets on June 19 in East Texas. I had been looking forward to this day ever since I first met Mama Sugar about four months before, while researching black cowboys and their foodways for a cowboy cookbook. Although you'd never know it from watching Hollywood Westerns, a significant number of Texas cowboys have been black. And African Texans take great pride in their western heritage.

When I quizzed black cowboys about cooking, they sent me to see Mama Sugar. Not only did she grow up raising cattle in East Texas, she is also a nominee for induction into the National Cowgirl Hall of Fame. But most importantly for my purposes, she is one hell of a cook. When I was through copying down her recipes and marveling over the downhome flavors of her food, I wangled an invitation to her famous Juneteenth party. With the possible exception of Christmas, Juneteenth is the biggest celebration in the Texas black cowboy community.

Juneteenth (short for June 19) commemorates the day in 1865 when Union general Gordon Granger arrived in Galveston and announced the freeing of the slaves. For more than a century, the occasion was marked by African Texans with parades, pageants, and barbecues. Because blacks were often barred from holding festivities in public parks, parties were held out in the country on private ranches. Horses and cowboy gear became a part of the tradition. Juneteenth had largely died out by the early 1960s, but it was revived on June 19, 1968, the final day of the Poor People's Campaign march on Washington, D.C., when the Reverend Ralph Abernathy called for people of all races to show solidarity. Since then, it has spread across the country, and Juneteenth became an official state holiday in Texas in 1980. The spirit of the holiday combines elements of Martin Luther King Jr. Day, Passover, and the Fourth of July: It's a celebration of African American heritage (including Emancipation) and a barbecue blowout.

With the threat of rain over, Mama Sugar's husband, Ron Sugar, set up the sound system, and soon the 1980s disco hit "Funkytown" was blaring from the nightclub-size speakers on the big wooden front porch. Country, jazz, soul, and pop would boom out over the ranch for the rest of the afternoon and into the night. Gathered on the lawn were some of the early arrivals. While their mothers were busy cooking and setting up the buffet, a gaggle of teenage granddaughters were roaring with laughter at the expense of their cousin Nathan Sanders, a tall, muscular young man of nineteen. The girls were all dressed western-style in blue jeans and cotton shirts, some with cowboy hats. They were making fun of Nathan's hip-hop outfit of chartreuse baggy shorts and matching shirt accented with a backward ball cap.

I asked LaDraun Campbell, a friend of the family who was manning the two barbecue trailers parked under the carport, what all the hilarity was about. "Nathan don't rodeo," he said. "He thinks he's a big-city boy now," he teased in a loud voice that made Nathan roll his eyes and the girls laugh even harder.

City boy or not, Nathan is one of the most fearless riders in the family. Mama Sugar and most of her guests belong to the Southwest Trail Riders Association, an umbrella organization for black saddle clubs. Mama Sugar's gang, the Sugar Shack Trailblazers Riding Rodeo Club, was formed in 1983. Her kids all ride, and her grandchildren grew up on horseback.

At my request, the barbecue man opened the steel doors of the five-foot smoker and showed me what he had going on. "I always barbecue on Juneteenth," Campbell said as we checked out the smoked meats. He grew up in Lane City, a small farming community about half an hour southwest of Houston. He's been barbecuing since the age of eleven and now runs a company called L&D BBQ and Catering, in Missouri City, Texas. Campbell showed me Mama Sugar's "Margarita ribs," which are rubbed with tequila, then marinated in Margarita mix. We cut off a couple of pieces of meat from the skinny end of the rack. The pork was still a little tough, but the tart and peppery flavor made my cheeks tingle.

In the big trailer, there were a whole lot of briskets—I couldn't count them for all the thick smoke. Campbell had rubbed them with a commercial seasoning called Fiesta Brisket Rub, and he was smoking them for five hours, fat side up, at around three hundred degrees. The wood was mostly oak, with some pecan added for its sweeter flavor, he said. After smoking, the briskets would be wrapped in aluminum foil to keep the meat from getting too dark; it would also trap escaping steam, accelerating the cooking and making the beef fall-apart tender.

As the skies cleared, cars and pickup trucks started arriving, and soon there were people milling around on the broad expanse of St. Augustine grass that surrounds Mama Sugar's house. Three men walked over to the side yard to drink their Budweisers and admire a beautiful five-month-old tan-and-white paint colt named Duke. To the delight of a dozen or so small children, Ron Sugar led the two gentlest horses out of the barn and parked them under a shade tree. He threw a saddle on the Morgan called Ole Black and tightened the girth until the leather creaked. While he was at it, the kids gathered around the horses to pet them. One of the girls climbed up on the sorrel named Frisky and lay flat on her back. The bigger kids got to ride first, then put the littler ones in the saddle in front of them. Soon, an older boy was charging around at a gallop. "This is all these kids want to do out here," said Ron Sugar with a laugh.

Energized by the arrival of family and friends, Mama Sugar buzzed around, supervising the cooking. She moved pretty fast for a large woman with a cane. The okra in the pot on the porch had come from the grocery store, she said, but she needed some more for the purple-hull peas. I followed her as she waded into the green sea of her garden, walking in between the rows. Gently pushing the spiked leaves of young okra plants back and forth, she found some fuzzy baby okra pods and snapped them off their stems. "I usually let them get bigger than this," she said, rolling them in her palm. But the tender little pods would be perfect as an accent for the peas. She also picked a bright green corkscrew-shaped cayenne to cut up for the pea pot.

Mama Sugar, whose formal name is Nathan Jean Whitaker Sanders, has been celebrating Juneteenth since she was a small child. She was brought up from the age of six by her aunt and uncle on a cattle ranch and farm in the tiny community of County Line. They raised hogs and chickens as well as cattle. Watermelon, tomatoes, and peanuts were sold for cash in town. The family also harvested corn, okra, sweet potatoes, black-eyed peas, pole beans, and ribbon cane for their home kitchen. The ribbon cane was taken to a local mill where it was crushed and cooked down into syrup. Cane syrup was the only sweetener available, and Mama Sugar grew up using it for everything. Today, when she cooks sweet potatoes, she still sweetens them with cane syrup. And when she can't find it in the store, she makes her own with cane sugar and water.

I asked her what Juneteenth had been like in her childhood. "We did the same thing we're doing here, except we did it at County Line Baptist Church," Mama Sugar said, looking out over her front lawn. Between 100 and 200 people came to those church gatherings. "My uncle would kill a goat, clean it, and hang it in a tree until it was time for the barbecue," Mama Sugar remembered. She fondly recalled the desserts, which she ticked off on her fingers: "peach cobbler, banana pudding, cakes, pecan pie, sweet-potato pie, and sweet-potato cobbler—nobody makes that anymore!"

"What did the preacher at County Line Baptist say Juneteenth was about?" I asked Mama Sugar. "He said it was about being delivered from slavery," she replied. "About how we used to work in the fields and eat outside all the time."

I asked her how she explained it to her kids and grandkids, and she said she used stories from her own life. After she graduated from high school, she moved to Houston and worked in restaurants and as a maid in people's homes while raising five daughters. One moment in her life made her understand emancipation and equality. "I remember the first day a woman I worked for asked me to sit down at the table with them. I had my own dishes there and I always ate in the kitchen. But then one day she just changed her mind.

"I tell the kids Juneteenth is about how we don't have to go to the back door at white folks' houses anymore. I think they understand."

As dinnertime approached, LaDraun Campbell started bringing barbecue meats up to the porch so Mama Sugar could do the carving. She unwrapped a brisket from its foil and put it on a cutting board she had set up on a card table, so she could carve while sitting down. I managed to sneak a few tidbits of brisket when she wasn't looking. The meat was juicy, with a deep smoke flavor. Mama Sugar cut it into nice thin slices with her favorite carving knife, but you probably could have carved this brisket with a butter knife. The buffet, set out on a pair of tables, included her okra and homegrown tomatoes and those purple-hull peas with baby okra, peppers, and ham hocks, but there were also green beans, pintos, smoked corn on the cob, white bread, jalapeño cornbread, pickles, onions, and barbecue sauce. Dessert—three sweet-potato pies, one pecan pie, and a huge container of banana pudding—stood ready as well.

There were patches of blue in the sky by the time the sun started to set, and the party was in full swing. Suddenly the music stopped and Ron Sugar came over the sound system asking, "Are you ready to bless the food?"

The kids in line to ride the horses were shushed. The men holding Budweisers over by the barbecue smokers bowed their cowboy hats. The domino players at the card table under the porch paused and put down their tiles.

"Heavenly and most gracious Father, we come to you on this day that you have glorified . . ." the Reverend Ron Sugar's eloquent invocation for Juneteenth began. When he said "amen," at the end, everyone in earshot gave a loud "amen" in response. Then he said, "Let's eat!"

Sweet-Potato Cobbler

Mama Sugar says this dish was common at Juneteenth celebrations years ago but is now seldom seen.

Serves 8 to 10.

For Filling

2½ pounds sweet potatoes
1 quart water
¾ cup pure cane syrup
½ cup packed light brown sugar
1 teaspoon ground cinnamon

½ teaspoon ground allspice
¼ teaspoon salt
2 tablespoons unsalted butter
1 teaspoon pure vanilla extract

For Biscuit Dough

3 cups all-purpose flour
4½ teaspoons baking powder
¾ teaspoon salt

¾ stick (6 tablespoons) cold
  unsalted butter, cut into
  ½-inch cubes
1¼ cups whole milk

Make filling: Peel sweet potatoes, then halve lengthwise and slice crosswise ¼ inch thick. Combine potatoes with remaining filling ingredients in a wide 4- to 5-quart pot and simmer, covered, until potatoes are almost tender, 6 to 8 minutes. Transfer potatoes with a slotted spoon to a bowl and boil liquid, uncovered, until reduced to about 2 cups (it will become syrupy), 20 to 25 minutes.

Make dough and bake cobbler: Put oven rack in middle position and preheat oven to 375 degrees. Whisk together flour, baking powder, and salt in a bowl. Blend in butter with your fingertips or a pastry blender until mixture resembles coarse meal. Stir in milk with a fork until a dough forms. Gather dough into a ball, then turn out onto a lightly floured surface and gently knead 7 or 8 times. Divide dough into 2 pieces, then form each into a disk. Roll out 1 disk with a floured rolling pin into a 14-inch round (about 1/8 inch thick) and fit into bottom and about halfway up side of Dutch oven, pressing against side to help it adhere. Roll out remaining dough into another 14-inch round, then trim to a 12-inch round with a paring knife, reserving trimmings.

Spoon half of sweet potatoes evenly into dough-lined Dutch oven, then top with 1 layer dough trimmings, cutting and fitting trimmings to almost cover potatoes. Add remaining potatoes, then pour syrup over potatoes and cover with 12-inch dough round, pressing edges together to seal. Cut 3 steam vents in top with paring knife.

Bake cobbler until top is golden, 40 to 45 minutes. Cool to warm before serving, about 30 minutes (dough will absorb most of syrup).

Adapted from Nathan Jean Whitaker Sanders.

The Sacred Feast

Kathryn Eastburn

I set out from Nashville on the first day of July, driving southeast along a winding, climbing road through a spectacle of green hillsides, then heading down just outside Chattanooga and entering Alabama. The roadsides were crowded with plywood fireworks stands, each claiming to have the best prices for "black cats" and bottle rockets, as I drove toward Henagar—a tiny settlement on Sand Mountain, a rocky hump rising directly across from heavily forested and river-laced Lookout Mountain, in Alabama's DeKalb County—a part of the state called, for obvious reasons, the highlands.

I was on my way to the annual Henagar-Union Convention, two days of gospel fueled by a potluck feast each day at noon. I was introduced to this weekend of all-day singing and "dinner on the grounds" three years before when I began researching the Baptist hymns of my Kentucky childhood (at age ten, I was the piano player at my grandfather's little church in Bowling Green). What I found at Henagar's Liberty Baptist Church was something different from what I'd grown up with: Many of the hymns were the same, but they were sung a cappella, in the haunting four-part harmonies known as Sacred Harp.

Sacred Harp is a form of shape-note singing, based on music written not according to conventional notation but with triangles, ovals, squares, and diamonds representing the musical syllables fa, sol, la, and mi. The practice uses a four-note system created in England and brought in the eighteenth century to America, where it was popularized by prolific New England tune-smiths and evolved into its present form. Shape-note singing traveled south and west in the early nineteenth century with itinerant music teachers who visited small rural churches to teach the simplified method of sight reading to the untrained. *The Sacred Harp*, a collection of hymns and anthems first published in Georgia in 1844, remains the songbook most widely used in the tradition, and the Sacred Harp Publishing Company continues to revise and publish new editions to this day.

Until the mid-twentieth century, Sacred Harp's stronghold was the rural Deep South, in places like Henagar. But as families dispersed to larger cities and other parts of the country, and as a preference for religious music accompanied by organ and piano developed, the singings dwindled in number and popularity. The form has enjoyed a revival of interest in recent years, as university music departments and folksingers have embraced it, and regular singings are held in community centers, living rooms, churches, and classrooms across the United States.

On Sand Mountain, families like the Woottens, the Iveys, and the Lacys have been singing Sacred Harp for over a hundred years. When I arrive in Henagar—a place that has become legendary among Sacred Harp enthusiasts because of its community of singers, the acoustics of its small Liberty Baptist Church, and the remarkable midday spread of foods at its singing get-togethers—I head first to the home of Tony and Sandy Ivey, who are busy preparing their dishes for the next day's potluck. Tony is the current pastor of Liberty Baptist, and he and his wife, both in their mid-forties, are lifelong singers. "I started singing Sacred Harp when I was six or seven," he says. "I stayed at my granddad's as much as I could and went to singings with him." Sandy also grew up visiting her grandparents and singing on Sand Mountain. The Iveys' son Scott and daughter Rachel carry on the tradition. "I guess Scott could sing by the time he could talk," Sandy says with a laugh.

When I arrive, Tony, a quiet man with a shy smile, has cranked up his brand-new smoker to cook four Boston butt pork roasts, rubbed with his signature dry mix of salt, sugar, black pepper, cayenne, paprika, lemon peel, and Accent. He tends to the smoker from a lawn chair beneath a stand of tall cypress trees, occasionally throwing sticks of apple, pecan, and hickory wood—all from local trees—onto the fire. Meanwhile, inside the house, Sandy is fixing chicken and dumplings the way her grandmother taught her (the dumplings hand-rolled as thin as noodles). There is already a pot of baked beans—topped with strips of thick, smoked bacon—simmering in the oven, and the heady smell of yeast rolls, rising on the side counter beneath a tea towel, fills the comfortable kitchen, cluttered with Sandy's collection of old dishes. "The recipe for the rolls came from the women of my church," she says. "When Tony and I got married, they made up a cookbook of all their favorite recipes."

As dusk settles, lightning bugs rise from the lace cap and oak leaf hydrangeas surrounding the Ivey home. Crickets sing loudly. Tony settles in to tend his barbecue. He'll let it smoke all night, he says. It should be just right by morning.

I arrive at the church early on Saturday morning as an assortment of pickup trucks, vans, and rental cars with license plates from as far afield as Michigan and New York begins to pull into the parking lot. A large crowd of Iveys, Woottens, and other Sand Mountain singers slap backs, hug, and shake hands in greeting. The men of the church set out tables beneath towering oak trees and around the outdoor tabernacle where church picnics are held. A few visitors wander through the tidy church cemetery, as the damp morning air softens the outlines of the tombstones and of the abundant, brightly colored flower arrangements adorning them.

Tony Ivey's grandparents Esther and Andrew, better known as Mommy and Poppy, are buried here. Their family headstone is engraved with names and dates and a slogan that speaks to all who come to Henagar: SINGING IN A BETTER LAND. Other headstones echo the sentiment: HOW CAN I KEEP FROM SINGING? asks one; SINGING PRAISES WITH THE LORD, reads another.

Inside the church, every pew is crammed, shoulder to shoulder. At the front, where the pulpit would normally stand, chairs have been arranged in four sections—for tenors, basses, altos, and trebles—facing inward, forming the "hollow square," in Sacred Harp terminology. In the middle of the square, a volunteer leader calls out the first song number, and the singing rapidly commences. Many singers turn to the announced page but rarely, if ever, look at their books; they know the notes and words by heart.

Outside, Willard Wright, an older man in a knit shirt and a mesh baseball cap, has pulled his truck up onto the lawn, the flatbed loaded with nine ice cream freezers and the fixings for seven different kinds of homemade ice cream, including peach, blueberry, and peanut butter. Throughout the morning, as the singing goes on inside, he pours rock salt over ice while the electric freezers whir. His favorite flavor is the peach, he says, made with fruit grown in Alabama—along with his "secret ingredient," a touch of Nehi peach soda. I sample a bite of the smooth concoction, which slides down sweet and tingly.

Betty Wright helps her husband manage his ice cream freezers and often brings a special fruit punch made from a recipe that dates to the pre–Civil War era. "It looks like lemonade until you drink it," she says. Wright was working in a pharmacy when a friend came in and asked for citric acid and tartaric acid, called for in an old family punch recipe. "I asked her for the recipe and then wrote it down on the back of a paper bag. The flavor blossoms after it sits in the refrigerator a few days, and it freezes well. I just pull it out of the freezer and add water whenever the grandkids come over."

As noon approaches, women start to drift out of the church to unload ice chests and baskets. Soon they have covered one long table, stretching end to end beneath the tabernacle roof, with pots and bowls and casserole dishes. Coy Ivey, a local farmer, and his son Rodney put out large aluminum roasting pans packed to the top with Coy's famed oven-cooked pulled pork barbecue. The tender meat is sweet and wet, with a slight cayenne kick. Another huge roasting pan is piled high with deep-fried chicken livers—coated with egg and buttermilk, then rolled in seasoned flour (nothing but White Lily flour will do, says Coy), and fried in vegetable oil in an industrial-size deep fryer. The livers are crisp and brown on the outside, soft and steamy inside.

At one end of the table, Rilla Greeson unveils her coconut layer cake, glowing with a thick coating of glossy white frosting. The creation stands at least six inches tall, commanding attention. Surrounding it are fruit pies, cream pies, meringue pies, and brownies. Reba Dell Windom—who grew up on Sand Mountain but now lives in Brant, Michigan—lays out her rum bundt cake, golden brown and drizzled with a buttery rum and sugar glaze. "Mother always brought that rum cake to the singing, until she passed away," says Reba. "A little extra rum in the icing makes us sing better in the afternoon," she adds with a wink.

At high noon, singers pour out through the open church doorway and form a long line leading to the buffet table. There is a steady buzz of conversation, punctuated by sharp laughs and the trill of a mockingbird overhead, as they load their plates. I try everything—vinegary coleslaw, Sandy's tangy beans, sweet squash casserole, smoky green beans simmered with ham hocks, Coy Ivey's chicken livers and barbecue—trying to save room for Rilla Greeson's coconut cake, whose marshmallow frosting is melting into an ambrosial puddle in the midday sun.

When dinner is over, the dishes are quickly put away and the singing resumes for the afternoon. We turn to number 340 in our books, a hymn called "Odem," written by T. J. Denson in 1935. The voices rise strong, renewed by the feast. Singers stir the air with cardboard fans and sing: "Give me the roses while I live, / Something to cheer me on, / Useless the flowers you may give, / After the soul is gone."

On Sunday morning, Betty Lacy Shepherd, a fit and outgoing sixty-six-year-old, is one of the first to arrive at the church, carrying an ice chest of food, including her signature dish, poor man's caviar—a cold salad of marinated black-eyed peas, bell peppers, and green onions. Betty's mother was an Ivey, and her father, Leonard Lacy, better known as Uncle Leonard, taught many of the Henagar singers how to read shape-note music when they were young children. "I thought everybody sang together and ate like this, until I joined the Air Force and saw the world," says Betty in a raspy alto voice. Having left Alabama at the age of eighteen, Betty returned forty-three years later, to the place where, as she says, "people are so good to me." She now lives in the larger town of Fort Payne, down the mountain, and for many years worked as a cook on a riverboat on the Tennessee River.

Some of the singers from other states have headed home, so the crowd is a bit smaller today and notably more dressed up. There is no sermon—just the singing—but Sunday best is the custom: Ladies have pulled out their hats and men their ties. Sandy Ivey sports a straw hat and a low-waisted cotton dress, a yard sale treasure, imprinted with the stars and stripes of the American flag. She wears it with equal amounts of pride and good humor. We open with song number 278, "Love Shall Never Die," a mournful tune, written in a minor key and sung slowly, but with surprisingly affirmative lyrics. The room vibrates with the tapping of shoe soles on the hardwood floor and the volume of mixed voices.

Before we break for dinner, a memorial service is held for those singers who have passed away in the last year, and a song is offered for the sick and shut-in, led by Alison Ivey, Coy's tall, blond granddaughter, a graduate student at Auburn University studying audiology. Alison's father, David, a well-known teacher of Sacred Harp singing, is the chairman of this annual convention. His wife, Karen, petite and perky, has brought her sweet potato cobbler to the dinner. "I got the recipe from Mrs. Alma Lambert of Oneonta, Alabama," Karen recalls, as she uncovers her enormous enamel dish. Firm slices of bright orange sweet potato, fragrant with nutmeg, mingle with soft dough beneath the top crust. "I wrote the recipe right in the back of my songbook."

At the edge of the crowd, eighty-year-old Loyd Ivey crouches over an old washtub in the back of his pickup truck. He has squeezed some two hundred lemons by hand to provide lemonade for the singing. He makes a mixture from a gallon of pure lemon juice, ten pounds of sugar, and approximately five gallons of water. "No chemicals or nothing," he says; "just water from the well." When the mixture tastes right, he begins to put in ice, stirring the lemonade all the while with a big ladle. At the end of the singing, Loyd takes his washtub home, oils it, and hangs it up on the back porch, where it will stay until the next singing.

A cup of lemonade in hand, I fill my plate from the bowls of pole beans, butter beans, cucumbers, tomatoes, and Gazell Parker's homemade hominy. That rare treat calls for hickory cane corn, which Gazell grows in her garden. An elaborate washing and soaking process involving lye softens and swells the hard corn kernels, which are then cooked at a slow boil. The flavor is unforgettable, smoky and earthbound.

Just as the singers begin to relish the food on their plates, a huge burst of thunder shatters the sky overhead, and a heavy rain begins to come down. Everyone moves into the tabernacle, crowding around the table, as the men of the church unroll plastic sheeting to make temporary walls. A few folks escape into the church, their plates piled with food. "The good thing is we always make it work," says David Ivey, his voice raised to be heard above the storm. He and Karen recall dinners inside the church before the outdoor tabernacle was built, when sheets of plywood were stretched across the pew tops to form tables. No one seems to miss a bite as thunder crashes outside the makeshift dining room. Finally, the rain calms, the tables are cleared, and the afternoon singing commences.

"We had a good dinner again today," says David, leafing through his book toward the song he has chosen to lead. A long round of applause ensues—praise for the meal and those who cooked it. After two more hours of singing and the bittersweet final song, the rain has stopped completely. The clouds have cleared, and mist rises off the broad green field across from the church as the singers say their long good-byes.

The Henagar-Union Convention is over for the eighty-ninth time. Cars are loaded, and the church lot empties, as tired singers head home, their hearts already inclined toward next year's sacred feast.

Sandy's Baked Beans

Before she bakes them in an old-fashioned stoneware bean pot,
Sandy Ivey enlivens her beans with juice from her
"under the sink" homemade sweet pickles.

Serves 8 to 10.

2 28-ounce cans pork and beans
1½ cups light brown sugar
1 cup ketchup
½ cup yellow mustard
½ cup molasses or sorghum

¼ cup juice from a jar of sweet pickles
1 small yellow onion, thinly sliced
4 strips bacon, halved crosswise

Preheat oven to 400 degrees. Put the pork and beans, brown sugar, ketchup, mustard, molasses, and pickle juice into a large ovenproof pot or bean pot and stir well to combine.

Top the bean mixture with onion slices and lay the bacon over the top in a single layer. Bake, uncovered, until the bacon is crisp and the beans are hot and bubbling, about 1 hour. Remove from the oven and allow to cool slightly. Stir the onions and bacon into the beans before serving.

Fresh Peach Ice Cream

"We try to make nine gallons of homemade ice cream for the July singing at Liberty Church every year," says Willard Wright. "The peach is the favorite."

Makes about 1 quart.

1 cup sugar
⅔ cup evaporated milk
1½ cups whole milk, divided
2 eggs

1 large peach, pitted, skinned, and puréed
½ cup peach soda, preferably Nehi
Pinch of salt

Put sugar, evaporated milk, ½ cup of the whole milk, and eggs into a medium saucepan and whisk until well combined. Cook over medium-low heat, stirring constantly, until thickened, about 30 minutes. Strain the mixture through a fine-mesh sieve into a large bowl and set aside to let cool.

Once mixture has cooled, add puréed peach, peach soda, remaining whole milk, and a pinch of salt and stir well.

Pour mixture into an ice cream maker and process according to the manufacturer's directions. Transfer ice cream to a sealable, freezer-safe container and freeze.

Open City

Jessica B. Harris

On the night before Thanksgiving 2007, I paid a visit to the home of my friends the Costas, just as the New Orleans night scents of jasmine and tea olive were beginning to waft in through their kitchen windows. Mary Len Costa was chopping onions for the dressing with a burnt matchstick in her mouth to keep the tears at bay. Her husband, Lou, was puréeing sweet potatoes, and I was happy to roll up my sleeves and pitch in, swirling the orange purée around beige rutabagas and topping the mix with pecan halves to create the casserole that is one of the family's holiday standbys. Their postdebutante daughter, Lenora, on her way to a holiday ball, entered the kitchen in a floor-length formal gown and strapped on an apron to lend a hand for a few minutes.

For more than a decade, I have spent Thanksgiving in New Orleans. It began when my mother and I tired of the turkey-for-two meals we'd grown accustomed to at her Queens, New York, home after my father died. We decided to try something new, and after a rainy time in Barbados and a few New York misses, we found that the Crescent City suited us perfectly, with its rich history, diverse mix of cultures, and bustling restaurant community. The Thanksgiving meals we had were distinctly of this place: elegant, easygoing, and featuring the racy Cajun and rich Creole flavors that distinguish the local cuisine.

Friends in the city, like the Costas, always had space at the table and a warm welcome for my mother and me. One of the warmest came from Leah Chase, a New Orleans culinary icon and co-owner, with her husband Edgar "Dooky" Chase II, of the Dooky Chase restaurant. I'd met Mrs. Chase on my first trip to the city, more than thirty years ago, and over time she became a good friend to my mother and "Aunt Leah" to me.

After my mother's death in 2000, I was left without any living relatives; I longed for the comfort and ritual of a shared family meal. Again, New Orleans came to my aid. In this convivial city, Thanksgiving visits to friends and neighbors are de rigueur, at least among all the people I know. Now I spend the day making my way from house to restaurant to house: appetizers at one place, turkey at another, desserts somewhere else. In the absence of family, traveling around the city like this reminds me of my good fortune in having a large and welcoming family of friends.

I now own a house in the Fauborg Marigny area of the city, and I spend as much time there as I can. Most of my neighborhood was dry ground after Hurricane Katrina, but when I returned for Thanksgiving in 2005, the devastation across the city was nevertheless heartbreaking. Some friends had not returned; others had only just begun rebuilding. Yet those of us who were able gathered around a communal table in the home of my friend Jan Bradford and were thankful for being there. The city had not been spared, but our tradition had; in this we found hope. As for Thanksgiving 2006, it has already receded in memory into a blur of changed plans, halting recuperation, and bruised hopes in the face of a slow recovery and governmental red tape. But progress was in evidence: new traffic lights and street signs in an outlying neighborhood, more tourists in the Quarter, and the return of the Saturday Crescent City Farmers Market. By November 2007 we were inching toward a new normal. In fact, today, after yet another hurricane (Gustav), I look back on that year's Thanksgiving as one of the most memorable of my life.

In the years before Katrina, my New Orleans Thanksgiving always began at breakfast, with a visit from my old friend Kerry Moody. Kerry grew up doing all the baking for his family, which he finally decided was just about enough for a whole lifetime. Now he bakes only once a year, on Thanksgiving. His fluffy yeast rolls, made with a copious quantity of Irish butter, have earned a glowing reputation, and every year, it seems, more friends are angling for a batch. So, Kerry typically starts baking at three o'clock in the morning and spends part of the day delivering piping-hot rolls wrapped in cotton towels to his neighbors and loved ones.

According to our established routine, Kerry awakens me on Thanksgiving with my own allotment of yeast rolls. We sit at my tiny kitchen table, sip chicory-flavored café au lait from mismatched antique porcelain cups, and savor the rolls Kerry has brought over from his kitchen. But in 2007, Kerry, like many of my friends, was still in the midst of renovation. Always resourceful, he'd made arrangements to cook in the kitchen of our friend Patrick Dunne, who lives around the block from me.

Patrick, a dealer in culinary antiques and a decorator, has one of my favorite New Orleans kitchens. Copper pots of all sizes gleam on the shelves in a setting seemingly transported from nineteenth-century Paris. I sat down at a small table in front of the kitchen hearth surrounded by Patrick's friends and his ever-present English bulldog, Clovis; the warmth of the oven and the aroma of the baking rolls put us in a festive mood. As we waited for the rolls, Patrick and I reminisced about our mothers, who had met years ago at a memorable luncheon at Galatoire's. Soon everyone was breaking apart the golden rolls, slathering them with butter, and relishing their chewy crust and slight sweetness. It's always the same: one bite, and memories begin flooding my mind; two, and I know the holiday has arrived.

The Costas are an integral part of my New Orleans extended family, and it is usually at their house, in the lower Garden District neighborhood known as the Muses, that I settle in for my holiday turkey. Their snug unit of mother, father, and only daughter calls to mind my own family; it's an arrangement that makes me feel at home. In 2007, the Costas, too, were still recovering from the storm, their dining room festooned with water stains and falling plaster, and so they were celebrating Thanksgiving around the corner, at the home of their neighbors and good friends the Strachans, whose antebellum house had a dining room large enough for the two tables they needed to accommodate the extra-large assemblage of families and friends. I noted the pinecone baskets and other decorations from Mary Len Costa's collection that were on loan for the day to brighten the room.

Sandy and Eric, the Strachans' adult sons, had decided to be true to Louisiana tradition and fry the turkey. The fryer was set up out in the side yard, and they lowered in a plump bird seasoned with a spicy marinade. The weather had turned seasonably chilly, and after chatting outside with other guests for a while, I checked my watch and gauged that I had just enough time to steal away for appetizers at the home of another friend, Lauren Anderson.

A transplanted Northeasterner like me, Lauren has flourished in our adopted city. Her family had arrived from up and down the eastern seaboard to celebrate Thanksgiving at her home, a Victorian gem shaded by two massive magnolia trees, in the Irish Channel neighborhood, near the Garden District. I brought French saucisson sec and olives, as well as a dish of the spiced pecans I offer guests at my own house. A pinch of Spanish smoked paprika gives them a smoky flavor, while a dash of cinnamon adds an exotic note. They've got just enough heat to make a convincing case for another glass of champagne.

In Lauren's large open kitchen, everyone looked on enthusiastically as our host set out shrimp cocktail and green tomato relish, brought down from Connecticut by Lauren's mother, Betty, and served with cream cheese. Spread on crackers, the sweet-tart tomato mingled perfectly with the mild cheese. When I asked Betty whether her relish came from an old New England recipe, she smiled and said that it was actually the work of local chef Emeril Lagasse. The influence of New Orleans's culinary traditions obviously extends to Thanksgiving tables far beyond the city limits.

By the time I got back to the Strachans', the turkey had just emerged from the fryer; its skin had crisped beautifully and turned a dark caramel color. Mary Len had also brought a bird, which she'd roasted in the oven to a pale gold and decorated with slices of satsuma, a petite, orange-skinned citrus fruit, to go with the satsuma-cranberry relish that is a highlight of the Costas' yearly meal. In Louisiana, the arrival of satsumas signals the start of the holiday season; for a little over a month, in the late fall, satsumas are everywhere. I like them early on, when they're a little tart, but as the season progresses they sweeten, and by Christmas they have a rounder, honeyed flavor.

As turkey-carving time approached, Mary Len and Lenora turned their attention to assembling the first course: creamy, aromatic oyster stew, a Thanksgiving favorite in New Orleans homes as well as at classic restaurants such as Antoine's and Brennan's. Once the oyster stew was ready, the twenty of us took our seats, bowed our heads, and joined hands to say grace. A toast went up to departed friends and family members. The Strachans were spending their first Thanksgiving without the family patriarch, and I realized that the Costas were helping their friends through their sadness in the same generous way that they'd helped me after the death of my mother.

And now the feasting began in earnest. The oyster stew disappeared rapidly as the appointed carver, a family friend, set to work. A spirited debate commenced over whether what we were eating should be referred to as stuffing or as dressing, with a giggle at the fact that the fry boys had used Stove Top brand for their bird. After the main course, Lenora brought out a cushaw pie, prepared from an old recipe she had found in the 1901 edition of the *Picayune's Creole Cook Book.* Cushaw, a crookneck squash that grows throughout the South in the summer and fall, is synonymous with Thanksgiving for many New Orleanians. With its pale, peach-colored flesh, it makes for a delicate variation on the familiar pumpkin pie theme. After another flute of champagne to punctuate the meal, it was time to head out again into the dusk to see Aunt Leah.

Leah Chase's restaurant is in the Tremé neighborhood, the historic heart of New Orleans's African American and Creole culture. Dooky Chase had not fully reopened after Katrina, but when I arrived, Mrs. Chase, her daughter (also named Leah), and her granddaughter Chase were finishing their own meal after a day of serving dinner to a restaurant filled with customers. Dooky Chase is a Thanksgiving institution for many New Orleanians, and the Chases couldn't dream of turning them away on this, of all days. Far as I was into my itinerant feast, I still had room for a few bites of Mrs. Chase's famously moist turkey, which she serves with her equally renowned hashed turnips. Turnips were childhood favorites of mine; my mother's, flavored with bacon drippings, were served only once a year, at Thanksgiving. The crisp, autumnal sweetness of Mrs. Chase's simply prepared turnips, bolstered with savory bits of pork, took me right back to long-ago family celebrations.

It's always a blessing, on Thanksgiving in particular, to know a first-class baker of pies and cakes. Ken Smith, the chef at Upperline, a restaurant on the edge of the Garden District, is a great buddy of mine and an even greater baker. On Thanksgiving, when his restaurant is closed, he welcomes friends to his home for dessert. He outdid himself on this Thanksgiving day. His dining room table was crowded with pecan pies, two kinds of pound cake, the fluffy coconut cake with boiled icing that was my childhood birthday party favorite, and gâteau de sirop, the lush Louisiana cake made with dark cane syrup and tinged with ginger and cloves. Ken had sprinkled powdered sugar on top of his and served it with a bright-tasting satsuma sauce.

Once again, champagne corks popped. Ken had gathered many of our mutual friends, including Patrick and Kerry, with whom I'd started the day. We raised a final glass to the magnificent, resilient Crescent City, which was recovering, yes, but doing so in its own fashion, with characteristic spirit and verve. It felt like a fitting end to a Thanksgiving celebration that was equal parts tradition and improvisation, bittersweet nostalgia and abiding hope.

Red Velvet Revisited

Neely Barnwell Dykshorn

Racy yet regal with just a hint of redneck, red velvet cake is wrapped in pedigree but remains queen of the comfort food. Its origins stretch back to the 1920s, when it's said to have been invented at the Waldorf Astoria Hotel, created for a red velvet-themed wedding. Another story at the Waldorf, less poetic, says the hotel charged a patron who requested the recipe one hundred dollars for it. Probably neither is true.

Today red velvet cake still turns up as far north as the West Village, where New Yorkers wait in line for Magnolia Bakery's pastel-iced, homey cupcake version. So, if the Waldorf Astoria launched it and modern-day Manhattan is still in hot pursuit, then what—besides a blockbuster cameo as an armadillo-shaped groom's cake in the film *Steel Magnolias*—makes the red velvet cake seem so Southern?

"They were cakes people made for each other," says Ted Lee, coauthor of *The Lee Bros. Southern Cookbook*. "Probably a doctored Duncan Hines—I wonder if it even had cocoa."

The book features a red velvet cake in the cover photo and a recipe for an orange zest–tinged, cream cheese–iced version inside. "We had one from a bakery in Harlem that had orange extract—it was like 'chocolate-plus,'" says Ted. The Lees' favorite bakery red velvet comes from Kudzu Bakery in Georgetown, South Carolina, and launched an attempt to replicate its mayonnaise-spiked formula. "I thought it's what gave it moisture, but I tried making a red velvet cake with mayonnaise and it was appalling," he says.

The cake in the Lees' book is something of an anomaly. Red velvet recipes don't turn up in Rose Levy Beranbaum's *The Cake Bible* or even *The Joy of Cooking*; they were more in the domain of shared recipe cards and church cookbooks. A classic example is found in Richmond, Virginia, in Grace & Holy

Trinity's *Cooking with Grace*. That recipe embraces a full two ounces of red food coloring and eschews cream cheese frosting in favor of a Crisco buttercream, and it's tough to argue with the unabashed Southernness of that.

Chef Greg Johnson of downtown Richmond's Chez Foushee, where red velvet cake rotates on and off the menu, traces the cake the farthest back and the farthest south. Johnson's research led to the Acadians who settled in Louisiana after the British kicked them out of Nova Scotia. "There [Louisiana], they made their own beet flour and were using it in baking for its sugar content," says Johnson.

The debate remains as to whether red velvet cake came from Bayou beet flour or the ballrooms of the Waldorf Astoria. "Whatever the origins are, I think it's Southern now," says Matt Lee. "It could have been invented in Bangladesh, but we've adopted it."

Grace's Red Velvet Cake

Serves 10 to 12.

Cake:

½ cup Crisco

1½ cups sugar

2 eggs

1 tablespoon cocoa

2 ounces red food coloring

2 cups flour

½ teaspoon salt

1 cup buttermilk

1 teaspoon vanilla

1 teaspoon baking soda

1 tablespoon vinegar

Cream Crisco and sugar. Add eggs and beat thoroughly. Add cocoa and food coloring and beat until well mixed. In separate bowl, add salt to flour. Add flour mixture alternating with buttermilk to the Crisco mixture. Add vanilla and mix well. Stir soda into vinegar and add immediately to above mixture. Fold in carefully. Bake in two greased and floured 8-inch round pans at 350 degrees for 30 minutes. Test cakes for doneness.

Icing:

1 cup whole milk

¼ cup flour

Pinch of salt

½ cup Crisco

1 stick butter

1 cup sugar

1 teaspoon vanilla

Cook milk, flour, and salt to pudding stage—it must be thick. Cool until cold. Cream together Crisco, butter, sugar, and vanilla. Add milk and flour mixture and beat until very smooth, about 5 minutes. Frost cake. Keep covered in refrigerator.

From Cooking with Grace, *Grace & Holy Trinity Church, Richmond, Virginia, 2005.*

The Food and Music Pantheon

Roy Blount Jr.

If music be the food of love . . . Or is it the love of food? Salsa is hot sauce,
zydeco comes from *les haricots*, and jazz was invented (at least according to
the man himself, Jelly Roll Morton) by a man named Jelly Roll. Rock groups
have had food-associated names from Cream to Korn. Many people call an
ocarina a sweet potato. The African "juba beat," one of the most essential riffs
of rock and roll, has been more popularly known as the *hambone*. How would
we talk about jazz without the use of *chops, cooking, tasty*, and *jam*? And if
you don't think "jam" as in "jam session" has anything to do with food, you're
forgetting Fats Waller's *Black Raspberry Jam* and his verbal asides thereto, like,
"Spread that jam around, yehhhhh."

Waller is the fourth most prolific recorder of food-related music. If you
want to challenge that statement, show me your database. Mine, gathered
over a period of eight years, is ninety-seven tapes, comprising 2,949 different recordings of food-related songs. Fats appears, singing and playing the
organ or piano, on twenty-five of them, including three different versions of
what I venture to call the most-recorded food song ever, *Honeysuckle Rose*.
I have thirty-five versions of that song, three of them featuring Fats himself.
He wrote the music, Andy Razaf wrote the lyrics:

> Don't buy sugar,
> You just have to touch my cup.
> You're my sugar,
> It's sweet when you stir it up.
> When I take a sip
> From your tasty lips,

The honey fairly drips.
You're perfection, goodness knows,
Honeysuckle Rose.

Fats smacks his lips over them like nobody else. And yes, to get this out of the way, food songs *do* tend to be about sex. But they're also about food. Waller's propensity for swaying women's thinking along the lines of one of his songs, *You're My Dish*, got him into plenty of trouble, but his appetite for food was what killed him at thirty-nine. (Well, for food and drink. The eight fingers of whiskey he took in the morning, four before shaving and four after, he called "my liquid ham and eggs.") Once, while dining with orchestra leader Fletcher Henderson, the story goes, Fats ate nine hamburgers and found he had no money. Pay for the burgers, he told Henderson, and I'll write you nine songs. Henderson agreed. Waller called for paper and dashed off the melodies right there at the table.

Among the food songs Fats recorded are *You're Not the Only Oyster in the Stew* (nor "the only wrinkle on the prune"), *Rump Roast Serenade*, *Hold Tight (I Want Some Seafood, Mama)*, and *Eep, Ipe, Wanna Piece of Pie*. If his music—the rolling-thunder left hand, the right hand like a band of pixies, and the comparably wicked-ingenuous, meaty-sweetie range of manner and voice—were food, it would be a roast rack of lamb with plenty of au jus and mint.

Perhaps Bulee "Slim" Gaillard—who ranks fifth in food-music production, with twenty-four recordings—was jiving when he said, "I invented the word *groovy*." But he did make up a language, called "Vout," which consisted largely of the word *vout*, other words that resembled *vout*, and the widely applied suffix *o'roony*. And the following are cold facts: that a copy of his first hit song, *Cement Mixer, Putty, Putty*, was buried along with *Stars and Stripes Forever* and *Rhapsody in Blue* in a time capsule at the 1939 New York World's Fair; that he appears in the Jack Kerouac novel *On the Road* as someone whom the arch-hipster character Dean Moriarty regards as God; and that—more to the point here—he was composer and coperformer of *Avocado Seed Soup Symphony* (in two parts) and many other songs that one critic characterized as "musical mixtures of avocado, chicken, rice, lamb, and grape leaves garnished with Greek and Arabic speech patterns" and other elements.

We don't know how much of what we know about Gaillard's life is true. He claimed Cuba as his birthplace, but apparently Detroit (in 1916) is more likely. His father, a steward on a steamship, took twelve-year-old Slim along on a round-the-world cruise and accidentally left him on the isle of Crete. There the boy is said to have remained for a year or so, broadening his horizons culinarily and otherwise, before finding his way to (or back to) Detroit, where he was adopted by an Algerian family. Somewhere along the way, he picked up smatterings of Yiddish, which stood him in good stead when he came to compose *Matzoh Balls*, *Drei Six Cents*, and *Dunkin' Bagel*. That last number, as recorded by the Slim Gaillard Quartet, moves from an initial tango feel, with a backdrop of sort-of-African-sounding drums, through lots of noodly piano arpeggios, a dash of snake-charmer/hootchy-kootchy, and lyrics along the lines of these:

> Dunkin' bagel.
> Dunkin' bagel.
> Dunkin' bagel.
> *Splash*! in the coffee.
> Matzoh balls! Gefilte fish!
> Pickled herring!
> Lox *o'roony*!

Of Louis Jordan's twenty-six food-song records, at least four topped the rhythm-and-blues charts in the forties and early fifties: *Ain't Nobody Here But Us Chickens*, *Boogie Woogie Blue Plate*, *Beans and Cornbread*, and *Saturday Night Fish Fry*. He sang and danced, played strong alto sax, and led his own bands with an iron hand, but most notably he was a caper-cutting showman. From his small-town Arkansas background and early experience in both minstrel shows and serious jazz, he developed hospitable jump-shuffle rhythms that helped pave the popular way for several genres of African American music: Nat King Cole, Ray Charles, Chuck Berry, and James Brown have all cited him as a primary influence. Perhaps, it must be said, his identification with food music overshadowed his greater contributions. Describing one of Jordan's late albums, his biographer, John Chilton (who is English), reveals a certain exasperation:

> On "Chicken Back," Louis again struts around the barnyard, but this time ends up in the kitchen to present another "food" song, sharing vocal duties with Dottie Smith. Dottie also joins Louis on "Texas Stew," which at least has tastier lyrics than many of Louis's other culinary offerings. The gormandizing ends with "Bananas," which has a charming, light calypso feel. Several of the songs are spiced with rock-and-roll seasoning, but are mercifully not connected with food.

But you just track down a recording of his jumping lament *I Get the Back of the Chicken* and see if that doesn't make you want to hop up and go looking for breasts and legs and wings.

The only one of the top five food-musicians who was not African American was, however, thought to be so, both by white club owners in New York who at first refused to hire him in the segregated thirties, and by black audiences, at the Apollo for instance, who took to his singing and horn-playing right away. What he was, was New Orleans French Quarter Sicilian American. By 1923, when he was twelve, he was an established local jazz trumpeter. By 1969, when a stroke forced him to retire, he was a longtime Vegas headliner whom some called the primogenitor of the lounge act.

When Louis Prima appeared at the Strand Theatre in New York, fans streamed down the center of the aisle to lay pizzas and pans of lasagna at his feet. I have him on twenty-nine food songs, from *Banana Split for My Baby* to *Please Don't Squeeza da Banana.*

And now we come to the greatest food musician of them all, who happens, fittingly, to be the twentieth century's greatest musician. It's a cliché to discuss the culture of New Orleans in terms of gumbo, but Louis Armstrong, who came from that city, does call that improvisational dish to mind. There are many kinds of gumbo, and within each kind, many levels: Gumbo can be down-and-muddy and also too finely ambrosial to be deserved, and both things are going on in the same bowl.

Certainly no one who fails to appreciate New Orleans food can be regarded as having any taste in American music. When James Lincoln Collier's absurdly condescending biography of Armstrong came out, jazz scholar Dan Morgenstern busted it on that basis. Satchmo generally signed his letters "red beans and ricely yours." This, wrote Morgenstern, "is proof to Collier that he was 'obsessive' about food. Armstrong's favorite dish is dismissed by Collier, who has already demolished gumbo and fishhead stew, with 'and red beans and rice are—well, beans and rice.' Quite so. And wine is fermented grape juice."

Even for a New Orleanian, though, Armstrong was more than averagely focused on eating and digestion. Here's how he recalled falling in love with Lucille, who would become his fourth and ultimate wife:

> "After all [she said], I'm just a little small chorus girl, lucky to come in contact with a bunch of lovely, well-hipped people." That's when I stopped her from talking by slowly reaching for her cute little beautifully manicured hand, and said to her, "Can you cook red beans and rice?" which amused her very much. Then it dawned on her that I was very serious.

Early in his career, after watching a fellow musician nearly starve himself trying to save money, Armstrong resolved that "I'll probably never be rich, but I will be a fat man." As he grew older, and portlier, he developed firm ideas about dieting as well. He swore by orange juice, which "softens fat," and an herbal laxative called Swiss Kriss.

He recorded at least thirty-seven songs significantly involving food—in their titles (three of his greatest instrumentals, *Potato Head Blues, Struttin' With Some Barbecue,* and *Chinese Chop Suey*), their lyrics, or both (*Big Butter and Egg Man, All That Meat and No Potatoes*). With Ella Fitzgerald (who is the sixth most prolific food-song recorder, and with whom Louis Jordan cut a tasty version of *Patootie Pie*), he recorded five great food duets: *Frim Fram Sauce, I'm Putting All My Eggs in One Basket, Strawberry Woman's Call* from *Porgy and Bess, Let's Call the Whole Thing Off,* and *A Fine Romance.*

What do these food-music immortals have in common? All their careers, aside from Gaillard's low-profile comeback in the eighties, were encompassed by the period between 1914, when Armstrong got a steady red-light-district gig at the age of thirteen, and 1971, when Armstrong died. They were all fine musicians, great comedians, and enormous hams. They all liked to roll words and subverbal enunciations around in their mouths—Prima laid claim to "gleeby rhythm," Jordan had a big hit with *Choo Choo Ch'Boogie,* and Armstrong was the first great scat singer. Each of them recorded *Honeysuckle Rose.* Slim was the only thin one; the others were all good, funny dancers; Slim was perhaps too laid back. Except for Jordan, who was brought up by his father, and perhaps Gaillard, who for all we know was not of woman born, each of them was extremely, fondly attached to his mother and her downhome cooking. And yet every one of them was out in the world, performing and exploring, before he was old enough to shave.

All of them helped shape jazz in the twenties, thirties, forties, and fif- ties, when it was about making cultural history, yes, and tasting sips from lots of tasty lips, yes, but also about getting fed. Up in Harlem great players jammed on Monday nights at Minton's Playhouse and after hours at Monroe's Uptown House because Minton and Monroe were good to musicians—didn't pay them, but did lay on plenty of ribs and chicken. On the road the same musicians, playing for cheering white people, were often hearing their own stomachs growl for lack of a restaurant that would serve black people, even take-out.

They all had appeal that notably crossed racial lines. There is something universal about each of them. See if you can supply the f-word I've left out of what the *New York Post* once quoted Gaillard as telling an audience: "F— is such a pleasure to enjoy. I think f— is a good invention."

Nope, it was "fun." But "food" would have fit just as well.

Recollections

A Fine Virginian

Lucretia Bingham

Buried beneath layers of buttons, World War I badges, and loose papers, my great-aunt Fan's journal was weathered when I found it in 1971, as a young adult. It was in an old leather box that was left to me by Aunt Fan's sister, my grandmother Rebecca. She and Aunt Fan had moved, in their eighties, to a tiny room in an assisted-living facility in Waynesboro, Virginia. At the time of my grandmother's death, two years after Aunt Fan's passing, I'd gone to Waynesboro to help my mother sort through both women's belongings.

Though the cover was faded and the string bindings frayed, as I began to flip through the journal I could tell at once that its contents glowed as fresh as the spring jonquils of which my great-aunt sometimes wrote. The small book was crammed with poems jotted down from memory, typed genealogical charts, receipts from the sale of the family's farm-raised turkeys, and handwritten recipes for, among other things, pecan cake and eggnog. Its pages were golden with age, as delicate and as browned along the edges as a cookie left in the oven too long.

Because I never had the chance to spend much time with Aunt Fan, her journal took on a deeper meaning. In the mid-1950s, when my brother and I were small children, my mother swept us off from Florida to a remote island in the Bahamas, so we first got to know Aunt Fan through the frequent letters that came in on the mail boat. My mother would read them aloud to us, and I could hear my aunt's refined voice long before I was ever in the same room with her. I think Aunt Fan was afraid that our sojourn in the islands would turn us into uncouth children, and she was determined to teach us, if only through her words, about mores and manners. "Don't you ever forget," she wrote, "that you come from a long line of fine Virginians."

It was my father who finally took my brother Russell and me to Charlottesville to meet her, when I was about ten years old. As we entered the house that she shared with my grandmother, both of them fussed around us before retreating to the kitchen. Hot waffles with chipped beef soon appeared, and they sat to watch us eat, Aunt Fan smiling as if our every bite were the most entertaining thing she'd ever seen.

Miss Frances Norris—as Aunt Fan was known to others—was born in 1881 in Mitchells, Virginia, only a few years after family estates in the area had suffered under what she called "Yankee depredations." Carpetbaggers had seized Rosemont, the family's Greek Revival mansion, and her father had just enough money left to buy a small country house and farm in Culpeper County. Aunt Fan, who never married, and her brother, George, lived and worked there for the first six decades of their lives.

In the early years of the twentieth century, while Northerners were developing a taste for dining out, Virginians were still cultivating the art of hospitality at home. Aunt Fan was gracious about entertaining in a way that belied how hard she worked; my mother even recalled once seeing her run full-speed across a field to catch a turkey, skirt flying. And though she might have "perspired" (Only horses sweat, don't you know! she often said) as she saw to her work, by the end of the afternoon, when guests came calling, Aunt Fan was fresh and scrubbed and ready to serve up plates of home-cured Virginia ham, tart chutney, sweet pickles, and rich devil's food cake, all to be enjoyed with homemade elderberry wine.

My discovery of her journal made me want to know even more about her, and for that I turned to my mother, who spent most of her childhood summers on the family farm in Mitchells. As on every farm, time was marked by the seasons and the many kitchen rituals that accompanied them, like the pickling and canning that went on most of the summer.

My mother recalled Aunt Fan's low-ceilinged kitchen as being about twelve feet square, with enormous rafters and a couple of windows. Beneath them was a long, oilcloth-covered table where most of the prep work took place. Cooking there was never a lonely pursuit. "There would be laughter and talk about all the goings-on," she said. Next to the stove was a square hole where the farm cats came in and went out. In the corner, a "safe" with screened doors held perishables and cooked food, like Aunt Fan's delectable cakes.

"Every year," my mother told me, "there was a big Sunday-school picnic, in front of an old pillared colonial, all ramshackle, way off in nowhere." Tables were set out, laden with food supplied by local ladies. "Aunt Fan's cake was always demanded. 'We just like Miss Fanny's cake,' people would say. It disappeared very quickly."

The ability to bake superb cakes was not her only talent; she was also an accomplished hostess. When guests came, the activity would shift from kitchen to dining room, where the table was always polished to a high shine. Behind it was a sideboard covered with silver tea services and candlesticks—all that was left of the old family silver.

"Most of the silver had been buried during the years of the war so that the Union army wouldn't find it," my mother said, recalling a story that Aunt Fan had told her. The silver had to share space in patches of earth around the farm with jars of brandied peaches, which were also stowed underground for safekeeping. According to Aunt Fan, when a farmworker couldn't recall where the peaches were, a few family members had "duck fits."

Later, after the Mitchells farm had been sold, Aunt Fan and my grandmother moved to Charlottesville; that marked the beginning of the period from which my most vivid remembrances of her are drawn. She was always charming as she greeted her callers, a steady stream of elderly ladies in hats and gentlemen in rumpled seersucker. As she offered them food, she would talk—oh, how she would talk!—stories and facts pouring out of her as haphazardly as the shiny strands of hair that she despaired of ever holding back in a bun. She would smile shyly at her guests as she launched into a soliloquy on the family's original estate. Or she might expound on the colors of Florentine frescoes as if she had been to Italy to see them herself, though she had not.

Just as she counted on her visitors' pleasure on hearing her stories, Aunt Fan took for granted that they'd be delighted by another piece of cake, as they usually were. "Just one more," she'd say. "I'll be devastated if you don't, just devastated!" If I refused thirds, the sudden droop of her smile conveyed her disappointment.

Shortly after acquiring her journal in the 1970s, I began cooking her dishes. One by one, they started appearing at my holiday meals and, sometimes, at my everyday ones. I was paying homage in a way that surely would have pleased her.

Despite all her readings and musings, Aunt Fan rarely left the borders of her Virginia farm, and yet, as she often assured me in her letters, her life was rich and satisfying. She also begged me to send her detailed descriptions of every little thing I did. Perhaps that explains why the following Emily Dickinson poem shows up three times in her journal, twice written out by hand (near a note about washing blankets and also alongside a recipe for watermelon pickle) and once in the form of an old newspaper clipping:

I never saw a moor,
I never saw the sea;

Yet know I how the heather looks,
And what a wave must be.

I never spoke with God,
Nor visited in heaven;
Yet certain am I of the spot
As if the chart were given

Though I never saw the kitchen in Mitchells, where all that canning and baking went on, Aunt Fan's journal has given me a window into the soul of the place, a vision of that long kitchen table and of that passionate cook with the heart of a poet.

Chapel Hill Eats
and a Chef Remembers

Ben Barker

I am two generations removed from the farm. My grandparents on both sides ended up in Burlington, North Carolina, in the early 1930s, seeking opportunity. As children of a dental student—and soon-to-be young faculty member—and a stay-at-home mom raising three babies born within six years, we didn't have many restaurant experiences. Going out to eat meant driving to northern Alamance County to the old King home place on Sundays and gathering around the table with the extended family. We were surely restaurant neophytes.

I was ten or eleven when I realized the magic of the ritual of "going out for supper." Dinah Washington was on the stereo, singing "Heart and Soul," while my dad prepared himself a "toter," his euphemism for a cocktail for the road, wrapped in a brown paper bag. My sisters and I piled into our tan Chevy Bel Air station wagon, giddy with excitement to celebrate Mom's birthday at the Pines, Chapel Hill's establishment restaurant for University of North Carolina alumni and locals. By the time we arrived, we were nearly intoxicated by the comingling of aromas: Aqua Velva, Beefeater's and quinine, Newport menthols, Joy eau de parfum. Mrs. Merritt, the proprietress, greeted everyone at the door by name: "How are you, Dr. Bennie? And happy birthday, Mrs. Barker!" We were seated at a red damask-covered table. Mixers were delivered for Daddy and the first of limitless sweet teas for us. Menus were perused even though we each already knew our order: shrimp cocktail, prime rib "rare" with salty au jus and baked potato, and strawberry shortcake or ice cream. Occasionally the exotic Mr. Merritt, who drove a Carolina blue

Corvette Stingray, would come by the table for a backslap exchange with Daddy. There, in the honeyed glow of knotty pine paneling, my image of fine dining was firmly established.

When I was growing up in 1960s Chapel Hill, still genuinely a village then, there were several institutions that defined our dining. A five-mile bike ride, the last mile up torturous Stroud Hill, was rewarded with a cherry Coke and a grilled pimento cheese sandwich at Sutton's Drug Store. The Port Hole, with its fabulous, just-baked Parker House rolls, burnished with butter, provided a solid base to many fraternity boys embarking on a night of Ancient Age or the bottomless Purple Jesus. At the Carolina Coffee Shop, those same boys would struggle in, long past time for their first class, to seek salvation in fried eggs, biscuits, and country sausage. At Leo's, our only Greek restaurant, Mr. Eliadis would reward good behavior with a sliver of halvah, and you might spot Larry Miller or Billy Cunningham, Carolina basketball stars, tucked lankily into a booth in the back.

The iconic Danziger family owned a conglomerate of restaurants. The Rathskeller had a subterranean aura. Gracious and witty black waiters delivered sizzling cast-iron skillets of mysterious sliced pepper steak, barely discernible in the gloom. It was the Zoom Zoom for pizzas and baked spaghetti, and the Ranch House for personally selected, hand-cut steak grilled on an open pit fire in the center of the dining room, flames illuminating the gleaming faces of solemn black cooks in tall red chef's toques. And there was the oh-so-sophisticated Villa Teo, presenting the essence of Continental cuisine in a Tuscan villa filled with antiques, statuary, and one of the great entrances in all of the restaurant kingdom, down a curved stone staircase with cast-iron balustrade.

Rock-solid, always reliable Brady's was located behind the Rock Pile, where the Siena Hotel now stands. Its fundamental fried chicken was always righteous, but my birthday choice was a seafood platter with fried oysters.

My first job at thirteen was bussing tables at the Carolina Inn cafeteria. I was a cook's assistant at Mom & Pop's Ham House, where they'd converted the bowling alley at Eastgate Shopping Center into a "Southern" restaurant. Chef Sam taught me on the loading dock to add a large slug of scotch to a half-pint carton of sweet milk so the boss couldn't smell it and it went down easier. Keith Allen & Son's Barbecue was a five-minute drive from my high school— easily the best lunch venue outside the Four Seasons in Manhattan.

After several colleges and numerous restaurant jobs, I pursued a culinary degree. Rumors began to filter up to Hyde Park, New York, that someone in Chapel Hill was doing something special. A young couple had opened a provincial French restaurant out in the country, and the chefs were the owners. Cooking seasonally—with Julia Child, Richard Olney, Roger Vergé, and

Michel Guerard holding their hands—they were creating daily menus, and Bill Neal's food was turning heads.

And then the state legislature passed local option liquor by the drink, enabling individual counties to vote for or against the sale of alcohol in restaurants. Orange County, being populated by forward-thinking people, was among the first to pass the law, and the Neals' Restaurant La Residence moved from Chatham County to a charming white cottage on the corner of Rosemary and Church streets. Bill came to define the Chapel Hill restaurant dynamic through the power of his persona, his intellectual curiosity, his wine knowledge, and his ability to translate classical and contemporary dishes in the French vernacular and make them broadly appealing and delicious.

Nearly simultaneously and of equal impact, the Carrboro Farmers' Market was founded in 1979, led by a redoubtable group of hippies, back-to-the-land movement disciples, traditional farmers, and true visionaries like Ken Dawson of Maple Springs, Alex and Betsy Hitt of Peregrine Farm, and Bill Dow of Ayrshire Farm. It is difficult to convey fully the impact the market had on the restaurant community and how far-reaching it has been. The market stimulus formed the petri dish for the restaurant growth we've witnessed over the last generation. The growers were young and receptive to directives and requests to grow new products. The symbiosis was beneficial. The restaurant cooks created demand, the public with their burgeoning interest in cooking and procuring restaurant-quality ingredients amplified the demand, and more growers joined in to supply that demand. Both community center and political-kibitzing locale, the market provided the opportunity to pursue first-class ingredients that transformed menus and created an environment that taught us how to cook locally and seasonally.

This was the ideal scenario for a newly anointed chef to make a triumphant return home and learn from Bill Neal. I desperately wanted to work for this man, but he had a healthy skepticism of culinary school grads, preferring to impart his knowledge to those unscathed by classically structured training. His appearance in *Food & Wine* magazine as a rising star of the Southern culinary pantheon only aggravated my desire to have him mentor me in the restaurant business, to teach me about being a chef-proprietor.

Meanwhile "Mama Dip" Council and her daughters were delivering the best home-cooked soul food to the first of several generations of college students and academics who were too far removed from their mamas and the farm. R. B. and Jenny Fitch were developing the village of Fearrington, where the original La Residence would be reborn as Fearrington House, ultimately luring Edna Lewis to their stoves and forthwith to the cover of *Gourmet* magazine.

Circumstances forced Bill Neal from the restaurant and opened the door for Karen and me at La Residence. Our opportunity to learn from Cheri Klein, Bill Smith, and Nancy Brown, all disciples of Bill's but with extraordinary skill sets of their own, was incomparable. We shopped and then we created menus, handwriting them minutes before the doors opened. It was a magical and formative experience.

Meanwhile, Bill took over a rundown roadhouse on the edge of Carrboro to create Crook's Corner. Inspired by his Southern heritage, he refined his remarkable skills and demonstrated his extraordinary grasp of Southern idiomatic cooking. Craig Claiborne of the *New York Times* took notice and anointed Chapel Hill as the heartbeat of Southern cooking. Bill's innovative talents, sense of timing, and grasp of self-promotion will lead and inspire the next generation of cooks and restaurateurs.

After two successful years at La Res, Karen and I took over the kitchen at Fearrington House some six months after Edna Lewis returned to New York. The Fitches' innate sense of design and marketing made the restaurant an extraordinary venue for us to develop the cooking style and operational understanding we needed to open Magnolia Grill in Durham in 1986.

Chapel Hill's Siena Hotel, constructed in the small European hotel model, struggled to establish a food identity for years, until Brian Stapleton arrived. His total grasp of operational standards and quality methods, developed from years of heading Ritz-Carlton foodservice properties, transformed the Il Palio dining room, and he performed the same magic at the Carolina Inn, raising the bar for hotel dining in the community.

The wave of Mexican and Latin nationals who moved from the farms of North Carolina into the labor pool in the 1990s has dramatically affected the Chapel Hill restaurant scene, changing our cultural dynamic and diversifying our foodways from African American and Eurocentric to a panoply of new ingredients and relationships.

More entrepreneurs continue to expand our dining options. Bret Jennings took his experiences from Kinkead's in Washington, D.C., Magnolia Grill, and travel in Mexico and Europe to create Elaine's on Franklin, a union of worldly cooking and superb wines. Wisely, Gene Hamer convinced Bill Smith to take over the kitchen at Crook's Corner for the late Bill Neal. Mama Dip moved across the street to larger quarters and continues to sustain with fine collard greens and fried chicken.

Andrea Reusing brought a clear vision, strong talent, and a solid commitment to using local, sustainable meat and produce to create Lantern Restaurant. Up in the Courtyard, led by the mayor of West Franklin Street, Lex Alexander, 3 Cups provides great coffee next to Sandwhich, home of the penultimate roast beef grinder. Across the way, Chip Smith and Tina Vaughn at Bonne Soirée deliver refined contemporary cooking in a stylish, elegant dining room that has become the successor to the La Residence of the early 1980s, Chapel Hill's salon.

We will watch with great anticipation as new generations of cooks—black, white, and Latino—take our restaurant world to new heights and place their imprint on Chapel Hill.

Purdue

John Martin Taylor

My mother was an odd bird, at once very private and very social. Though she cooked three meals a day and did all of our voluminous laundry and house-cleaning herself, she managed to play bridge often (at one point, seven times a week!) and to attend church, garden club, circle, and PTA meetings regularly. She somehow found time to travel as well—to the shore on the weekends, to New York with her girlfriends in the fall, sailing in the Caribbean with my father, and on a big family trip each summer. We always spent the holidays together, either at home in South Carolina or visiting relatives in Tennessee. One year I was the first to arrive home from college at Christmas. I found my mother playing hymns and carols on the console piano in the living room. It was the first and last time that any of us heard her play.

When we lost her to leukemia on Thanksgiving in 1982, we were robbed of one of the last of the great old-fashioned homemakers. The holidays have never been the same. My parents were young when my mother died. Daddy had retired early so that they could spend their lives together aboard their sailboat. He was ill prepared for her demise. He started dating fairly soon after Mama's death; the women were much younger than he was. He wanted an energetic companion who could be his first mate, the way my mother had been. Before long Lila, a young woman just a little older than his oldest child, moved aboard with him. They seemed genuinely happy, though I've never seen two people more different.

Both of my parents were scientists by training, but Mother agreed to raise children while my father pursued his career. From the beginning of their marriage, she developed an almost fanatical interest in cooking. Though firmly rooted in her rural Southern upbringing, her repertoire came to include Spanish *paellas*, Viennese desserts, and French stews. Her adventurous palate was enhanced both by her reading and her travels. When fairy rings of agaric mushrooms appeared in our yard, for example, she harvested them, sautéed them, and added them to omelets.

Mother's first handwritten collection of some of her favorite recipes—a book we all called "Purdue" because it was recorded in an old chemistry department notebook from the university where my father had attended graduate school— was a source of both culinary knowledge and pride. Invariably, my siblings and I would call Daddy at Christmas, desperate for a cookie recipe—for while Mother was an exceptional cook, she never really taught us how.

Daddy had always shared Mother's enthusiasm for good food. When we traveled, we ate in the Duncan Hines– and *New York Times*–recommended restaurants. We even had a wine cellar in a small town in South Carolina in the 1950s! And while he had done the grilling at home, Mother had always been the cook. When she became ill, Daddy took to cooking the way he had to sailing. He's quite a home chef. I had just begun my career as a food writer, and he and I read through the literature of food together. We shared kitchen tips and tested each other's theories and recipes. Though he's slowed down a bit now, we still do.

When Daddy sold his house and moved aboard the boat, Lila joined him. I got Mother's collection of cookbooks—a thousand of them!—but Dad kept a few gems, most importantly, "Purdue." After a couple of years, he and Lila got married. Their prenuptial arrangement was a division of labor: He'd do the shopping and cooking, and she'd do the cleaning—an arrangement they've stuck with through the years. Eventually, when handling the boat became more work than fun, they bought a simple house on a canal in Florida.

Dad continued to cook elaborate meals, which Lila and their friends enjoyed, but she admits that her major culinary interests are good chocolate and even better coffee. We all felt even more honored and surprised, therefore, when, one landlocked Christmas, she and Daddy presented each of us—there are four kids—with the most thoughtful gift I've ever received. At seventy-two, my father had bought himself a computer, taught himself how to type, and painstakingly copied the fragile yellow pages of "Purdue," recipe by recipe, page by page, omitting some of the possible substitutions such as margarine, but remaining true to Mother's originals. By then, he had been the cook at home for over ten years, and he was used to testing recipes for me.

"Purdue" is a wonderful collection. In a concise foreword, Daddy wrote, "These recipes were collected and recorded beginning in 1942 and continuing for about ten years. They were by no means her repertoire but rather, I suspect, those not in cookbooks and those not committed to memory." While he transcribed, Lila baked. For Christmas that year we each received not only a copy of the marvelous recipes but also tins of cookies, a dozen each of a dozen varieties, each labeled with the recipe title and page number from the book. It was the most thoughtful gift that I've ever received, and I continue to find wonderful ideas among the recipes.

There are delicious Pecan Shells—buttery, nutty crusts that you drape while still warm over custard cups to hold your favorite ice cream, mousse, or pudding. There are hot cheese tarts enlivened with country ham. There are exotic breads such as *chapati* and a classic pizza with a slow-rise yeast dough, tomatoes, mozzarella, anchovies, Parmesan, and oregano. Mother's deviled crab, I found, has a roux made with cream. No wonder it tasted so good! Her gumbo included shrimp, ham, and crabmeat. Her Bourbon Balls are made with homemade shortbread instead of the more pedestrian Vanilla Wafers. There are even recipes from Lindy's and The Four Seasons.

"Purdue" also contains her lengthy and precise directions for making Danish pastry from scratch, which we always had first thing on Christmas morning, before we went outside for oysters and champagne—before the ham biscuits, the quail, the ambrosia, the cookies, and the eggnog. Now that I've got the recipes, I still don't see how she managed it all.

Bourbon Balls

Makes 3 to 4 dozen.

2 cups crushed shortbread
¾ cup confectioner's sugar, plus
⅓ cup for dredging
1¼ cups chopped pecans
¼ cup unsweetened cocoa
powder

¼ cup light corn syrup
⅓ cup bourbon or sour mash
whiskey (or dark rum if you
prefer)

Put all of the ingredients except the sugar for dredging in a food processor and process until blended together. Roll into ¾- to 1-inch balls, roll in the powdered sugar, and store in wax paper-lined tins. The balls will keep for about a month.

From "Purdue"

Platters and Permanence
Walk and Talk A-Plenty at
Spartanburg's Beacon

Susan Shelton

In the Appalachian upland of South Carolina some things are certain. The summers are hot, and the line will be moving along at the Beacon Drive-In. For over three generations, this pantheon of burgers and shakes has drawn the faithful from all of Spartanburg and the world beyond.

On Thanksgiving Day 1946, a young World War II veteran opened the door to a new eatery with the motto, "Where Food Is Always Good." Over the intervening years, the Beacon has become a local and national icon. The landmark lighthouse, rising three stories above the huge parking lot, tells the hungry hordes they have arrived. Lured by the expansive menu, which includes breakfast, lunch, and dinner, a varied customer base has enjoyed the Beacon's food for more than sixty years. A social salad of young and old, rich and poor, blue-collar and professional, regulars and tourists can be found huddled together in wide-open, noisy dining rooms where 350 people can eat at one time. It is an oasis of comfort, constancy, and companionship.

Founder John White had always enjoyed the reputation of being a generous and caring employer and community leader. Stories abound about his providing food to those in need, whether from natural disaster or hard times. On one occasion, he fed three hundred fellow sailors free of charge. In 1977, when a downtown Spartanburg building collapsed, killing five people, White rushed to the scene with a truckload of food and drink to support the recovery effort. In recognition of his contributions to the community, a four-mile portion of Reidsville Road, the location of the Beacon, was renamed John B. White, Sr. Boulevard in 1998.

The Beacon is not only a gathering place for the entire community, it has also become a mandatory stop in any politician's quest to drum up votes for a successful campaign. Local and state office-seekers make it a point to glad-hand in the eatery, and even presidential candidates—among them Jimmy Carter, Bob Dole, Ross Perot, John McCain, Howard Dean, and George W. Bush—have passed down the line for a cheeseburger-all-the-way.

Julia Roberts, Garrison Keillor, and the contestants of the television pro-gram "The Amazing Race" have eaten there. Miss South Carolina contestants are routinely paraded in during pageant week. On one memorable evening, the entire cast of the Broadway production of *Cats* arrived in full costume after a performance at the Spartanburg Memorial Auditorium. White treated all the feline diners to a complimentary banana split.

The Beacon menu has changed very little over the decades. The number-one-selling chili cheeseburger continues to reign supreme, with the ubiquitous beef hash following at a close second. Entrees ordered "a-plenty" come buried in a mountain of french fries and hand-breaded Vidalia onion rings. Each week, three tons of both potatoes and onions are consumed by the restaurant's patrons. The average weight of a burger platter comes in at over two pounds of deep-fried wonderment.

All burgers at the Beacon come fully equipped with lettuce, tomato, and mayonnaise—South Carolina's Duke's, of course. Mustard is available only in packet form, and ketchup is dispensed from one-gallon cans which are opened in the dining room with gigantic can openers like those on naval vessels or in prison kitchens. Two hundred such containers are emptied in a week's time.

The newest entry on the menu is the "Hushpopper," a puffy cornmeal hushpuppy stuffed with homemade jalapeño pimento cheese, served with a creamy chipotle dipping sauce.

The Beacon claims to serve more sweet tea than any other restaurant in the country. Longtime employee Robert Nash brews over twelve hundred gallons per week, sweetening it with more than three thousand pounds of sugar. Each of the four large dining halls is equipped with a huge vat of the syrupy nectar.

Satisfying and decadent food is not the only driving force behind the success of the Beacon. Among a team of some sixty employees, workplace turnover is virtually nonexistent. The average career at the Beacon spans twenty-eight years.

White's generosity toward his employees is well-documented. It was common for him to loan money with no expectation of repayment. Cars were provided to insure reliable transportation to work, college educations were financed, and even homes were provided to those in need. Such magnanimous gestures were repaid with utter loyalty, and that spirit of fidelity continues today.

The undisputed king of the Beacon is J. C. Stroble, who has worked there since age fourteen, despite being legally blind. Fifty years ago, he explains, there were few employment options for young black men. He chose carhopping over working in the peach orchards or being a caddy at the local golf club. Since there was no indoor dining in the early years, carhops were the main line of defense against the onslaught of diners who flocked to the Beacon.

These days, J. C., at sixty-six, is considered the "ambassador" of the Beacon, having been featured in numerous local and national publications as well as television shows. The most recognized person in the restaurant, he can be found every day at the head of the line, arriving promptly at eleven o'clock, dressed spotlessly in a starched white shirt and pants, a crisp white apron, and polished black shoes.

J. C. says his primary job is to keep the line moving, so you'd better have read the menu and know what you want before you appear at the head of the line. As diners approach, he greets them with his famous, "Walk and talk." He then bellows out the order to the prep crew waiting behind the counter, followed by "Call it." Each cook is attuned to the sound of J. C.'s chant, and those not receiving an order have learned to tune him out until the next order is called. In other words, the sandwich makers pay no attention as a burger order is shouted out, and the burger man doesn't listen when the order is for fried catfish. Amid the noise and chaos, somehow, miraculously, diners receive their orders correctly at the pickup area. Nothing is written down. It's just a well-rehearsed symphony of cooperation and food preparation.

J. C. receives compliments from those entering the line, which he graciously acknowledges with a "Thanks a lot" or "I love you, too, honey." He's never met a stranger.

Another indispensible member of the Beacon family is Betty McClurkin. Known to all as "Miss Betty," she has been at the restaurant for forty-two years and is in charge of the kitchen. Everything on the menu is made from scratch, and nearly all of the recipes are Betty's. She does all the baking and has been known to cater a meal for four hundred single-handedly. During Thanksgiving week, she roasts more than four hundred preordered turkeys. Never seen by the customers, Miss Betty is the secret force behind the homemade pimento cheese, chicken stew, and pecan pie. White always said that he once prayed for someone to run his kitchen, and Miss Betty was sent to him from God.

Ezell Jackson, who began at the Beacon in 1950, worked as a carhop for forty-six years, until he was ninety. Willie Farmer served for fifty-three years, starting on the second day of business in 1946. Thomas Byrd worked at the Beacon for fifty-two years. It was his first and only job. James Meadows started working at the Beacon in 1952, served for forty-seven years, and never missed a day of work.

Upon White's retirement in 1998, the Beacon was sold to three local businessmen who have dedicated themselves to keeping the time-honored traditions alive. Kenny Church, the current general manager, adheres to an "If it's not broken, don't fix it" policy. Like White, the new owners consider their employees the cornerstone of the Beacon's success. And while some items have been added to the menu, a website has been launched, and outside marketing of the trademark tea began a few years ago, the current owners have no plans to make sweeping changes. They intend always to pay tribute to the man who built a hamburger empire with nothing but a vision and his often-quoted philosophy: "Anybody can do the ordinary. The Beacon strives to do the impossible."

The Restaurant That Time Forgot

Lee Walburn

When I moved to Atlanta in the 1960s, the Hollywood version of the Old South, the romanticized *Gone with the Wind* version, the happy black folk Uncle Remus version, was slowly beginning to fade. Nevertheless, a phosphorous glow lingered from symbols that vaunted a regional reluctance to forget the past. Of course, in a city boasting it was too busy to hate (truth in advertising be damned), burgeoning commercial opportunities meant businesses over time would gradually grow hesitant to reflect reverence for "the old ways." For example, the *Atlanta Journal-Constitution* eliminated its long-standing *Dixie Living* section, and only in the newspaper's archives can be found the braggadocios motto, "Covers Dixie Like the Dew." In political arenas, flags flaunting the stars and bars that in 1960 might have helped elect a candidate were, by 1990, more likely to defeat one.

At the midpoint of the last century, restaurants became a conspicuous target for headline-grabbing protests and, especially after Lyndon Johnson signed the Civil Rights Act, for legal action. Yet, well into the late 1960s, quite a number of Atlanta eateries remained slow to realize that symbols of discrimination could attract social lightning bolts, even if random and more unpredictable than legal storms. Those establishments had freed up their diner stools and booths, if not their consciences, as sit-ins transitioned into sit-downs. The names of some of Atlanta's most popular restaurants might well have been subtitled, "Forgit, Hell!" There was Johnny Reb's, Mammy's Shanty, Lickskillet Farm, Pittypat's Porch, and, of course, Aunt Fanny's Cabin.

Yes, I ate at every one of them. I first visited Aunt Fanny's in 1966, the year the Braves moved from Milwaukee to Atlanta and hired me as press and promotions director. A man named Harvey Hester owned the restaurant.

He was a garrulous charlatan, Falstaffian in girth, and a longtime friend of Donald Davidson, the Braves' traveling secretary. Donald was not my boss technically, but I was a newcomer to both major league baseball and expense accounts and easily influenced as to the distribution of the team's entertainment dollars. Donald measured exactly forty-eight inches tall and taxed his tiny kidneys by seldom drinking from a glass that wasn't filled with Cutty Sark. His tongue sponsored a range of vulgarities that sometimes led to near physicality in bars and restaurants—one of the reasons he encouraged my company in his entourage. Naturally, the major league world considered Donald an irascible, lovable, and relatively harmless icon.

I elucidate Donald's august stature and resulting influence in this showering of the Braves' expense funds on Aunt Fanny's Cabin, not as a personal mea culpa—I've never favored ignorance and weak backbone as a disclaimer—but as an example of my hindsight awareness of mixed messages that pervaded an era diffused with irony. In corporate philosophy and in fact, the Braves, led by GM John McHale and aides Dick Cecil and Bill Lucas, would pioneer an admirable record for affirmative action in the front office and in the community. I recall with pride the Braves' enlightened view of their institutional responsibility in race relations, although I really can't remember if I personally felt any pangs of discomfort during the visits to Aunt Fanny's. Perhaps we . . . I . . . considered the restaurant a caricature, as far-fetched from actual zeitgeist as Amos and Andy on television.

In general, Atlanta . . . I . . . had not fully realized just how deeply symbols can penetrate hearts and minds. And that mindset was not exclusively Southern. Aunt Fanny's owner Harvey Hester apparently knew or was known by the majority of America's celebrities, judging by the autographed photos that covered the walls of his restaurant.

In reconsideration, the best that can be said for Aunt Fanny's is that it served the best fried chicken I've ever tasted, and perhaps that was the main reason even the more liberal of its clientele were able to reconcile digestion with the glorification of the South's legacy of slavery.

Hester had concocted the totally humbug legend that his establishment was named for a former slave famous for her cooking, who had lived past the age of one hundred in the very same cabin that housed the restaurant. Guests were greeted by a small boy who poked his head through a blackboard with the menu chalked on it. In sing-song he would warble, "Wekummmm to Aunt Fanny's Cab beeeen! Wot'll it be, fokes?" At some point in the evening black waitresses in period gowns gathered around the piano and sang haunting gospels. They shook jars and claimed they were collecting money for their church; white folks were more apt to turn loose change over to the church than tip African American performers.

Today, almost all of the Atlanta restaurants selling customers a South that Hollywood myths created are gone with the wind. Mammy's Shanty shocked native Atlantans and conventioneers by closing in 1971. No longer would we savor Willie B. Borders's chicken shortcake (a marriage of cream, milk, chicken fat, pepper, pimento, mushrooms, and chicken served over hot egg bread slices). One by one, other establishments with Old South themes collapsed. Aunt Fanny's shuttered in 1994.

Not long ago, while engaging a friend in intellectual sparring over the merits of fried chicken, we began to rank Atlanta's restaurants in terms of the South's favorite dish. I raised my verbal flag for Watershed in Decatur. A number of other restaurants—Quinones, Sweet Lowdown—have in the last decade championed Southern cooking with a sense of culinary heritage absent a sense of cultural nostalgia. I was admittedly startled when my friend said, "But have you eaten at Pittypat's Porch lately?"

"Frankly, my dear," I replied, "I didn't know Pittypat's was still in business, or even more frankly, if anyone gives a damn."

But it is indeed alive and vigorous. *Atlanta* magazine actually has its signature faintly scratched on the conceptual cornerstone of Pittypat's Porch. A. J. Anthony had intended to open an Italian restaurant, but he read in the magazine that the city lacked the cuisine and historical atmosphere a growing number of visitors expected. Anthony abandoned his plans for pasta and in 1967 introduced Pittypat's Porch, blatantly themed on *Gone with the Wind*. The book and movie towered above all others when the world thought about Atlanta (if it thought about Atlanta at all prior to the 1996 Olympics).

The evocation of Pittypat's Porch stimulated whatever nerve in me always seems to respond to incongruity. Hearing that, after four decades, it was indeed very much in business, I immediately reserved a table for four. And so it was I discovered that the restaurant, virtually unchanged in appearance from its 1967 inauguration, remains at what was once 25 Cain Street but is now 25 Andrew Young International Boulevard. Those who don't comprehend the irony of the address may also miss the discordance of the theme.

Anthony named the restaurant after Aunt Pittypat Hamilton, portrayed lovingly in Margaret Mitchell's book and more memorably in the 1939 movie as a gracious hostess and gifted cook, though prone to faint in shock at Scarlett's socially irresponsible attitude. Then as now, Pittypat's Porch is inconspicuous at street level, though once inside, a customer steps up to a gigantic front porch supposedly epitomizing those wrapped around plantation mansions. Ambience strives for a similar level of cliché. A greeter, African American, sits beneath a portrait of Aunt Pittypat's porcelain-white face.

Artwork reminders of "the way it was" cover the porch's perimeter walls. A painting of a cake walk calls attention to the blithe spirit of colorfully garbed, dancing, high-slapping black men. As I walked the circumference of the porch, I saw a portrait of Robert E. Lee and other legends of the Civil War, as well as Prissy, who famously didn't know nothin' 'bout birthin' babies, plus a variety of movie-gilded stereotypes.

On the stairs descending to the dining room, we passed a wall crowded with photos of recognizable faces inside plain, dark frames: Governor Lester Maddox, Representative John Lewis, and Mayor Maynard Jackson, to mention a portion of the paradoxical museum.

We were appointed seats next to a table occupied by an African American lady and two young men. A few minutes later, five black women took their seats at another table, and within half an hour, the number of African American diners reached fifteen. I counted white customers. Thirteen. That included the four in my party.

As the family at the nearby table was preparing to leave, I introduced myself and asked, "Did you like your meal?"

"Oh, yes," the woman replied. "Is this your restaurant?"

"No, just curious," I said. "I apologize for such a personal question, but does the theme, the décor of this restaurant offend you?"

"I really had not thought about it," she said. "I thought it would be a good idea to get some real Southern cooking. We don't have it in Los Angeles."

"I sorta thought about it," said the teenager, who was enrolling the next day at Morehouse College, a citadel of African American leadership.

Somewhat surprised by the answers, I moved over to the table of five ladies. Our server had volunteered the information that most of the clientele is from out of town, but these women said they lived in Atlanta. I asked the question I had presented to the visitors from Los Angeles.

"Offended?" one responded with a laugh. "That stuff is so long ago. We come here because the fried chicken is great."

Their responses inspired several nights of uncertain reflection. Could their relaxed presence at Pittypat's Porch mean that the sharp-edged promises of inalienable rights have begun to parry the daggers of symbolic insult? Those diners apparently come to Pittypat's Porch because . . . because they can . . . because they have the choice to express righteous anger at insensitivity—or to just turn a cheek that is munching on some mighty good fried chicken in a restaurant that time forgot.

Miss Congeliality

Julia Reed

Several years ago my mother had a four-day house party during which she served an almost exclusively gelatin-based menu. I don't think it was on purpose; she just wanted to make everything in advance so she could spend as much time as possible with her friends. But by the end of the second day, when the guests had already consumed a crabmeat mousse, a strawberry mousse, two kinds of tomato aspic, and a charlotte russe, one complained that he could not get up from the table. "I think," he said, "my blood has coagulated."

None of the rest of us saw anything funny about the food. This was in the Mississippi Delta, after all, where congealed items are a staple of our diets. In *Gourmet of the Delta*, a cookbook put together by the region's Episcopal churchwomen, there are seventy salad recipes, and fifty-one of them contain gelatin; in *The Memphis Cook Book*, twenty-three of the thirty-three salads are congealed. I didn't even bother to count the desserts. We congeal everything. Instead of serving Smithfield ham with hot mustard, we serve it with a shimmering hot mustard mousse. Rare roast beef gets horseradish mousse sliced and stacked with the beef on homemade yeast rolls. For hors d'oeuvres, we would rather offer a molded Roquefort ring (Roquefort, chopped pecans, cream, and cream cheese) than mere Roquefort. Then there are the endless variations on tomato aspic, including my favorite—tomato soup aspic, a Junior League cookbook perennial made with canned tomato soup, mayonnaise, cream cheese, and sliced green olives.

I had always assumed that the Southerner's proclivity toward anything made with gelatin derived from the heat. All those smooth and glistening aspics and mousses would have provided cool relief. In fact, it wasn't until the advent of refrigeration that we could enjoy them during most of the year. "Jellies should never be made in hot weather," Marion Cabell Tyree warns in

Housekeeping in Old Virginia, published in 1879. In *Dishes and Beverages of the Old South*, published in 1913, Martha McCulloch-Williams describes a typical wedding menu, adding that in cold weather, wine jelly "took the place of syllabub."

It turns out that our fondness for jelled foods comes from the British, who began making molded "jellies" as early as medieval times, when artistic cooks decorated them with edible gold and silver. Techniques for making them weren't perfected until toward the end of the eighteenth century when they became symbols of sophistication and status. No wonder. To make them was such a long and tedious process, only the wealthy could afford it. First, calves' feet and knuckles or hartshorn (deer antlers) were simmered in water for hours and allowed to cool, leaving a translucent jelly on the top. The jelly was further reduced by boiling, clarified with egg whites, and flavored with everything from fruit and wine or cream to ground meat or nuts. A typical example is "The Duchess of Montague's Receipt for Hartshorn Jelly" from an eighteenth-century manuscript found at Canons Ashby in Northamptonshire. In it, the cook is advised to "put in one gallon of water half a pound of Hartshorn. Let them boyl slowly till the Liquor is a pretty strong Jelly, then strain it off and put in . . . the peel of eight oranges and four lemons, cut very thin, boyl it a quarter of an hour, then put in the whites of 12 eggs . . . the Juice of the Oranges and Lemons, and a pound and a quarter of double refined Sugar, boyl it a little and then strain it through a Flannell Bagg."

In Colonial America, gelatin was not such an indicator of class. In her cookbook, Tyree points out that it was easy for "country housekeepers in particular to make this sort of jelly, as the materials generally are within their reach." Isinglass, a jelling agent made from the air bladders of sturgeon, was also popular, and by the 1860s, some crude commercial gelatins (sold in paper-thin "leaves") were available. Tyree was partial to Cox's Sparkling Gelatin and included it in recipes for blanc mange, Bavarian cream, charlotte russe, "meat jelly for boned turkey," and "lemon froth." However, Isinglass required almost as much boiling and straining as calves' feet and hartshorn, and the early leaf gelatin was not always foolproof. Finally, in 1890, the process for making granulated commercial gelatin was perfected by Charles Knox, a fact that made him so rich he bought the famous racehorse Anaconda and gave him the unfortunate new moniker "Gelatine King."

While gelatin is defined in *The New Food Lover's Companion* as "pure protein derived from beef and veal bones, cartilage, tendons, and other tissue," most commercial gelatin today is a by-product of pigskin. This information must be startling to those vegetarians who ingest commercial ice cream, yogurt, gummy bears, and the hundreds of other prepared foods containing gelatin, not to mention the "gel caps" that encase an increasing number of over-the-counter medicines. Since I am not a vegetarian I am grateful for those handy quarter-ounce envelopes of instant gelatin. My friends and I spent much of our teen years drinking dissolved Knox straight out of a glass in an effort to make our hair shiny and our nails strong. (These days there is a product called Knox for Nails.) But my devotion to Knox reached its apex just a few years ago, after I'd apparently lost my mind and tried jelling something the old-fashioned way.

I was in Bath, England, for the summer and in charge of organizing an enormous picnic to take to a country-house cricket match. One of the guests was originally from New Orleans and her favorite thing in life is daube glacé, a highly seasoned beef stew that is jellied and molded in a loaf pan. Served on crusty French bread with lots of homemade mayonnaise, it makes an extremely upscale and delicious New Orleans roast beef po-boy sandwich, and I was determined to show the Brits a thing or two. Maybe it was the English damp, or maybe it was all the hours of mind-numbing cricket I'd been forced to watch. At any rate I forgot all about Mr. Knox and followed the only recipe I could find in the Bath bookstore, which included plenty of calves' feet and veal knuckles but no granulated gelatin. It didn't work. After about eight hours of simmering and two days of refrigeration, it ended up a sort of glutinous beef soup, which I finally heated up and served over noodles the day after the picnic.

I have since learned to forgo the animal parts and add four envelopes of gelatin (one envelope usually will jell about two cups of liquid). Now that I have perfected my daube glacé I intend to serve it at my own next house party, where I'll have no qualms about thickening the blood of my guests. Over the course of the weekend I'll probably also offer a tomato aspic ring filled with lump crabmeat or a curried rice salad, a boozy charlotte russe with homemade ladyfingers, Julia Child's divine chicken mousse with foie gras and truffles, and maybe even some wine jelly, although that is most often served during the Christmas holidays, in keeping with its original seasonal roots.

While I cook, I'll entertain myself by listening to Rogers and Hart—specifically "I Wish I Were in Love Again," surely the only song ever written that successfully incorporates the verb "congeal" into its lyrics. "When love congeals," Lorenz Hart wrote in one of his archer moments, "it soon reveals the faint aroma of performing seals." I will also raise a glass to the rather gauche Mr. Knox, whose gelatin has no aroma whatsoever, and when it congeals the result is not dull or disastrous, as in the song, but shimmering and divine.

Opinion Stew

Salley Shannon

My first childhood memory is of dappled light on yellow-green grass, me in a metal stroller, and Mama saying, "Cover your ears, now, sweetheart. Mama's going to go bang-bang." And then the jolt of a shotgun firing twice in rapid succession, birds making a ruckus as they bolted from trees, and Mama trotting off to pick up the squirrels she's just shot for Hopkins County stew—as in Hopkins County, East Texas.

I don't know how old I was: old enough to know that something good, something cozy and full of flavor, was headed my way for supper, but not old enough to turn up my nose at the idea of eating squirrel, which I did later, to Mama's dismay. Mama considered squirrels to be tree-borne chickens with a few more brains and fur. "Good eating and there for the taking" was her assessment. Well, yes, if you are a deadeye shot and don't mind some skinning and eviscerating. My five-foot, one-half-inch mother—heaven help you if you forgot the half inch that made her taller than her sister—hunted and fished joyfully and easily. Not all her friends and female kin had her fine aim, but all of them were equally adept at preparing a meal from scratch in the days when "scratch" meant the meat was still mobile, onions had to be dug from the garden, and butter was churned from milk. They were as proud of their ability to manage foodstuffs as they were of their nice manners and handed-down silver teaspoons. So, Mama was matter-of-fact about cleaning the day's take, staunchly ignoring my "Euuuuuew!" as beneath her notice. I was just too nicey-nice. Didn't I know that somebody had to kill and prepare the meat we ate?

When I was little, in the 1950s, we lived in Weaver, Texas, population one-hundred-something, about ninety miles northeast of Dallas. We had a white frame house with fields and woods behind it full of hickory and short-leaf pine trees. Down the road was a small cemetery, where several generations of my mother's people awaited the general resurrection. They were early settlers in Hopkins County, having come from Tennessee and North Carolina but originally from Scotland, Ireland, and England.

Mama herself lies in that cemetery now, along with Daddy and a good many of the relatives whom I remember sitting on porches or under spreading pecan trees, arguing over the important things in life. Like water baptism versus sprinkling, the inerrancy of Scripture, and whether making Hopkins County stew with chicken was too sissified to be endured or whether it could be the real thing without okra.

On that last point, Mama and her sister would debate until their faces were red. "The children will just leave the okra in the dish," Aunt Beth would say. "They should learn to like it made right," Mama would counter, and off they'd go. Mama also maintained that no chicken, especially a "store chicken," would ever blight her Hopkins County stew.

The tradition of making the stew dates to the 1840s or a little earlier, when my people lived in wagons while land was being cleared and houses and barns raised. (My great-aunt Doll Sparks Stephenson was known for more than ninety years as "the wagon yard baby" because she was born during that time.) Families in the wagon yards would often pool their supplies and cook their meals together in big cast-iron pots hung over an open campfire. The dish they loved best—and probably had the wherewithal to make—evolved into Hopkins County stew. Perhaps some frontier cook had known about Brunswick stew, from Brunswick County, Virginia, which became popular after being served in 1828 at a political rally and also is made with squirrel and onions. Or maybe squirrels and onions were there in abundance, so they ate them cooked up in the tastiest way they could manage.

The dish saw a revival during the Depression because it was (and still is) an appealing, nourishing way to feed a crowd. Everything in it came out of the garden or canning jars, and if you were handy with a rifle, you didn't even have to kill one of your chickens.

When I was small, older relatives would tell of last-day-of-school parties at which a cauldron of Hopkins County stew simmered. Every family would bring something for the pot: tomatoes, potatoes, onions, corn, cleaned squirrels or chicken. Townspeople would stop by the store for a hunk of cheddar, called "rat-trap cheese," and some crackers from the barrel as their contribution to the meal. The proportions of the stew undoubtedly varied, but it was always delicious and filling, and it was something everybody had in common from "the old days." Over time, Hopkins County stew became the centerpiece of church and civic get-togethers.

Today, there is a Hopkins County stew cook-off every fall in the town of Sulphur Springs. Local families and newcomers alike cook up sixteen- or twenty-gallon pots of stew using old family recipes or try their hands at evolved versions that some folks have the temerity to make with garlic, paprika, and all sorts of gosh-durned foreign mush. Several thousand people gather in front of the Chamber of Commerce to eat Hopkins County stew and celebrate their pioneer heritage. What was originally settlers' survival fare has now developed cachet. A down-home-style band, Jupiter Coyote, even has a song called "Hopkins County Stew," which it has sung in clubs from Memphis to Tallahassee, and which begins, "Well Grandpa Taylor had a big black pot/Cooking out back of the house."

Personally, I believe the stew never would have become famous if folks hadn't started leaving out the okra. Nasty, slimy stuff. When I was growing up, you see, I took Aunt Beth's side of the argument. Also like her, I began putting creamed corn into my stew. Delicious! Sometimes I even threw in a few carrots—thorns in Mama's flesh.

Long before that, however, Mama had to eat her words about Hopkins County stew made with chicken. From Weaver we moved to Dallas, then to Amarillo, where I finished growing up. Because of the town's large size, no firearms could be discharged there. That meant Mama couldn't shoot the squirrels in our backyard or in a nearby park, however temptingly plump they looked. Also, our neighborhood was gentrified: no chicken coops. So, if we were going to have Hopkins County stew, it had to be made with store-bought chicken. Mama shrugged and made do—but she always offered saltines and rat-trap cheese on the side.

Hopkins County Stew

This is Salley Shannon's "sissified" version of her mother's stew:
She uses chicken instead of a backyard squirrel and, like her aunt,
leaves out the okra—but adds creamed corn.

Salt

1 3-pound chicken, quartered

3 cloves garlic, peeled and
   minced

3 large waxy potatoes, peeled
   and cubed

1 large yellow onion, peeled and
   chopped

1 28-ounce can diced tomatoes

2 14¾-ounce cans creamed corn

1 15¼-ounce can whole-kernel
   corn, drained

1¾ cups chicken stock

Freshly ground black pepper

1–2 tablespoons chili powder

Bring 5 cups of lightly salted water to a boil in a large wide pot over high heat. Add chicken and garlic and reduce heat to medium-low. Cover pot and simmer, skimming any foam that rises to the surface, until chicken is cooked through, 30–40 minutes. Transfer chicken to a bowl, setting pot with broth aside. When chicken is cool enough to handle, remove and discard skin and bones. Cut or tear chicken meat into bite-size pieces and set aside.

Add potatoes to pot with broth and cook over medium-high heat until just soft, about 15 minutes. Add chicken, onions, tomatoes, creamed corn, corn kernels, and chicken stock. Season to taste with salt, pepper, and chili powder. Reduce heat to medium-low. Simmer stew, covered, until flavors have melded, about 1½ hours. Serve with crusty bread or saltine crackers and sharp cheddar on the side, if you like.

This Recipe Is Remembrance

Michelle Healy

Family food traditions are as much a part of the holidays as wrapping paper and jingle bells. For Elbert Mackey, this means whipping up a batch of tea cakes—golden-brown, circle-shaped cookies with a hint of vanilla and nutmeg.

To be honest, Mackey says, he doesn't limit his much-loved recipe to the Christmas season. But in a time of year when preparing food also means sharing family stories and a bit of yourself, his passion for tea cakes takes on added meaning.

The owner of an Austin, Texas, medical equipment repair business, Mackey is trying to preserve the tea cake recipes that were often a favorite in African American homes before the advent of convenience foods. He also wants to collect stories, poems, and remembrances associated with this dessert. He launched the Tea Cake Project to solicit recipes and stories that he hopes to include in a cookbook.

"Occasionally in Southern cookbooks you see a recipe here or there, but nothing dedicated to tea cakes, and nothing unique to African Americans," Mackey says. "These little bites of heaven are disappearing."

Tea cakes were introduced to the Colonies by the British, who served sweet cookies or cakes with afternoon tea or with the more formal "high tea" later in the day, says Atlanta-based food editor and teatime historian Millie Coleman, author of *The South's Legendary Frances Virginia Tea Room Cookbook*.

During the 1800s, in regions of the South with a strong Scots-Irish or British background, the tea cake tradition carried on, except that the standard recipe became more of a sweet cookie, Coleman says. The term also expanded to include a variety of cookies and cakes served with tea, she explains.

Tea cakes were not a slave food, says food historian Jessica Harris, author of such books as *The Welcome Table: African-American Heritage Cooking*.

"The white flour is an ingredient that slaves would not have had access to. And when it's sweetened with refined white sugar, you know it's relatively recent," she says.

Still, over time and throughout the South, many African Americans adopted the food as their own, sometimes as a snack, other times as a treat for special occasions, especially Easter and Christmas, says Mackey.

Because the basic ingredients—flour, eggs, milk, sugar—were relatively inexpensive household staples, tea cakes could be enjoyed by families of limited economic means, he says. "Along the way, cooks would add their own special ingredients, such as molasses, grated lemon rind, various spices, and flavoring. Something simple was turned into something wonderful."

Today, tea cakes remain a little-known regional treat, says Harris. "There are areas where people go, 'What?' and other areas where they know it," she says.

High school and college students may only know the term because it's the nickname of the guitar-playing hero Vergible "Tea Cake" Woods in Zora Neale Hurston's classic novel *Their Eyes Were Watching God*.

The tea cakes common today are actually more of a shortbread-type cookie. Some recipes produce a soft cookie with a cakelike texture, while others produce a thin, crisp texture, similar to a sugar cookie.

Mackey came to know and love tea cakes growing up in tiny Minden, Louisiana, where his schoolteacher grandmother would share stories about her mother's wonderful tea cakes, butter rolls, and sweet potato pones. Although his grandmother made good tea cakes, it was her daughter, his Aunt Maggie, who had the golden touch. "Eating Aunt Maggie's tea cakes made our day," Mackey recalls.

It was his search for a tea cake recipe that replicated the texture and taste of Aunt Maggie's cookies that inspired Mackey to start the Tea Cake Project. "During my career in the Air Force, I would meet people from all parts of the United States and would often ask if they had a tea cake recipe or aunt or someone who might have a recipe," he says. "I was surprised by the number of people who got excited just talking about them."

Among the submissions to the Tea Cake Project are a story about using Royal Crown Cola bottles for rolling out the dough and a memory of picking up eggs from the henhouse to make the treats every Sunday morning. Mackey has told his granddaughter Adrionah his stories about afternoon drives down a dusty dirt road to Aunt Maggie and Uncle Son's house and watching his uncle churn milk for the cream that would go into his aunt's cakes.

He says he has come close to recreating and updating Aunt Maggie's tea cake but notes that recipes for everyday foods were often never recorded. "Lots of [African Americans] were illiterate and didn't know how to write, but cooked with a pinch of this, a pinch of that.

"That's why I want to preserve the legacy of tea cakes," Mackey says. "Tea cakes are just part of our history that's gradually fading away. I'm just trying to keep it alive."

North Louisiana Tea Cakes

Makes 1 dozen cookies.

½ cup butter, softened	1¾ cups all-purpose flour
1 tablespoon fat-free sour cream	¼ cup pastry flour
1 cup sugar	2 teaspoons baking powder
2 large eggs, lightly beaten	½ teaspoon ground nutmeg
2 teaspoons pure vanilla flavor	⅛ teaspoon ground coriander

Beat butter and sour cream at medium speed with electric mixer until creamy; gradually add sugar, beating well. Beat in eggs and vanilla until blended.

Combine flour, baking powder, nutmeg, and coriander. Add a small amount of dry ingredients at a time to butter mixture and beat until well blended. Scrape down sides of bowl. Cover bowl and chill for 30 minutes.

Oil a regular size ice cream scoop inside and out and fill with equal amounts of batter. With cleaned, floured hands, toss the dough from hand to hand to form a ball. Pat out each ball of dough into a ¼-inch round cookie and place on a lightly greased cookie sheet.

Bake in a 350-degree oven for 20–25 minutes until lightly brown. Tops will begin to crack. Remove from oven and let stand on cookie sheet for 5 minutes before removing to wire rack to cool down. Store in airtight container.

From The Tea Cake Roundup *by Elbert Mackey (Infinity, 2009).*

Knowing

Sylvia Woods

A child of Depression, blue-veined hands
map a life drawn from hilly acres, hands that
suckered tobacco, weeded corn, dug potatoes, endured
loss of child and man, palms open to help neighbors, kin.
On her front porch, she leans forward in painted chair,
breaks the tip of a half-runner, tugs string
down its spine. The pile grows like green spaghetti.
"Did you know the Chinese stir-fry green beans?"
asks a niece, the one who went to Europe junior year.
"And the French cut them slantwise with a knife."
"I simmer beans with a little fatback,
cook them hours, steam up the windows,
bake cornbread hot and crusty in the skillet
Mama left me." Mae says, "That is what I know."

Accents

Muffulettas and Meringue Pies
The Immigrant Experience in the South

A Photo Essay by Amy C. Evans

. . . . .

All photographs are by Amy C. Evans and are published by permission of Amy Evans, operating under the auspices of the Southern Foodways Alliance.

Abe's Bar-B-Q in Clarksdale, Mississippi, was opened by Lebanese immigrant Abraham "Abe" Davis in 1924.

Brothers Abe Jr. and Pat Davis oversee their late father's restaurant, Abe's Bar-B-Q, which is known for barbecue as well as Delta-style hot tamales.

A shelf of canned goods and Mexican religious candles for sale at Cliff's Meat Market in Carrboro, North Carolina.

Cliff Collins of Cliff's Meat Market in Carrboro, North Carolina, holding a tray of marinated pork used in *tacos al pastor*.

Florence Signa, better known as Aunt Florence, prepares a salad at Doe's Eat Place in Greenville, Mississippi.

The parchment-wrapped hot tamales at Doe's Eat Place in Greenville, Mississippi. Sicilian immigrant Dominick "Doe" Signa opened his namesake restaurant in 1941.

The Crystal Grill in Greenwood, Mississippi, is known for its extensive menu of Southern staples and Greek specialties, as well as its mile-high meringue pies.

Mike Ballas, who was born in Florida but raised in Greece, took the helm of the Crystal Grill in Greenwood, Mississippi, in the late 1940s.

A curtained booth at the original Giardina's in Greenwood, Mississippi, which was opened by Sicilian immigrant Joseph Giardina in 1936.

Brossi and Rosina Giardina with their son, Joseph. Together, they operated the original Giardina's restaurant in Greenwood, Mississippi, for more than sixty years.

Andy and Karen Pinkston, fourth-generation owners of Lusco's restaurant in Greenwood, Mississippi.

Opened in 1933 by Italian immigrants Charles and Marie Lusco, Lusco's is known for its hearty steaks, fresh pompano, and broiled shrimp.

The traditional New Orleans–style muffuletta that is served at the Pasquale's Hot Tamales stand in West Helena, Arkansas.

Joyce and Joe St. Columbia operate Pasquale's Hot Tamales in West Helena, Arkansas, a fairly recent incarnation of a business that was started by Joe's Sicilian grandfather almost a century ago.

Kathy Koutroulakis shows off her Greek heritage while working behind the counter at Pete's Famous, a legendary hot dog stand she runs with her husband, Gus Koutroulakis, in Birmingham, Alabama.

Gus Koutroulakis hands a hot dog and a Grapico across the counter at Pete's Famous in Birmingham, Alabama, where he has been grilling hot dogs every day since 1948.

Your Dekalb Farmers Market
Food and Ethnicity in Atlanta

Tore C. Olsson

In the summer of 1977, Robert Blazer opened a local farmers market in Decatur, Georgia, only a few miles from the heart of downtown Atlanta. The market began humbly in a former greenhouse with no refrigeration, and Blazer's operation initially served as a simple exchange point between local farmers and consumers. Born into a middle-class family of Italian descent, Blazer grew up in his father's variety store in Pawtucket, Rhode Island, and was quite familiar with the retail food industry. After securing a loan from his family, he moved south with plans to enter the grocery trade himself. His initial goal seemed simple: "to provide the people in the neighborhood with high quality product" and perhaps turn a bit of a profit along the way. In the city of Atlanta, Blazer saw a "traditional" community that reminded him of his New England roots, "especially when it came to cooking."

While the culinary atmosphere of 1977 Atlanta may have remained "traditional," the city itself was hardly reminiscent of the romantic world Margaret Mitchell depicted in her 1939 Civil War epic, *Gone With the Wind*. Having endured the racial turmoil of the Civil Rights Movement without the overt violent conflict that haunted some of its Southern neighbors, the Atlanta of the 1970s was a city obsessed with economic progress, and it would undergo tremendous expansion in the last decades of the twentieth century. Just as *Atlanta Constitution* editor Henry Grady had looked north for investment and support in the wake of the Civil War, the city's newest generation of boosters saw international dollars as the future for Atlanta and relentlessly promoted the city's hospitality, cheap labor force, and agreeable business climate.

But despite Atlanta's claims of being an "international city," most of its residents in the 1970s still affirmed stereotypical myths about the homogeneity of a Southern biracial society. Atlanta, like the rest of Georgia and the Southeast, had not experienced the massive influx of immigration that transformed Northern cities in the early twentieth century, and few tightly knit ethnic communities were noticeable within the city. Although some immigrant groups—notably Jews, Greeks, and, in the 1950s, Cuban refugees—had settled in Atlanta, their numbers were comparatively small, and many of them arrived with cultural and financial capital that eased their assimilation into an established society. In a state with nearly 5.5 million residents, Georgia was home in 1980 to fewer than 100,000 foreign-born individuals. Less than 1 percent of Georgians classified themselves as outside of the binary racial structure of black and white; in metro Atlanta this number was barely higher. In a matter of two decades, this homogeneity would be considerably upset.

Over the course of nearly thirty years, the "Your Dekalb Farmers Market," like the city itself, was wholly transformed by an immigration revolution that continues to redefine the dynamics of the urban South. What began as a roadside produce stand was a decade later one of the largest indoor food markets in the nation, occupying a facility of over 140,000 square feet and catering to a demographic group that had only recently settled in the region. In today's Dekalb Farmers Market, laden shopping carts collide in crowded aisles, hundreds of voices speaking dozens of languages blend into a jarring cacophony inside the refrigerated warehouse, and nearly two hundred flags from all corners of the globe hang from the rafters, reflecting the diversity of both the employees and the clientele.

Although the phrase "farmers market" brings to mind images of local growers peddling their produce, Blazer's operation is fully centralized, with all workers officially employed by the market. Out of these nearly 550 employees, no more than two dozen are native Southerners, black or white, and Blazer claims that his workforce hails from "every area that has a large immigration going on." The Dekalb Market's clientele is similarly diverse. The product line has also shifted to meet the preferences and tastes of its new customers, with bok choy, carp, and samosas for sale alongside okra and collard greens. The Dekalb Farmers Market has thus become an animated monument to a multicultural Atlanta.

While statistical figures can offer only a slice of reality, a comparative analysis of the 1980 and 2000 censuses is solid proof that Atlanta has undergone tremendous change. DeKalb County attracted thousands of immigrants during these two decades, due to the availability of cheap housing and access to public transportation. While the county grew 38 percent in total population between 1980 and 2000, the number of nonwhite and nonblack residents grew by 747 percent, from 1.5 to nearly 10 percent of the population. Comprised mainly of Asian and Latino immigrants and refugees, this wave of newcomers found homes in all of Atlanta's fast-growing communities. In some of the city's suburbs, this increase was especially noticeable. Chamblee, located in northern DeKalb County, was more than 92 percent white in 1980, but twenty years later this number had fallen to 46 percent. Chamblee's foreign-born population simultaneously increased from 6 to 64 percent of the total, eventually earning the suburb the derisive nickname of "Chambodia," although today Latinos are by far the area's largest immigrant group.

This demographic upheaval raises several important questions. How has the introduction of a large immigrant population reshaped Southern culture, long known for resisting outside influence? How does cultural and culinary diversity shape regional, ethnic, and racial self-awareness? And in looking at trends within the food industry and Atlanta cuisine, why did the Rebel Chef Drive-In, as an allegorical example, close, while the Thai Diner opened a second location? As demonstrated in the history of the Dekalb Farmers Market, ethnic food, its sale and consumption, was critical to both the dissolution and preservation of identities for both recent immigrants and native Southerners; and while the growth of the market was occasionally resisted by natives, it was more often embraced and promoted by those who saw ethnic and cultural diversity as vital to the making of a truly international and cosmopolitan city.

In the course of a quarter century, this tremendous immigrant influx internationalized Atlanta from the bottom up and deeply affected the way white and black Southerners eat, drink, and think about food and themselves. Atlanta's cultural transformation was exemplified in the rise of the Dekalb Farmers Market and has given a new spin to the adage "You are what you eat."

The explosion of immigration in the Sunbelt South is a rather new phenomenon, and our understanding of its significance is only now developing. Both journalists and historians are coming to grips with the social, political, economic, and cultural effects of recent immigrants and are finding the worn debate of the "melting pot" versus "multiculturalism" insufficient for fully explaining present issues. Recent publications acknowledge the downfall of the South's binary racial order and discuss the complications that this has brought. As historians and anthropologists recognize the tremendous cultural importance of food and its place within modern consumer societies, we gain an important tool in analyzing the effects of global migrations. Still, much of today's Southern food writing is cast in a framework of black and white, despite the addition of Latino, Asian, and African cuisines to the Southern diet.

When Robert Blazer opened Your Dekalb Farmers Market in the summer of 1977, however, non-Euro-American foods were fringe delicacies enjoyed only by a small percentage of Atlanta's population. Glancing through the 1977 Atlanta Yellow Pages reveals a city that had yet to be transformed by the proliferation of ethnic food: Only ninety-two out of approximately fifteen hundred restaurants could be classified as non-Euro-American. With forty-six

Chinese, fourteen Japanese, eighteen Mexican, and only two Thai restaurants, Atlanta was a city still characterized by "all-American" food such as that served at the Varsity and Chick-fil-A, two popular restaurants that both claim Atlanta as their birthplace. Blazer was therefore not incorrect in describing Atlanta's culinary atmosphere as "traditional" upon his arrival.

The very same year that Blazer relocated to Georgia, Herbert T. Jenkins, the former longtime police chief of Atlanta, published a short book on the history of the city's produce business. Titled *Food, Fairs and Farmers' Markets in Atlanta*, Jenkins's book portrayed a city whose food industry truly was as "traditional" as Blazer remembered. In describing the Atlanta State Farmers Market, which was then the largest such venue in the city, Jenkins writes of a "pleasant nostalgic scene" where Georgia farmers brought their harvest directly to local consumers. One annual celebration was the "popular and enduring" Watermelon Day, where free slices of watermelon and live country music were a "big highlight for the entire family." Though "esoteric produce" like "clementines, romaine, [and] shallots" were sold, they did "not comprise a typical Atlanta menu."

It was in this city of grits and greens that Your Dekalb Farmers Market opened on June 2, 1977, at Scott Boulevard and North Decatur Road in Decatur. The local community newspaper described the market as a "new business that will specialize in the sale of fresh fruits and vegetables." The *Decatur-DeKalb News/ Era* likened Blazer's new business to a "street market" where "nothing will be held over night" and any remaining produce was to be "sold at special prices just before closing." The range of food sold was "traditional," as well, "from apple[s] to a crate of greens." Two weeks later, the market ran an ad in the same paper, advertising "fresh fruit and vegetables direct from the farm to you!" The produce sold was primarily locally grown, as nearby Georgia, Tennessee, and South Carolina farmers brought their goods to the city. While Blazer's operation was primitive in comparison with today's warehouse and lacked its multicultural focus, the market was initially successful, in part because it faced little competition from similar vendors in the local neighborhood.

In the following months, the market quietly grew and built a consumer base in the city of Decatur and in DeKalb County, but February of 1979 brought an unplanned catastrophe: A buildup of ice and snow on the roof of the building caused a collapse, causing more than $100,000 in damage. Blazer went door-to-door in Decatur to raise nearly $25,000 to aid in rebuilding the market, and dedicated customers proved critical in financing the reconstruction. Blazer's brother and sister, Harry and Linda, also moved to Atlanta to help rebuild and to join the business, and Harry Blazer became general manager for several years.

The market's reinvention as an ethnic bazaar had its roots in these early years and was inspired not only by changing demographics but by food-industry trends as well. Throughout the 1980s, the commercial food retail industry underwent large-scale consolidation, and the massive supermarkets run by corporations such as Cincinnati's Kroger placed enormous pressure on smaller, independently run firms. To survive these "supermarket wars," a business like Blazer's needed a competitive edge, which came in an expanded selection of foods unavailable in mainstream grocery stores. The Dekalb Farmers Market was one of the first groceries to experiment with internationalizing their product line, though by the end of the decade, Blazer would have a score of followers. "The revolution is now," claimed one Atlanta food writer in 1988. "Atlanta's former beans-and-potatoes complacency is being subverted by cadres of strange and alien fruits, nuts and vegetables." Growing awareness about health foods and the benefits of a varied diet contributed to the market's popularity. In 1991 James Hood, editor of the supermarket trade publication *The Shelby Report*, praised Blazer's business as a "throwback to the old days of traditional markets." "We're seeing more of these places in response to consumer demand," he argued in an interview with the *Atlanta Journal-Constitution*.

With a new location, building, and an evolving business strategy, the market prospered as it began to attract a clientele that was quickly growing within Atlanta. The nonwhite and nonblack population of DeKalb County nearly tripled in the 1980s, and Asian and Hispanic immigrants flocked to the market as Blazer's business began catering to this new demographic influx. Connie Siu Guinn, the daughter of two Asian immigrant entrepreneurs who opened Golden China, one of the first Chinese restaurants in nearby Snellville, re-members shopping at the market throughout the eighties: "Going to the market was a ritual. Every Saturday my family would go. My mom would buy the produce and the products she missed so much, and my father would pick up wholesale items for the restaurant." In providing the raw materials for ethnic food vendors, the market facilitated the operation of dozens of restaurants like the Siu family's. The market also became a social experience for immigrants: "I knew I would not only get a Toblerone all to myself, but that I would get to see some 'nonwhite' kids," said one customer. "Many times it was a social place, too. My parents would see friends from the tightly knit Asian community." Atlanta immigrants began forming what historian Daniel Boorstin has called "communities of consumption," where "nearly all objects," certainly food, become "symbols and instruments of novel communities." These informal networks only multiplied as time passed.

Thousands of shoppers swarmed the cramped aisles on weekends, and increased growth soon became problematic at the Scott Boulevard location.

The food editor of the *Atlanta Journal-Constitution* quipped in 1986 that "if the three words 'Dekalb Farmers Market' leave a bad taste in your mouth, it's probably because three shopping carts pinned you in between the peppers and cucumbers one Saturday morning or a noisy, honking forklift chased you from the seafood to the cheese department." Spatial constraints necessitated a move, and in September of 1986 the market relocated to its current location, an expanded building on East Ponce De Leon Avenue in Decatur. Designed by Robert Blazer himself, the new facility was more than four times the size of the previous location and promised "the widest, cross-cultural array of seafood, produce, deli items and baked goods ever assembled in Atlanta."

At the same time, local residents near the old Scott Boulevard location, who had experienced firsthand the explosive growth of the market and its new customer base, were happy to see it go. Despite reassurances from the DeKalb County Health Department that the market violated no regulations, unhappy neighbors deemed it rodent-infested and malodorous; traffic flowing in and out of the market's undersized parking lot congested city streets. "Unfounded rumors of poisonous snakes in the produce" also plagued the market, reported an *Atlanta Journal-Constitution* writer in 1984, and it is apparent that not every Atlanta resident embraced the sudden introduction of foreign foods and cuisines into the city.

A bitter family feud disrupted the operation of the market in 1987, and Harry Blazer left the company after a personal dispute to undertake an independent venture, Harry's Farmers Markets. Eschewing the utilitarian focus and multiethnic clientele of his older brother's company, Harry opened stores in suburban Cobb and Gwinnett counties, which were becoming home to middle- and upper-class white-collar workers. Harry's Farmers Markets, while still selling products from all over the globe, had higher prices and immaculately decorated interiors that were far different from the wet concrete and fluorescent lighting of the Dekalb Market. As "the brothers are divided by their differences," reported the *Atlanta Journal-Constitution*, the two markets "divided shoppers as well." The visually pleasing Harry's Markets attracted well-to-do, native-born whites, while the Dekalb Market solidified the loyalty of its growing immigrant clientele. Many shoppers living in the suburban communities north of Atlanta stopped making the "long trip down" to Decatur, but not all believed Harry's gloss and sheen to be superior: "Harry's took the idea and made it commercial," one loyal Dekalb Farmers Market shopper insisted.

Robert Blazer assured reporters that while "the appearance of the [Dekalb] Market may not be spectacular, . . . when the smoke clears, Dekalb will still be around. I don't know what will happen with these other markets." The elder Blazer was right. Though initially successful, Harry's Farmers Markets never turned a profit after 1993; the stores were eventually bought out by the natural-foods giant Whole Foods Market in 2001. "Our aspirations have exceeded our grasp because of our performance," Harry Blazer told the media after the deal was finalized. While a buyout from a larger corporation was often financially lucrative for a smaller company, the Whole Foods deal was not negotiated entirely on Harry Blazer's terms: Several of the smaller Harry's in a Hurry stores were not included in the purchase. As Harry's Markets foundered, the Dekalb Market prospered.

In addition to fierce competition from Harry's and similar copycat grocery stores, the Dekalb Farmers Market faced opposition from native Southerners who did not see growing multiculturalism as a positive trend. During the first Persian Gulf War in 1991, more than one hundred war veterans, opposed to the presence of an Iraqi flag among the nearly two hundred others hanging from the rafters of the relocated East Ponce market, picketed and boycotted the store. Ten Atlanta Veterans of Foreign Wars posts organized the demonstration in response to Blazer's refusal to remove the flag, which had been hanging inside the market for more than three years. Despite receiving harassing phone calls and bomb threats, Blazer did not yield. "We said the flags represented the people, not the politics," Blazer recalled. Many Atlantans agreed, including one who wrote a letter to the editor of the *Atlanta Journal-Constitution*: "The notion of removing an enemy's flag in time of war reminds me of an emotional teenager tearing up the photograph of an ex-boyfriend or girlfriend." While the conflict was resolved without a major boycott, it was clear that not all native Atlantans viewed the all-inclusive, immigrant-friendly market positively.

Nevertheless, the flag protests, along with the earlier snake rumors and parking complaints, were isolated incidents. The market's popularity with both natives and newcomers grew enormously over the years. "As many as 10,000 people come to shop on weekends and hundreds of others come simply to marvel at the piles of fruits and vegetables and the attendant babel of languages," wrote an *Atlanta Journal-Constitution* reporter in 1984. As Atlanta's boosters actively promoted the city's "international" status, the market became an oft-mentioned symbol of Atlanta's diversity. "If Atlanta has any claim to world-class rankings," argued one 1991 editorial, "the market boosts that claim considerably." An *Atlanta Journal* writer described the market as "Atlanta's greatest cultural melting pot," and a 1988 *National Geographic Magazine* feature on Atlanta's "energy and optimism" singled out the Dekalb Market as "something Atlantans like to brag about," as it was "an international city in itself." As many Atlanta residents enthusiastically lionized the market and incorporated it into the city's mythology, it seemed Southern culture was more flexible and adaptive than previously thought.

Popularity and growth brought internal problems, however, and interactions between different immigrant groups and market management occasionally proved difficult. In December 1988 eight former employees of various nationalities, both native and foreign-born, sued the market in federal court over questionable training practices involving the "Forum," an alleged "New Age quasi-religious cult" that allegedly subjected employees to "harassment, humiliation and interrogation." In 1987 Robert Blazer joined the "human potential program" founded by New Age philosopher Werner Erhard in the early seventies. Blazer allegedly forced employees to attend group training sessions, and workers later protested that the sessions violated their right to religious freedom "under the guise of 'management training.'" With eventual American Civil Liberties Union involvement, the case received significant national publicity but was eventually settled out of court in June of 1989.

This would not be the last dispute between labor and management: In June 1991 twenty-eight Ethiopian employees were fired for leaving work to attend a protest in Atlanta against U.S. foreign policy in their home country. A misunderstanding arose when several workers believed they had received permission to attend while Blazer denied having granted any such request. "They decided that they would much rather be at a demonstration than keep their jobs," Blazer told the media. "We love our jobs, but we love our country, too," countered a former employee. Both the lawsuit and the 1991 firings demonstrated that the assimilation of immigrants into the market's workforce was not without its problems.

Despite competition, opposition, and internal division, by the mid-1990s the market had established itself as a permanent institution for incoming Atlanta immigrants, particularly as a source of employment. "With waves of immigration, we absorb those people," Blazer said of the often-shifting workforce. "Some will stay, because they really like the business, but others will just pass through. But they get their start here: thousands and thousands of people." Welcoming refugees from around the world into its growing workforce, the market began to assume almost a charitable, philanthropic position in the burgeoning immigrant community; the *Atlanta Journal-Constitution* even described Blazer as "do[ing] his small share in helping race relations." Mekonnen Yayne, an Ethiopian refugee who arrived in Atlanta in 1987 after fleeing an oppressive regime in his home country, expressed his gratitude: "I am very grateful to the Dekalb Farmers Market for the opportunity to support myself in my new life. I miss [my family] greatly but get comfort from the family I've developed here at the market." Each time a member from a large immigrant family was hired, he or she made possible the relocation of more relatives to Atlanta.

Once in Atlanta, recent immigrants found that the wide selection of ethnic foods at the market facilitated retention of their ethnic identities. Because of the market's rapid product turnover and large clientele, Blazer has been able to order foods from all over the globe. "A guy like me can foster all this product coming in, but it's not easy to find," Blazer says. Despite this difficulty, Blazer's efforts have paid off for Juan Bautista, a Dekalb Market employee for more than twenty years and a native of Puerto Rico: "Everything is here. No matter what country you come from, you'll always find the stuff you need." Connie Siu Guinn agrees: "You are not going to find beef tongue, tripe, fresh made samosa, or rice candy at your local Kroger." Since "food was [her] parents' way to hold onto memories and pass on traditions," Connie and her family found the market to be critical in preserving their memories, traditions, and identities.

While many older immigrants clung to native foodways and shunned American mass-market hamburgers and hot dogs, their children were often drawn to the mystique of a new culture. Wendimu Abeb, a young Ethiopian who worked at the market for two years after fleeing his homeland, admitted that he shopped at Ethiopian restaurants for a year before going to Chinese restaurants and then on to "try new things." Robert Blazer also saw younger immigrants "branching out, and start[ing to] cook different things for their families," whereas the older generation was "not going to change much." As children of immigrants forego their traditional identities, or "get caught up in the nonsense," as Bautista says, their community suffers. "They need to stay together to continue to develop their cultures." As the children of immigrants immerse themselves in mainstream American culture, the once-rigid boundaries between ethnic cuisines and cultures will continue to blur and break down.

The market was not alone in providing ethnic food to recent immigrants. Atlanta's restaurant industry experienced an explosive growth in the numbers of non-European eateries. From 92 ethnic restaurants in 1977, Atlanta in 2005 could claim 579, with nearly 200 Chinese, 162 Mexican, and more than 50 Thai restaurants. These numerical estimates may even be low, as many smaller restaurants operating with solely immigrant clienteles are not listed in the Yellow Pages.

While Your Dekalb Farmers Market may be the largest, it is only one of many ethnic food retailers in Atlanta. Equally famous is the Buford Highway Corridor, a six-mile stretch of highway that spans three counties and was home to more than seven hundred immigrant-owned businesses in 1998. This "real international boulevard," as the *Atlanta Journal-Constitution* has called it, also features a food market that is a copycat of Blazer's Decatur market, the Buford Highway Farmers Market. In addition, former Dekalb Market employees founded the nearby International Farmers Market in Chamblee, which offers similar products. As Atlanta's immigration increased over the years, more and more newcomers became food entrepreneurs, providing their compatriots with an opportunity to preserve culinary traditions.

Atlanta's new ethnic restaurants and markets did not cater solely to immigrant communities. White and black Southerners alike became regular shoppers and consumers of these newly introduced cuisines. As immigration historian Donna Gabaccia has noted in examining the impact of ethnic food in the early twentieth century, owners of "enclave markets" that catered exclusively to fellow immigrants came to realize that their consumer base "provided a rather fragile financial foundation." By reaching "beyond the boundaries of ethnic communities," immigrant entrepreneurs attempted to expand their horizons in catering to native Southerners. The process was difficult at first, as rigid ethnic identities made for strictly defined tastes and preferences. "Many of my colleagues advised me not to experiment with things that were too authentic because American customers were not used to them," said a Chinese restaurant owner who arrived in Atlanta in 1977.

With some adaptation by those who prepared the food and those who consumed it, cross-cultural eating became ubiquitous over time, despite initial misgivings on both sides. The "novelty, entertainment and a sense of partaking in the excitement of big city life," Gabaccia argues, drew Americans to eating outside their traditional culture. Food consumption, as historian Andrew Heinze has noted in his examination of European Jews in America, became a "bridge between cultures," capable of signifying "one's attitude toward and place within society." Reflecting modern Atlanta's culinary mélange, John Kessler, a food writer for the *Atlanta Journal-Constitution*, described his intimate relationship with the Dekalb Farmers Market: "I love the thrilling strangeness of the place, the feeling that *this*—right here, right now—is my culture."

As immigrants remade Atlanta into a truly international city, Robert Blazer capitalized on this nascent consumer base, and eventually the Dekalb Farmers Market became symbolic of a multicultural Atlanta. The process was neither simple nor speedy but perfectly reflects the profound demographic changes that are giving rise to what historian Leon Fink has termed the "Nuevo New South." As Atlanta lost its reputation as a city cast solely in black and white, ethnic food became the vanguard of cultural interaction, increasingly blurring the lines between foreign and native cultures and cuisines.

The history of Blazer's market also undermines the long-held popular interpretation of Southern culture as reactionary, stagnant, and resistant to change. The interaction of native and foreign cultures in the last decades of the twentieth century was less of a "clash" than a slow intermingling that melded the exotic with the "downhome." Historian James C. Cobb described Southern identity as "not a story of continuity *versus* change, but continuity *within* it." The same can be said for trends within foodways and ethnic cuisine, as witnessed in the eventual eagerness of Atlanta residents to experiment with their foodways. Grits and fried chicken won't disappear, but perhaps future Southerners will enjoy them with a side of rice noodles or enchilada sauce.

At the entrance of Your Dekalb Farmers Market hangs a plaque with Robert Blazer's motivational philosophy titled "Our Stand":

> We declare the world is designed to work.
> We are responsible for what does not work.
> We make the difference.
>
> No matter how technologically advanced we become,
> we cannot escape our fundamental relationship with food
> and each other. The possibility of these relationships is the
> world market. In this context, the world works for
> everyone free of scarcity and suffering.
>
> We commit ourselves to the possibility this world market
> is for the future generations of this planet.

As customers of all races, nationalities, and cultures pass the sign by the thousands, I doubt that many stand in awe and contemplate the meaning of both this declaration and the larger market. But in the capital of the Sunbelt South, the quiet revolution of immigration and food continues to upset and redefine the meanings of local, regional, and global identity.

Descendants of Greek Immigrants Aren't Pining for Pita

John T. Edge

A clump of feta, tucked in a salad of iceberg and cucumbers. A stipple of oregano on a broiled snapper fillet. A streusel of baklava atop a cheesecake. At the Bright Star in Bessemer, Alabama, thirteen miles southwest of Birmingham, the vestiges of Greece are few.

Greek immigrants built the Bright Star, a vintage dining hall of intricately patterned tile floors, nicotine-patinaed woodwork, and brass chandeliers. It's a 300-seat behemoth of a restaurant, the civic and culinary anchor of a one-time industrial town, named for Henry Bessemer, the Brit who pioneered processes for forging pig iron into steel.

In 2007 the Bright Star turned one hundred. That means it's just two years younger than Galatoire's, the New Orleans restaurant of great renown and even greater soufflé potatoes. Like Galatoire's, the Bright Star remains a family-focused enterprise.

Descendants of Bright Star founding fathers—1906 arrival Tom Bonduris, a native of the farming village of Peleta in the mountainous Peloponnesus region, and his cousin, Bill Koikos, who followed from Peleta in 1920—still work the floor each and every day.

But the Bright Star is not hyphenated. It's not Greek-Southern. Or even Greek-American. The restaurant and, more to the point, the family who owns it, have ceased pining for pita.

They are fully realized residents of the South, lifelong students of the crusty art of cornbread. And so is the long-tenured crew of cooks, waiters, and busboys who work for present-day proprietors Jimmy Koikos and brother Nicky.

"We got some olive oil back in the kitchen," says lead lunch cook Robert Moore, a veteran of nearly twenty-five years, a man home-schooled in the traditions of soul food cookery. "We use that for our squash, but for everything else, bacon grease gets the job done."

Civic boosters once touted Birmingham as the Magic City, a reference to its boomtown industrial beginnings. Advocates of Bessemer dubbed their burg the Marvel City. Both places, birthed in the years following the Civil War, did not follow traditional Southern patterns, wherein a city grew wealthy by way of agricultural sales and commodity trading.

Instead, Bessemer and Birmingham built soot-belching furnaces and factories, heavy industrial enterprises that earned the area yet another nickname: "Pittsburgh of the South." And the promise of industry drew job seekers. Some were farmers, born and bred Southerners who pastured their draft horses in exchange for paychecks and pensions.

Others, from beyond these shores, followed relatives who had already blazed a trail, in search of a shot at the American dream. Greek natives came in droves. Propelled by wars with Turkey and goaded by crop failures and bungled agricultural initiatives, more than 400,000 Greeks made landfall in America between 1890 and 1910, the proximate decades during which Bessemer and Birmingham muscled their way to industrial might.

Those industrial workers, many of whom arrived without spouses or children, clamored to wolf down lunch-break sandwiches from portable canteens, to dine in cafés, to drink and carouse in taverns. And Greek immigrants met those needs.

Their entrepreneurial motivations were many. The restaurant business required minimal startup capital and offered a great deal of liquidity, factors likely to appeal to new immigrants. And the chance to interact with the public across a counter, across a table, promised on-the-job lessons in English.

Or maybe it was all kismet, fueled by cousin-to-cousin connections, wherein each family hire abetted another.

No matter. Greeks quickly came to set the restaurant industry standard in Bessemer and Birmingham. Much the same proved true in other Southern cities. Like Columbia, where the Elite Epicurean Restaurant was much beloved. And Knoxville, where the Greek-founded steakhouse Regas still bakes the city's favorite red velvet cake.

Atlanta lacked Birmingham's density of Greek-owned restaurants, but it did boast the Peachtree Café, co-owned by Charles Keramidas, described in a 1911 directory as having "already given himself up to the melting pot." (In more recent years, the hash-slinging Majestic Diner on Ponce de Leon Avenue was in its heyday when owned by K. A. Kliossis. On the opposite end of the economic spectrum, Panos Karatassos, a proprietor of Kyma, today's haute Greek destination, is the man who sold 1970s-era Atlanta on battered and fried lobster tails and the art of fine dining.)

Keramidas's move to fold into the multiethnic whole was the rule. Adoption of the South's mores and cookery was an early imperative of Greek life in a region that was, for the longest time, famously inhospitable to outlanders. Most famously, in the early years of the twentieth century, the Ku Klux Klan went on a xenophobic bender, intent upon running out "foreigners." Assimilation was the safe tack to take. And a diner counter or six-burner stove provided just the buffer a new immigrant required.

"Our mother belonged to both," says Nicky Koikos, the shorter and quieter of the brothers. "She went to the Greek Orthodox Church in Birmingham," he says, sipping a cup of coffee, watching the Bright Star lunch rush subside. "And the Episcopal Church in Bessemer."

Fried red snapper throats, priced at $10.75 and house-cut from whole Gulf fish, were on the menu this day. Okra in a cornmeal crust, too. And field peas with snaps. And that odd marriage of angel hair cabbage and almost Russian dressing that devotees call John's slaw, in tribute to the Greek-owned Birmingham restaurant that popularized it. Not to mention cornbread and pull-apart rolls that arrived in a wicker basket.

That's a pretty typical lunch roster at the Bright Star. The sort of midday repast that, five decades before, Tasia Koikos, mother of Jimmy and Nicky, would have eaten after the Episcopal Church released Sunday morning parishioners into the Bessemer streets.

Those snapper throats owe a debt to Greek fishing acumen and frugality. But much of the rest of the menu reads like a greatest-hits playlist from the Southern farm-to-table soundtrack.

Tasia Koikos came of age in a day when Greek-born citizens of the American South were working hard to prove fidelity to their adopted home. They formed civic groups like the American Hellenic Educational Progressive Association. ("Loyalty to the United States and love for its ideals" were, in the words of a 1931 newspaper account, the goals.)

These Hellenic sons and daughters tucked away recipes for olive oil–roasted leg of lamb. They cooked collards with fatback. And sweet potatoes slicked with butter and brown sugar. They learned to wrest smoky goodness from a cider vinegar–doused pork shoulder. They opened cafés with curious and somehow localized monikers such as Happy John Bollas's Barbecue Gardens.

They went native.

On this late winter day, Jim Middlebrook, a buyer and seller of heavy trucks who sat down to his first Bright Star meal in 1979, is eating beef short ribs. With sweet potatoes. And baby butter beans.

"I don't expect the black-eyed peas and the collard greens to be Greek," he says. "I expect them to be good. The snapper has some Greek in it. Personally, I like the Greek. But it's not for everybody."

Middlebrook takes a last swig of his sweet tea. He waves to Jimmy Koikos, seated, if only for a moment, at the bar. Jimmy worked the floor at lunch, wearing a pink button-down and a rep tie, directing dining room traffic like a Hartsfield vet. They did four hundred covers today. With dinner yet to come.

With a colleague, Jimmy goes over the play-by-play of lunch service, taking note of which regulars were in attendance, what dishes were at their best. A wall-mounted television flashes with the latest presidential primary poll. He looks up for a moment, then readdresses his plate, forking in a mouthful of peas.

In due time, Jimmy Koikos will reach across the bar for a bottle of Pompeian olive oil, the fat of his fathers, his family stash. With a steady stream of extra-virgin, he will douse those ruby pickled beets, tucked alongside that slab of gravy-drenched country fried steak.

For now, though, his mouth is full of the South.

From Barbecue to Baklava
The Delta's Culinary Crossroads

Amy C. Evans

Chafik Chamoun serves fried catfish. Kim Wong sells pork rinds. Pat and Abe Davis make barbecue. All over the Mississippi Delta, immigrants are embracing and interpreting Southern food. These three examples happen to exist only a stone's throw from the intersection of highways 61 and 49 in Clarksdale, the spot where, as the legend goes, bluesman Robert Johnson sold his soul to the devil in exchange for guitar virtuosity.

But at Chamoun's Rest Haven, Chafik Chamoun also serves baklava. At Kim's Pork Rinds, Kim Wong cooks the rinds in woks. At Abe's Bar-B-Q, the Davis brothers have hot tamales on the menu.

For generations the seasonal flooding of the Mississippi River has enriched the soil of the Delta. So, too, have the waves of immigrants that have put down roots in this part of the American South, bringing their homelands' culinary traditions with them. The Davis family of Clarksdale is part of this legacy. Abraham "Abe" Davis arrived in Clarksdale from Lebanon in the early part of the twentieth century, a time when tamales—a food with its origins in Latin America—were peddled on street corners.

Perhaps Abe recognized the tamale's similarity to a dish from his native land, stuffed grape leaves. Both are portable foods made with a meat and a starch and then rolled in small packages for convenience. "And maybe that's why my dad even started making hot tamales back then," says one of Abe's sons, Pat Davis Sr. "Because he used to love to make grape leaves and cabbage rolls and all, and then he just probably heard about hot tamales and then said, 'Yeah, I believe I can do that.'"

By the mid-1930s, Abe was in the restaurant business. Deltans still enjoy the Davis family's brand of barbecue and hot tamales that they have had for more than seventy years. At home, Pat Davis Sr. still makes Lebanese stuffed grape leaves.

In Greenville, Mississippi, a small Sicilian grocery store evolved into the iconic Doe's Eat Place, owned and operated by the Signa family. The sale of hot tamales propelled the Signas into the restaurant business in the 1940s. As cans of tamales sailed out the door, customers started coming back for the homemade spaghetti and meatballs that Mamie Signa made for her family. Today, of course, Doe's has an international clientele, and the steaks and tamales are the main attractions. But you can still get a plate of spaghetti made from Mamie Signa's recipe.

Traditional family recipes even make their way to the dining room of KC's Restaurant in Cleveland, Mississippi, from time to time. Owned and operated by the Joe family, KC's is celebrated for its modern American cuisine, but the Joe family's food philosophy is based in their Asian heritage. Chef Wally Joe has made a name for himself by creating contemporary American cuisine with Asian undertones for his family's restaurant, as well as his namesake restaurant in Memphis.

Sicilians as well as Greeks have made their culinary mark in Greenwood, Mississippi. The Lusco and Giardina families assimilated their Sicilian culinary heritage with that of the Delta, as marinara and meatballs gave way to prime steaks and pond-raised catfish. At the new Giardina's Restaurant, though, Frank Leflore celebrates his Sicilian roots, offering an Italian sausage on the menu that is made from his grandmother's recipe. At the Crystal Grill, the Ballas family incorporates a couple of nods to their Greek lineage on the expansive menu, but the restaurant's reputation is built on the quality and variety of Southern favorites. A typical meal there can consist of a Greek salad, fried chicken livers, and coconut pie.

Even the ubiquitous coconut pie we take for granted as a traditionally Southern dessert has other origins. The tropical coconut was once a hard-to-find delicacy imported from faraway places, and it was a special occasion when a whole one was meticulously shaved by hand for use in a cake or pie. Today, coconut appears in all kinds of recipes, including sweet potato casserole. Many Southern versions of the casserole include marshmallows, a food with roots going back to ancient Egypt.

So what is Southern food? More than ingredients and origins, it is about tradition and family. Many Delta families incorporate hot tamales into their Christmas holiday menu. Others insist that a coconut pie from Chamoun's Rest Haven or the Crystal Grill grace the table at Thanksgiving. Greek or Sicilian, Asian or Lebanese, the Mississippi Delta is a wonderful illustration of how ethnicity has embraced Southern food and how Southern food has embraced ethnicity. Let us all gather at the crossroads.

Lebanese Stuffed Grape Leaves or Warak Enab

Serves 30.

2 pounds ground chuck
Half a jar of Orlando or other
　brand grape leaves (about 90
　leaves)
1¼ cups rice, uncooked

2 teaspoons salt
1 teaspoon black pepper
½ cup lemon juice, divided
　(or more to taste)

Wash grape leaves well in warm water. Drain. Mix all other ingredients together. (Lemon juice, ¼ cup, will keep meat from sticking together.) Place single grape leaf flat on plate, greener side down; place heaping tablespoon of mixture near stem, which is closer to you, and roll, tucking both ends in.

　　Place in 2–3-quart boiler, covering the bottom of boiler in one direction. Alternate the next row, leaving a little room between each roll for expansion of rice. Place small plate on top of leaves to keep them in place. Add enough water to cover the plate. Then add ¼ cup more of lemon juice. If you like a tangier flavor, add another ¼ cup of lemon juice. Bring to a boil and then simmer for 30 minutes. Turn off heat and let rolls rest for 15 minutes.

From Pat Davis Sr., Abe's Bar-B-Q, Clarksdale, Mississippi.

The Delta Hot Tamale
Save Those Coffee Cans

Martha Hall Foose

Sam the Tamale Man had a vision twenty-two years ago while recovering from a stroke. He was moved by these apparitions to build a truly moveable feast. From his well-appointed truck he has found his way to a contented spot on the shoulder of Highway 49 in the Mississippi Delta. He sells catfish and buffalo fish and some shrimp, too, but as the bold hand-printed sign advertises, hot tamales are the main attraction. He stays open until sunset every day, then cranks up his restaurant and heads home.

Every little honky-tonking town throughout the Delta has at least one hot tamale stand. You'll see these first cousins of Mexican tamales individually wrapped in traditional cornhusks, as well as an assortment of other wrappers like coffee filters and waxed paper. They are most often bundled in threes, tied with butcher's twine, and swaddled in newspaper for eating right then, or packed in lard buckets or #10 cans recycled out of necessity for travel.

Dozens and dozens of tamale transactions take place every day from outfitted trucks, roadside stands, and out-the-back screen doors of neighbors' kitchens, creating a thriving tamale economy. Delta tamale theory holds that African American farmworkers met migrant Mexican workers in the field. These two disparate groups both brought lunches featuring cornmeal from home, and the tamale assimilated into this area of the country. Whoever brought a love of hot tamales to the Delta, the Signas began meeting the demand.

Like many Delta dining establishments, Doe's Eat Place began as a grocery store. It opened in 1903. Carmel Signa sailed from Sicily and somehow made his way to the Mississippi River town of Greenville. With the family's living quarters in the back, the store—called "Papa's Store" by the Signa family—flourished until the flood of 1927. To help the family recover from their loss, Carmel's son Dominic, or Big Doe, started bootlegging whiskey. Several years later, he sold his still for $300 and a Model-T Ford. Big Doe worked in the cafeteria at the Air Force base in Greenville and was given a hot tamale recipe by one of the enlisted men.

Mamie, Big Doe's wife, improved on the initial recipe and began selling tamales from her kitchen. They were popular, and soon the Signa women and children were rolling tamales together, frequently to sell to the families who showed up with coffee cans and pots to get some of their spicy, saucy red hot tamales for their dinner.

Doe's is still going strong and still sells hot tamales at the table or by the coffee can. The Signa family was recently honored with a James Beard Award. To understand the economic and social history of the Mississippi Delta from the 1920s up to today, all you need to do is follow the tamale.

In the Doe's Kitchen with Aunt Florence

Anne Martin

Born in 1926 in Boyle, Mississippi, Florence Signa says she has no intention of retiring anytime soon. Florence grew up in the country outside of Greenville. She and her late husband Frank have four children, thirteen grandchildren, and three great-grandchildren. She says she doesn't smoke, drink, or gamble, doesn't read much or watch a lot of TV. Meeting all of the people who come into Doe's Eat Place in Greenville over the years is something she looks forward to every day. Her secret to a long, productive life, she says, is going to Mass every day at five-thirty in the morning.

Anne Martin: *I understand you've been working at Doe's since before you married Frank Signa in 1948.*

Aunt Florence: I always said I wasn't going to marry but after seeing Frank at a Catholic carnival in Shaw, I changed my mind. This good-looking man wearing gold pants and a maroon jacket came up to me and asked if I wanted to play one of his chance cards at the carnival. I said no. A few days later he asked my sister-in-law if I would date him. He called and asked me to the Greenville High School football game. I told him I would think about it and call back. I was playing hard to get. We had our first date on Halloween night. He worked at Doe's during oyster season and asked if I would help fry potatoes on the weekends. It was the only way we could see each other. He courted me through the window that separated the oyster shucking from the potato frying.

How did you end up with the job of making Doe's salads?

I had graduated from potatoes to waiting on tables where I got to visit with so many people. Frank's sisters helped out; his entire family worked there. One night one of the sisters got sick, and the one who was making the salads moved over to making some of the side dishes. They asked me to do the salads that night, and I've been doing that ever since.

Tell me about the legendary wooden salad bowl.

You mean bowls! We've been through a few of those bowls over the years. They have to be seasoned just right; it adds to the flavor of the salad. They will crack on the side and dry out if you don't keep them seasoned well. We have two new ones we are seasoning now. We've even had people bring in their own wooden bowls and ask us to season them. Mike Boyd, a Greenville attorney, brought in a bowl we kept for two or three years. We even had a man from Indiana mail us his bowl so we could season it.

Is there a secret to curing the bowl?

Rub it with garlic every night. But the best way is to make salad in it and let the garlic, oil, and lemon juice soak in. Those flavors just build up. That's why a wooden bowl is so much better than a metal one.

How have you adjusted the salad recipe over the years?

I haven't changed a thing. This is the same recipe Mamie (wife of original owner Big Doe Signa) was using in 1941. It's good, no need to change it. People like it.

One Friday night, I sat in the kitchen and watched you make salad. I lost count of how many bowls you made.

An average is about fifteen bowls a night. Out of that we can serve up about fifteen people. All of the ingredients—lettuce, tomato, onion—are cut up before we open. I only use fresh squeezed lemon juice. Everything is measured out, except the oil and salt, before the customers get there, so all I have to do is put it in the bowl and mix it up—between seating customers and answering the phone.

Who are some of the famous folks who have walked through the doors over the years?

Liza Minnelli came in one Sunday night with a group of folks from Arkansas. Frank's sister Rosalie came and told me. I didn't believe her, so I went and asked her. The man with her asked if I wanted her to sing for her supper. I got her autograph that night. Then a few years later I was in New York and she was singing at a convention. I walked past security, told her who I was, and asked if she remembered me. She said she did.

One day Willie Nelson came in and sat by the side door. We didn't make a big to-do about it; he just wanted to enjoy his meal. President Clinton came in when he was governor of Arkansas. His daughter Chelsea and her boyfriend Ian Klass have been here, and they are vegetarian! They ate everything but the steak. Oh, and the Ambassador of Great Britain, writers Willie Morris, Julia Reed, and several of the governors have been here, too.

What are some fun things that have taken place over the years?

Jesse Brent would bring a group of folks in, and after all of the customers would leave, we all would sit around and sing. One night, some customers were staying longer than Jesse thought they should; he was ready to have some fun. He asked Mamie if she could encourage them to finish up. She began to sing "Goodnight Irene." They got the hint, left, and the real party began.

Do you mind that most everyone who walks through the doors calls you Aunt Florence?

Oh, no. When folks walk in and say they want a table, Doe tells them to go see Aunt Florence. So they ask for Aunt Florence. Folks I've never seen before in my life call me Aunt Florence. We're one big family and like to make everyone feel at home.

Home Cooking
East Meets South at a Delta Table

Joan Nathan

In the Mississippi Delta town of Clarksdale, home of the blues and Muddy Waters, cooks are sizzling catfish and collards and crayfish every day and night. But you don't expect to find those home chefs stir-frying them or steaming them in a giant backyard wok.

But the Chow family, like the other hundred or so Chinese Americans here with Delta roots going back a century or more, use the ingredients at hand and the techniques passed on for generations.

"What we eat connects us so that we know we are both Chinese and Mississippi Delta folks," Gilroy Chow said in his thick Southern drawl as he cooked crayfish Cantonese style in an outdoor wok.

Near the crayfish, an eight-pound catfish was cooking in another wok. The fish, too big for a poacher, was a gift to the Chows from a fellow member of the local Baptist church. He had caught it that morning in the Mississippi, and now it was simmering in the giant wok. Covered with aluminum foil and balanced on a large propane burner, the wok is a family heirloom brought over from China.

The recipe is an heirloom from China as well, although with a couple of adjustments. After the fish was cooked, it would be seasoned with soy sauce, then garnished with garlic, ginger, scallions, and crisply sliced strips of bacon.

"The bacon is something that we have incorporated," Chow's wife, Sally, said. "It's the same with our fried rice. I don't think many Chinese would make fried rice with bacon, as we do."

The Chinese first came to the Delta during Reconstruction, when plantation owners, looking for cheap labor and worried that black workers were acting like free people rather than slaves, lured the immigrants with promises of jobs, said James W. Loewen, author of *The Mississippi Chinese: Between Black and White.* "But the Chinese immediately found that they had been lied to," Loewen said. "They could never make money and send any home competing against America's lowest-paid work force, blacks in the Mississippi Delta, so they opened grocery stores. Ninety-five percent of the Chinese operated grocery stores, mostly for black clientele."

Most Chinese who came to the South settled in the Delta, Loewen said. The 2000 census listed 689 in the Delta counties, but local Chinese Americans say there are more than twice that many.

The Chows came after the first wave. "My father settled in Cleveland, Mississippi, in 1912," said Gilroy Chow, an engineer. "Later, he opened a grocery store in Greenville."

Like many other Chinese in the South, the Chows lived above their grocery store and grew Chinese vegetables in their backyard. In a segregated society, they maintained distinctiveness from blacks and whites, having their own schools and Chinese Baptist churches. Today they are more integrated into society. The Chows are active in the Oakhurst Baptist Church, the largest in Clarksdale, and Sally Chow is its organist.

"We were all born in the Delta," said Gilroy, one of six children. "My father was an entrepreneur and was traveling, selling meat throughout the South." After making commercial contacts in the North, Chow's father moved the family to Forest Hills, Queens, New York, in 1947. He exported cotton and tobacco to China and imported tea, silk goods, and Chinese figurines to the Delta. But two years later the Communist Revolution put an end to that business, and he opened a restaurant in Manhattan.

While his family stayed in Queens, Gilroy Chow studied engineering at Mississippi State University, where he roomed with a cousin and met his future wife, also named Chow, a common name among Chinese Americans in the Delta.

Sally Chow's grandfather grew up in Marks, Mississippi, twenty miles from Clarksdale. "In the rich alluvial soil of the Delta, he had a grocery store and grew Chinese vegetables to send up to Chicago," she said. Family and friends would also share the bok choy, winter melon, Chinese broccoli, mustard, and radish, grown at home. These days, the garden is tended by Sally's uncle, L. K. Pang, who lives with them. He grows tomatoes, okra, beans, squash, and Chinese vegetables. The family also leases one thousand acres of farmland south of town, where it grows rice, cotton, soybeans, and wheat.

Collards have become a Chow family favorite. They demonstrated their version, stir-fried collards with oyster sauce and garlic, on the National Mall at the Smithsonian Folklife Festival in Washington in 1997, after being selected by local folklorists.

The recipe was adapted by Sally Chow from Yung Chow, a sister-in-law. With no garden and unable to find local Chinese greens like bok choy or Chinese broccoli, she substituted the Southern staple.

When the Chows' son, Bradley, was studying at Mississippi State University in Starkville, he tasted the collards at his aunt's home in nearby Columbus. Because he liked the dish so much, it has become a family favorite. Now his wife, Jennifer, makes it for him at their home in nearby Memphis.

As conversation in the South often does, the discussion of collards turned to the difficult task of ridding greens of grit.

"My aunt puts turnip greens in the gentle cycle of the washing machine," Sally Chow said. Another guest said she did, too, but also used a little mesh bag.

Even though Chinese ingredients are much more available everywhere nowadays, the Mississippi Chinese still like to blend the best of America with their traditional Chinese cooking.

Back in China, the family would have made chicken wings or a whole Peking duck. The Chows have adapted this recipe into a simple but delicious whole roasted chicken caramelized with hoisin sauce. Instead of displaying it whole on the table, like most of their neighbors would do with a roast bird, they cut it into pieces.

On the other hand, memories of China season an asparagus stir-fry with tofu and thinly sliced beef.

"When we got married thirty-three years ago, all Chinese staples came in from California or New York," Gilroy Chow said. "Twenty years ago we could go to Dallas or Houston for Chinese groceries. Now we can go to Memphis, where you can find lots of Chinese grocery stores." Sally listed baby bok choy, tofu, five-spice powder, hoisin, chicken fat, hog maw, and tripe—"things you wouldn't find at Kroger's." Once, they did buy oyster sauce, a condiment often used in vegetable stir-fries, at Kroger's, the grocery chain. "It tasted like cough syrup," Sally said. "It wasn't anything like we get in the Chinese stores."

As they do almost every week, the extended Chow family—Sally's brothers are pharmacists here—gathered at her home to cook. "We do it on Mondays because we are so involved in our church on Sundays," she said, checking the catfish.

Judging by her schedule, she is involved throughout the week. A teacher who mainstreams special education students into the regular curriculum at Coahoma County High School, Sally is also known locally for her little sideline, Chow Cakes, a special-occasion cake business she and Alice Chow, another sister-in-law, run.

She was even a finalist in 1996 for the new image of Betty Crocker, that great symbol of traditional America. She was nominated by her husband in a contest sponsored by the company. Today, though, Sally was relaxing with her family.

Three generations of Chows held hands around the table and said grace. "When you're living day to day," Sally said, "routine can blind you to your heritage. I think it's important to retain our traditions and pass them on to our children."

And yet, the Chows are Southern.

"You hurry back," Sally said as I left after dinner. "Next time we'll cook y'all some turnip greens and cornbread."

Stir-Fried Collards
Serves 6 to 8.

3 bunches tender collard greens
  (about 2½ to 3 pounds total)
Dash salt
2 tablespoons peanut or
  canola oil

6 cloves garlic, chopped
A few grinds of fresh peppercorns
2 to 3 tablespoons oyster sauce
½ teaspoon sugar

Bring a pot of water to a boil, and have a bowl of cold water ready. Wash and trim greens, and cut into 2-by-3-inch pieces. Blanch collards in boiling water for 1 minute, then immediately place in cold water. Drain well and pat dry.

Heat wok, then add salt; let salt brown lightly. Add oil. When oil is hot, add garlic and stir until lightly brown. Add greens and a dash of pepper and stir constantly a couple of minutes. Then stir in oyster sauce and sugar. Taste and adjust seasoning. Serve immediately.

Adapted from Yung Chow.

Virginia Is for Wontons

Mei Chin

Maybe it's a mutual love of pork and peanuts. Maybe it's because the hard, salty Virginia country ham bears a resemblance to the famous ham of Jinhua, in Zhejiang province. Or maybe it's because both the Chinese and Southerners understand pigs' trotters, vinegar, and crabs sucked from their shells. Belly and shoulder are the cuts of choice where pork is concerned; chicken breasts are pushed aside in favor of legs and thighs; and *skinless* is a dirty word. For whatever reason, the Chinese have long been drawn to the American South, even fighting on the Confederate side during the Civil War. Fifty years ago, my Chinese grandparents settled in Richmond, Virginia.

The Chins came to the States from Taiwan when Grandpa Chin was offered a job at a local architecture firm. I can clearly remember the Mondrian-inspired coop he built in the backyard for his collection of pigeons. Grandma Chin supplemented his income by opening Oriental Village, a shop that sold mother-of-pearl screens, painted fans, and spices. In many ways, the Chin kids (my mother was the third of five) experienced a normal childhood in their white neighborhoods and their white schools. They were taught to respect the Stars and Bars and to sing "Dixie Land" at homecoming games. They ate fried chicken, collard greens, and Jell-O salad.

The Chins were not without their social blunders, though, notably when Grandma Chin showed up at the cafeteria with the other school mothers in a cherry-red cheongsam slit up to her thigh. There is also shame: The parents went to great lengths to separate their children from those still referred to in Richmond as "the Coloreds." Back in the day, if you were Chinese you were going to be considered either black or white. "Black" Chinese ran laundries and cleaned houses. "White" Chinese worked in offices and sent their children to good schools where they wouldn't be teased.

The Chins lived downtown, on West Grace Street. The house was nine-teenth-century, with prewar trimmings—fireplaces, tall ceilings, steep staircases, and columns. Roses and damson plum trees were tangled in the backyard that adjoined elegant Monument Avenue. Across the street lived Miz Jenkins, who quickly became Grandma Chin's best friend. She was a spry woman, who navigated the neighborhood with a birdlike quickness in a gingham shirt and jeans.

On the Chins' first Thanksgiving, Miz Jenkins showed up at their door-step with an expertly carved turkey and a plate of stuffing. The Chins ate the stuffing but had to throw the turkey away. The bird's slightly gamy flavor is something that many Chinese cannot abide. But as Miz Jenkins continued the tradition every year, the Chins started eating turkey and liking it.

In 1963, at the height of the Civil Rights Movement, a sweet-eyed Sha Chin (one of my mother's sisters) fell in love with a handsome Chinese doctor by the name of Ed Sung, thereby uniting the Chins with a family just as different from them as America itself. (The Sungs had their own family crest.)

Still, the Chins loved the Sungs, especially Grandma Sung, a flamboyant woman who used to pamper me with sticky rice snacks. When Ed's parents (who had come from Hong Kong) opened a restaurant, it was an ambitious venture—with white tablecloths, real silver, and a separate banquet room. I believe the grandeur had something to do with Grandma Sung, who enter-tained a vision of herself as a doyenne, stuffing twenty-dollar bills into the palms of astonished McDonald's cashiers. If she was going to open a restau-rant, she was going to do it in style. Even now, her grandson Herbie speaks of the Sung restaurant as if he were reciting a creation myth. Grandma Sung, he says, went to Peking, where she learned imperial, ancient techniques, including the most revered recipe of them all: sweet-and-sour pork with maraschino cherries and pickles.

Considerably busier than the Sungs' restaurant was the kitchen at the Chins' house. Back in Taiwan, where Grandpa Chin taught at the local university, there was always a revolving roster of students and Grandma Chin's broth-ers on army leave. They would come for dinner, and then, a few hours later, Grandpa Chin would make late-night snacks of wonton soup. In Richmond, the Chins introduced a steady stream of friends to soft buns stuffed with pork and chives, ginger-spiced meatballs, and sticky rice steamed with dates.

Grandpa Chin was the head of the kitchen. A hot-tempered perfection-ist, he was inventive with humble and precious ingredients alike—julienned potatoes, velvety smooth and sautéed with beef; dumplings with bright crab roe. He deep-fried his meatballs not once but twice, for maximum crunch. His pigs' trotters were my favorite food, especially the sticky glazed fat and skin. (I ignored their meat altogether.) Their dark, sweet soy perfume is still, to me, the scent of Christmas.

In Grandpa Chin's opinion, his wife's greatest inventions were her tofu fritters. They're essentially Asian hush puppies. Tofu, scallions, and bread crumbs are mixed with a splash of sesame oil and plenty of bacon, molded between two spoons, and fried until they puff. The contradictory pairing of tofu and bacon is crisp, naughty, and completely addictive.

Both he and Grandma Chin integrated Southern ingredients into their cooking: bacon and bok choy, barbecued spareribs stir-fried with scallions. But Grandpa Chin never really developed a taste for Western food, and until the end of his life he ate everything—including ice cream—with chopsticks. Even when Grandpa Chin was dying, tofu fritters were something he called for over and over again.

Today, Richmond is a proud city but one that has been beaten down. Time there is syrup slow. Casual house calls can swallow entire afternoons. Grandma Chin's shop has become a chic café that whips up lattes, but when my cousin Jay and I stopped in not long ago, we could see where the beaded curtain used to hang. The smell of Oriental Village—sandalwood fans, mothballs, and anise seed—came back to us in an instant. The smell of Grandma Chin came back, too, like silk that had been kept for years in a cedar chest.

Bozo's

George Motz

Bozo's is not the kind of place where you'd expect to find a great burger. The restaurant is a destination for fresh oysters and excellent fried seafood, and the burger is listed at the bottom of the menu. Southern food writer and friend John T. Edge led me to Bozo's, calling their burger a "sleeper." Nevertheless, Bozo's has sold the same amazing hamburger po-boy for almost eighty years.

Bozo's sits in a fairly nondescript industrial neighborhood in Metairie, a half block from Louisiana's Lake Pontchartrain Causeway. The low wooden building is set back from the street with a large parking lot in front. If you didn't know what you were looking for, you'd drive right past. No ostentatious signage or loud neon here—just a small stained-glass window with the name Bozo's subtly painted on it. The dining room is pure function, clean and well-lit with wood-grain Formica tables and sturdy industrial seating. The only real decoration is a floor-to-ceiling mural of two fishing boats near a dock. "Those were two of my dad's boats," second-generation owner and septuagenarian chef Chris Vodanovich pointed out to me.

Yugoslavian immigrant Chris "Bozo" Vodanovich Sr. opened Bozo's Oyster House on St. Ann Street in New Orleans in 1928. At one point Bozo had a fleet of eight boats to service the needs of his restaurant. Fresh oysters, shrimp, and catfish were the reasons most locals patronized the tiny restaurant, but from the beginning, Bozo offered a hamburger po-boy as an alternative to seafood.

The burger at Bozo's is a combination of almost eighty years of experience, a proprietary mixture of meat and onions, and a twist on a regional specialty, the po-boy sandwich. Among those for whom the perfect po-boy is a passion, it is understood that the bread used is as important as what goes on it. Chris uses only the best—French bread from Leidenheimer Bakery, an institution in New Orleans for over a century.

I asked Chris how big the burger was and he didn't know. "We just make them to fit the bread," he told me, smiling. The bread is not small, making this hamburger po-boy a filling meal. The fresh ground beef has onions and "other spices" mixed in before being hand-pattied and cooked on a flattop griddle. The combination of the perfectly cooked burger and the pillowy bread makes for a great regional hamburger experience.

Chris inherited Bozo's and moved his father's business out of downtown New Orleans to Metairie in 1979 because, as he put it, "the neighborhood was getting rough." The Metairie location was expanded to accommodate 120 diners in two dining rooms separated by a large bar.

While I talked to Chris, every patron said "Thanks, Mr. Chris" as they paid their tabs and left. He speaks with a gentle Louisiana twang and has piercing blue eyes and wavy gray hair. I asked him, "Why Bozo?"

"In the old country, *Bozo* was the word for Christ," he told me, "and my name is Chris."

Currying Flavor

Brett Anderson

Roughly two hours after the Neville Brothers' assault on "Big Chief" provided the 2008 Jazzfest its suitably funky coda, Irfan Khan and his staff rushed to feed Sunday dinner to a set of families overflowing two booths in Salt 'n' Pepper restaurant.

Located in the French Quarter—around the corner from the House of Blues, down the street from Acme Oyster House, and within striking distance of the naked entertainment at the Artist Café—Salt 'n' Pepper can seem a tad out of context. While the restaurant serves its share of po-boys and pizza slices, the menu item listed below the fried oyster and shrimp platters is fish curry, and the families appeared to be enjoying examples of their native cuisine: plates of handmade paratha, the whole-wheat flour flatbread, and chicken tikka, a dish of marinated, hot-baked bird indigenous to the Punjab region straddling India and Pakistan; charred rods of ground beef formed with chiles, onion, and spices; and servings of samosa, the vegetable-stuffed pastries that one woman mashed to feed her toddler.

I was dipping pieces of my paratha in a dish of cilantro-yogurt dressing when my entrée arrived: stewed goat on the bone, a house specialty. The meat was spoon-tender, melting into a dark gravy, and as fiercely seasoned as any vindaloo I've ever had. Thankfully I'd fetched an Abita Amber from a bar down the street to cool my throat.

Irfan Khan, who was born in Pakistan, opened Salt 'n' Pepper in late 2001. "I always wanted to have a business of my own," he said. "And there were not many Indian-Pakistani places in New Orleans."

There still aren't. New Orleanians with a taste for north Indian cuisine, which is very similar to Pakistani, have for many years had little more than two options: Taj Mahal, the longest-tenured Indian restaurant in the area, and

Nirvana, Taj Mahal's Uptown spinoff. Both are owned by the Keswani family, but their similarities go beyond proprietorship. Every metropolitan area in America has a restaurant very much like one of them: the slightly faded storefront with the affordable lunch buffet, the wailing Indian folk music, and the kitchen churning out blistered naan, red-tinted tandoori chicken, and coriander-scented biryanis.

The pickings beyond these mainstays are so slim that when That Indian Place opened in the Place St. Charles Food Court after Katrina, it actually was something to write about—and is again now that the menu includes dosas, the delicate south Indian rice crepes.

The area's newest Indian restaurant is actually not new at all. It's called Tandoori Chicken: Singh Indian Cuisine, the new location of an old restaurant that for years occupied a secluded second-story space in the Central Business District. Its roster of curries, biryanis, and tandoori-fired meats shouldn't puzzle anyone who has indulged in traditional Indian cuisine, which the Singh family treats respectfully. On my two visits, the restaurant's naan never tasted as if it had suffered the indignities of a heat lamp, and Sukhdarshan Singh, a warm presence in the dining room, is justifiably proud of her chicken tikka masala. The mild, creamy curry is a resilient example of early fusion cooking: Legend has it that the dish was born when an Indian chef tried to satisfy a British diner's desire for gravy with his meat.

Located in a strip mall next to Peedy's Place saloon, the single dining room isn't a place where you'll find anyone toasting corporate mergers, yet still it's an upgrade from the old spot, where I once remember shielding my lunch from the dust stirred up by a floor fan.

Sara's is the only restaurant in New Orleans where one can enjoy Indian or Pakistani cuisine without sacrificing a bit of luxury and a reasonably good choice in wine—only Sara's is neither Indian nor Pakistani, at least not entirely. It's an Asian-fusion place that happens to serve shrimp vindaloo and really good saag paneer.

I do not mean to suggest that the scruffiness of New Orleans' traditional Indian restaurants correlates to the quality of food you'll find in them. But it is evidence that this cuisine still stays on our culture's fringe, and the situation is overdue for correction.

Of all the great Asian cuisines that have taken root locally—Vietnamese, Chinese, Japanese, Thai, and, most recently, Korean—Indian is the only one that has not noticeably affected the vocabulary of our best local chefs. And Sara's is the only local example of a chef or restaurant taking Indian cooking beyond its traditional roots, either by providing it elegant surroundings or by testing the inspirational potential of the elements—the dizzying array of chutneys and spice blends, the deep repertoire of stews, the tandoori oven—that make it so exciting.

Compared with so many of the afflictions harming this region, New Orleans' curry conundrum is not an urgent matter. But when talk turns to multiculturalism in south Louisiana, it does strike me as interesting that such a conundrum exists.

It certainly doesn't in a lot of other major culinary destinations. Floyd Cardoz became one of the most respected chefs in Manhattan at Tabla, a modern Indian restaurant that showcases, among other things, Louisiana shrimp. One of the most talked about chefs in Houston is Anita Jaisinghani of Indika, where the bar menu includes tamarind lamb ribs, pani poori, and Indian whiskey. One of the best restaurant meals I've eaten in the past couple of years—a salad of fried spinach lightly coated in chickpea batter and wild boar vindaloo perfectly paired with a pinot gris—was in Washington, D.C., at Rasika. It's the brainchild of the talented India-born restaurateur Ashok Bajaj.

That Indian culture is ascendant in general is undeniable, and I'm not talking about the folks who often answer when you call for directory assistance and technical support.

Jumpha Lahiri has become the rare serious writer to pen best sellers exclusively about the modern immigrant experience through the eyes of Indian Americans. Thanks to her appearances on the Food Network and "Top Chef," Padma Lakshmi, who was born in the Indian state of Kerala, has given the celebrity chef zeitgeist its very own Cindy Crawford. The rhythms of bhangra, the Punjabi folk music, are now commonplace in American hip-hop and dance music.

You could hear them at the 2008 Jazzfest when M.I.A., the Sri Lanka–born singer-rapper-whatever ("Can't stereotype my thing yo/I salt and pepper my mango!") played to a packed house in a Faubourg Marigny warehouse. It was the most powerful set I saw during the whole Jazzfest marathon. At some point around four o'clock in the morning, it felt like she had the whole town chanting "Blaze to blaze, galang a lang alanga"—an intoxicating bit of dancehall nonsense that sounds like a celebration of galangal, a gingerlike rhizome that Indian chefs often mix into their curry.

Louisiana's reputation for provincialism is dated. After all, we recently elected as governor Bobby Jindal, a man whose parents immigrated to Baton Rouge from the Punjabi village of Khanpura.

The governor is not one to emphasize his Indian roots. Indeed, when I contacted his office to ask if he had a favorite Indian restaurant in Louisiana, his spokesman called back to inform me that his favorite restaurant is McDonald's.

Great leadership does not require a great palate, but Jindal has been boosting Louisiana's national profile in part because outside observers regard him as a refreshing symbol of cultural progress in the Deep South.

Jay Leno fawned over him on "The Tonight Show." Jindal fielded questions about his parents, politely tolerated the host's caricature of Indian accents, and assured the audience, "We like to say we're changing everything in Louisiana but the food."

Of course, keeping the gumbo pot open to everyone's spoon is supposed to be the foundation of what makes Louisiana cuisine—and music—the stuff of festivals. Its inclusiveness is why no one can resist using it as a metaphor explaining everything that's admirable about where we are.

If Jindal's tenure stimulated a local renaissance in the cooking of his parents, it would be a reflection of the best aspects of Louisiana tradition. It would also be, in this season of supposed political change, an example of how Louisiana has, in one small but delicious way, become more like everyplace else.

Cooking for a Sunday Day

Corby Kummer

The best food, especially ethnic food, is made at home. All well and good to hear, but not so easy to find when traveling in a new country. Or a new town.

Irma's, an improbable mixture of politico hangout, tourist magnet, and kitsch extravaganza, is in Houston, but it serves home-style Mexican food of a freshness and quality hard to find on either side of the border. All the food is cooked by four or five Mexican mothers and grandmothers, using the skill bred into their hands and the kinds of modest tools and pots and pans you'd find in a Mexican home kitchen. The recipes are their family specialties and those of Irma Galvan, who keeps a watchful eye on her cooks and on everyone who comes in and out of the place.

The food is a dream of how, say, tamales and enchiladas would taste if you were invited to a long, loud family lunch. It was mine, at least, and a reminder that in the right hands, usually women's, Mexico's is one of the world's great cuisines—sophisticated and subtle yet utterly satisfying. In 2008 the James Beard Foundation gave the restaurant its America's Classic award; Irma's could soon become something of a national destination.

The chile rellenos were a particular surprise, with the look and delicacy of stuffed zucchini blossoms. The thin-walled fresh poblano peppers, first roasted and peeled, had the just-picked, vegetal flavor of squash blossoms, and the filling of soft white chihuahua cheese and onions, one of three the restaurant offers, was not far from the usual ricotta-and-herb mixture with which Italian cooks stuff squash blossoms. Each filling (the other two are picadillo—ground meat cooked with tomatoes, onions, and garlic—and shredded chicken with fresh tomato sauce) is flavored with dried chiles and fresh herbs like cilantro and parsley. But none is terribly hot, so you can actually taste and appreciate the different chile powders. The frying in a delicate egg-white batter is so quick and skillful, it could be Japanese. I was transported.

Revelations like this are usually the result of the real simplicity that comes of long experience and long preparation. "It takes forever to make chile relleno, okay?" the owner told me when I asked how the cooks did it. "Like tamale"—the other dish Irma's redefined for me.

Irma's may serve home cooking, but it doesn't feel like home, or not like (probably) yours. The lively hodgepodge makes sense only when Galvan or her daughter Monica or son Tony, the two of her four children who work there, explains what's on the menu. They have to, because there isn't one. This keeps the feel as personal as the somewhat relentless decor, and is a shrewd businesswoman's way of warmly dodging the question of prices. Galvan charges a fair price for the labor that goes into those seemingly simple dishes—prices most people aren't used to paying for Mexican food.

Galvan didn't go into the restaurant business by choice. On New Year's Eve of 1981 her husband, Louis, a cancer researcher at Baylor, was murdered in a random mugging. He was forty-one and Irma thirty-nine, and she became the sole support of their children, then aged five to fourteen. Friends had long urged her to open a restaurant: When she was growing up, in Brownsville and then Houston, she was the main cook for her two siblings (their mother, a single parent, worked), and Sundays were spent cooking with female relatives for an extended family that could number as many as sixty.

I asked Galvan whether she considered the food she learned and now serves to be Tex-Mex or Mexican—a malleable distinction. She replied that she prefers to avoid the question by calling it "home-cooked authentic" or "authentic poor people's food." Her mother and most of her family came from Matehuala, a town between Guadalajara and Monterrey; the women she hires come from states such as Veracruz, which is renowned for its cuisine. She tells them to cook "like you cook for your family on a Sunday day," for occasions like "a wedding, a baptism."

Irma's is in an odd part of town, far from many of the city's trendy and expensive restaurants—the "Warehouse District," the kind of no-man's-land that real-estate brokers officially name when abandoned buildings get turned into lofts. Today it is a prime spot for a restaurant, a stone's throw from Minute Maid Park, home of the Astros, which opened in 2000. But it wasn't in 1989, when Galvan opened Irma's. She knew the neighborhood well, having worked across the street from the building for several years; she planned to cater to warehouse workers, and featured deli-style sandwiches. They didn't sell and she didn't like making them, so after a week she switched to delivering tacos to office workers in the nearby county courthouse, using pots and pans she carted from home.

The Mexican dishes caught on, and customers started coming in, eating at the one table, also carted from home, for breakfast and lunch (even today, the restaurant, open only on weekdays, closes at three o'clock, except on game nights, when it stays open until seven). For a while, all four children worked in the restaurant, and one son, Louis, opened his own, which he called Irma's Southwest Grill. As part of her innate loyalty-building strategy, Galvan taped up the business cards of seemingly everyone who ever came in, and glossies of every local figure and demi-celebrity she could talk into giving her one. Today the 1970s walnut-look paneling is (mercifully) almost completely covered with them. Her natural hospitality won her a devoted political following. She was a frequent speaker at community hearings to encourage neighborhood improvement and strongly supported the building of the stadium. (Galvan bought the building for $25,000 in 1989; she kept adding on as business increased, and over the next decade she bought up the two square blocks around it.)

Galvan filled the dining rooms with antiques that took her fancy, and more or less anything else, too. Mismatched shelves and glass cabinets display collections of plastic dolls, old typewriters and radios, neon beer signs, beer bottles, souvenir china, Christmas ornaments, and Mardi Gras beads. Wildly colorful floral oilcloths are the brightest reminders of Mexican folk art.

But it is the food that made Irma's a local landmark and the reason I wanted to go back right away—despite having just taken vigorous part in a huge group lunch with a posse of national restaurant critics. We were there at the behest of Alison Cook, the critic for the *Houston Chronicle*, who had regaled us for years with tales of Irma's and of Irma. We immediately saw why. Galvan, who has the carriage of a dancer, waited on us, wearing her usual sweatshirt and boldly patterned tights (and, that day, combat boots). She bears plates over her head, and she stretches her arms out theatrically to get the attention of a whole table and signal waitresses to bring more of her signature lemonade (a tropical-fruit punch tasting more of strawberry, orange, and papaya than of lemon)—gestures perhaps acquired over a lifetime of compensating for low stature. Dishes arrive in a flash after she commands her small fleet of cooks to produce them. "She orders me around, too," Alison Cook, a staunch loyalist from the beginning, admitted.

I kept asking for more napkin-lined baskets of handmade corn tortillas, made every morning and warmed to order (they are impossible to find in Boston, where I live, and hard enough to find even in Houston), which make every enchilada noteworthy. Most popular are tortillas rolled around spinach sautéed with garlic so quickly that the leaves, shiny with olive oil, are barely wilted. They come in a fresh tomatillo sauce, yellow-green and lightly acidic and oniony, and topped with melted jalapeño jack cheese or mozzarella.

Galvan makes fresh flour tortillas, too, one of several Tex-Mex staples she did not grow up eating ("I called them gringo tortillas") but has mastered anyway—like salsa and chips, which she never saw in a Mexican home or restaurant. Now salsa and chips come to the table, and both are predictably fresh: quick-fried chips from her own homemade tortillas, with bright-flavored salsa made daily. The guacamole, too, is made by hand, and meticulously; it draws people from all over Houston.

As in all the best home cooking, small details make the dish—and in the best Mexican cooking, those require painstaking labor. For the tamale filling, cubed pork is simmered with whole heads of garlic and onions; the meat is hand-chopped and warmed with a "salsa"—really a thick paste of ancho (dried poblanos) and cascabel chiles, reconstituted and slowly sautéed with garlic and onions—until the moderate heat of the chiles permeates the meat. The masa, or white cornmeal paste that goes into cornhusk wrappers along with the meat, is made with the garlicky stock from boiling the pork and softened with the secret ingredient too few Mexican cooks dare use but more of them should: *manteca*. "You don't want to hear" what she uses, Galvan told me. Of course I did and was extremely glad to hear the answer, "pure lard"—most cooks use insipid shortening. The texture is pillowy, the flavor deep and subtle.

We visited on a Thursday, the one day Irma's offers homemade *tres leches* cake, which has recently become something of an obsession for sweets lovers, a group of which I am a proud member. For her recipe for "three milks," which many jealous bakers would refuse to reveal, Galvan uses whole, Carnation evaporated, and Lechera-brand condensed milks. The wet, rich goodness comes from an overnight soaking of homemade white sponge cake with a mixture of the milks, and from an icing of *cajeta*, the caramelized milk that has become popular as *dulce de leche*, mixed with honey, cinnamon, and pecans. It sounds rich, and is, but tastes as airy as the whipped cream on top. That was sprayed from a can. It didn't stop me from ordering a second portion.

I told Cook after lunch that I couldn't imagine preferring another restaurant (and I did manage to sample a number of the others she recommended in town). She replied that Irma's is the place she wishes she could go whenever she eats out, instead of a new restaurant—that place every food critic keeps in the back of her or his mind. If I lived in Houston, it would be mine, too.

Welcome to Cuban Sandwich City

Andrew Huse

Cigar City Magazine could have easily been named after the Cuban sandwich. These days, Tampa, Florida, can be more easily identified by that savory creation than the cigar. Like Cuban cigars, it can be mighty difficult to find a fine Cuban sandwich. Unlike Cuban cigars, one could argue that the so-called Cuban sandwich is more Tampa than Havana.

People in Miami often talk as if they invented the Cuban sandwich, but they are pretenders to the throne. In the early 1900s, workers in Cuba brought simple "*mixto*" sandwiches to work or bought them at cafés. These cold-cut concoctions took on a new character in Tampa, influenced by Ybor City's vibrant mix of immigrant cultures. By the 1920s, the old "*mixtos*" coalesced into something more distinct—the Cuban sandwich, an original Tampa creation.

Beginning in 1886, immigrants from Spain, Italy, and Cuba fled poverty and warfare to seek new lives in Tampa. But the tumultuous cigar industry provided some shocks of its own, with violence, strikes, and work stoppages in the cigar factories. An erratic cycle of feast and famine continued in Ybor City for fifty years. The Cuban sandwich rose in popularity during the 1920s, when electric sandwich presses and toasters became more common. During the Great Depression, the filling sandwiches served as a Latin-flavored equivalent of the New Orleans po-boy.

During tough times, Ybor City had the example of Cuban bread to follow. When Cuba struggled for independence from Spain in the late 1800s, citizens there faced hunger and hardship. Cuban bakers responded by stretching their bread into long, thin loaves to provide small slices for rationing. The practice never changed in Tampa, but today, bread in Cuba is generally short and more round.

Ybor City's struggling immigrants turned misfortune to their advantage. Tampa's most famous sandwich would not be possible without the stretched Cuban loaf. Ybor City cooks split the loaf and filled it with mojo roast pork, sugar-cured ham, salami, Swiss cheese, pickles, and mustard. Each of the main ingredients came from Ybor City's dominant ethnic groups: The Spaniards supplied fine glazed ham, bread and mojo pork came from the Cubans, and the Italians contributed salami.

The sandwich's popularity elevated the Silver Ring Café from a front for Bolita (illegal lottery) sales to a destination for hungry workers and tourists. That café was one among several to set the standard for Cuban sandwiches in the Tampa area. I enjoyed my first Cuban sandwich there fifteen years ago.

Many of the sandwiches I have had in recent years disappoint me, and I am not alone. On the food-related website Chowhound.com, a curious web surfer asked, "What is the deal with Cuban sandwiches?" After going to one of Tampa's most respected sandwich stands, she said, "It just tasted like a ham sandwich to me."

Not every restaurant owner invests the same amount of work into their sandwiches, but the other half of the problem is people who expect gourmet quality for a mere three dollars. When one examines the labor that went into making an old-fashioned Cuban, it is more understandable that today's sandwiches fall short so often. Like so many simple things in early Ybor City, the Cuban sandwich was elevated to an art and craft. Restaurateurs prepared every ingredient in painstaking fashion. When modern sandwich slingers take short cuts, their profits may not suffer, but the cult of the Cuban does.

Tampa's Cuban sandwich is a dying culinary breed. By the time it became a recognized and revered tradition in the 1940s, the real thing was already fading fast. The true Cuban sandwich—conceived in Cuba and perfected in Tampa—lived and died with Ybor City, which itself died between the Great Depression and urban renewal's bulldozers in 1965.

Wet, cheap, boiled ham and processed pork loaves give little indication of what a real Cuban sandwich should taste like. It doesn't help that most places pile on lettuce, mayonnaise, and tomato, which dilute the flavor. When done right, the sandwich showcases the contrast between the dry crust of Cuban bread and the rich mingling of melted fats within. The bold combination of salty ham and salami, the garlic and vinegar undertones of the roast pork, and the sharp taste of pickle and mustard are all married by the bread and Swiss cheese.

In 1957, Manuel Torres, a longtime Ybor City restaurant worker, volunteered to make Cuban sandwiches for a reporter in what even then was known as the "old-fashioned way." Torres soaked a select pork roast overnight in a mojo marinade of lemon juice, salt, fresh garlic, oregano, and vinegar. He then parboiled the pork with onions, celery, and garlic and roasted it. A whole smoked ham was parboiled in the same mixture. Torres trimmed excess fat and coated the ham in sugar, which he melted onto the meat with a hot iron. Drawn by the irresistible aroma, salivating onlookers gathered around the storefront as the sugar transformed into a thin amber glaze.

Torres carved the meat into thin slices: pork, ham, and peppered Genoa salami. Imported Swiss cheese, sour dill pickles, mustard, and Cuban bread rounded out the sandwich. He layered the ingredients onto the bread in traditional order: first the ham, then pork, salami, cheese, pickle, and mustard, spread only on the top slice of the bread. "It is always done that way," Torres said.

Richard Gonzmart, fourth-generation president of the legendary Columbia Restaurant in Ybor City, dug deep into his family's past to make the best Cuban sandwich I've had in recent memory. The kitchen bakes and glazes the ham, marinates and roasts the pork, and imports special salami. In taste and proportion, the sandwich is beyond reproach, especially after a good press that toasts the bread, melts the cheese, and renders the fat. The sandwich is a fine testament to the Columbia's place in Florida's culinary history.

Global Cornbreads
The Whole World in a Pan

Crescent Dragonwagon

Where corn has grown, so, inevitably, has cornbread. Corn has always traveled. First, with the careful, observant help of indigenous people, it crossbred itself into existence around 3000 B.C., in Mexico's Balsas River Basin region. But from there it quickly spread throughout southwestern North America and then farther, into Central America, then South America. When, about A.D. 1000, Native Americans began to migrate from the southwest to the north and east, they took corn with them and, by selection, developed corn strains adapted to colder climates. Corn was global long, long before corporations, pop stars, and the brand names we now call "global" even remotely existed. But unlike McDonald's, Wal-Mart, or Pepsi, corn did not force uniformity wherever it landed. On the contrary, adaptability to the region in which it found itself was its secret. Corn, with human help, adapted and modified; it could, and did, grow almost anywhere. And with each regional border crossing, corn intermarried with local foodways, ingredients, and traditions.

When we say "cornbread" in America today, our first thoughts are of skillet-sizzled, buttermilk-moistened Southern cornbread; sweet cake-like Northern cornbread; spicy, smoky Southwestern cornbread. But global cornbreads go in some other directions.

Just below the border, in Mexico, we encounter the closest cousins of contemporary North American cornbreads. *Pan de elote* (literally "bread of corn") has recognizable similarities, incorporating wheat flour and fresh corn kernels. Then we spin off into the sweet-savory pudding-like *budins* and into the leaf-wrapped meal-in-a-casing-of-steamed-cornbread, tamales. We find *humitas*, also steamed, in Colombia, Peru, and Bolivia. And *arepas*, similar to our hoecakes, are the definitive daily bread of Colombia and adjacent Latin American countries.

From South America we trace corn's transit to Europe, which began when the ships of Columbus's first fleet returned to Spain in 1499. The Spaniards, who had originally sought more profitable trade routes to the East Indies spice islands, wound up achieving something quite different. First, they carried new ingredients, most importantly corn—but definitely not the spices that had prompted their journey—back to Europe. But second, they introduced some of those very same spices *to* the New World, such as the soft canela (Ceylon) cinnamon and black pepper for which they'd originally set sail. Through the years, these flavors, as well as haunting Middle Eastern anise, mixed with native New World ingredients, creating singular dishes that spoke uniquely of place and time.

Meanwhile, New World corn began to take root in Old World Europe. And so we meet Portuguese cornbread, called *broa*—yeast-risen, round, dense— which seems made to soak up the big garlicky flavors of *caldo verde*, that country's national soup. The Italians took to cornmeal as polenta and the Romanians as *mamaliga*—in both cases, cornmeal mush, not bread—and the French shunned corn except as cattle fodder. But it was used in a very simple Cretan flat bread until quite recently, and in time the Greek army began to use fifteen or 20 percent cornmeal in the soldiers' bread. And, though the Greeks were slow to incorporate it into their home baking, Greek bakeries have started to carry cornmeal-laced breads with notes of olive, walnuts, feta cheese, and greens.

When Portuguese traders carried maize to India in the late 1500s, it was adapted immediately, becoming the griddled flat bread *makki ki roti*. This is served with deeply spiced *sarson ka saag*, an irresistible dish of slow-cooked mustard greens, a combination that echoes, in a different accent, the American South's beloved cornbread and greens.

Around the same time, Turkish traders introduced cornmeal to Africa. There it was widely accepted, though it was mainly used as mush. But the Southern part of the continent created a moist, simple, steam-cooked staple bread. And thus our last stop on our global cornbread tour is South African *mealiebrod*. Although it is far from American cornbreads in taste, flavor, and texture, it is another example of cornbread's significant global role.

Baked, griddled, leaf-wrapped, steamed . . . cornbread anywhere, any time, any way is an honest and earthy gift of sustenance, carried from the Americas to the whole round world.

Demystifying Grits for the Northern Palate

John S. Forrester

Some Southerners don't need the Mason-Dixon Line to tell them when they've crossed into the North. They know they've entered Yankee territory as soon as the roadside diners start serving hash browns instead of grits.

While plenty of families in the Northeast eat grits, ask a native New Englander about them and you'll probably get a look of befuddlement and a mention of gruel. Fried chicken, barbecue, and other quintessentially Southern foods have gained popularity here, but grits have remained somewhat of a mystery to the Northern palate.

That may be changing. Hash browns and home fries continue to be the favorites at Boston breakfasts, but grits are beginning to appear on some menus, as breakfast sides and in dinner entrées, showing that area chefs and their patrons are willing to give the humble grain a try.

In some cases, chefs seem to be merely searching for a diversion from the same old starch accompanying roasted or braised meats. "It's a little bit different than putting mashed potatoes with everything," said Tom Fosnot, executive chef at blu restaurant. "That gets a bit repetitive."

The treatments lift grits squarely into haute cuisine territory. Recently, blu's menu featured a slow-roasted Berkshire pork shoulder served over grits, with braised greens and baby carrots, and topped with red onion marmalade. Spire has braised short ribs with grits, black truffles, maitake (a Japanese mushroom), pickled red onion, and bacon. Rialto's Jody Adams recently paired her "gypsy rabbit" dish with grits.

Like polenta and cornmeal, grits, which are linked to Native Americans, come from dried and milled corn. Grits are the coarsest remains of the milling process and come in three types: yellow (made from unhulled corn), white (from hulled corn), and hominy (from corn soaked in lye to remove the hull and the outer germ).

Even though Quaker Oats sells quick-cooking grits in supermarkets, restaurant chefs favor organic, stone-milled grits made with unique or indigenous corn, a product that requires more time and attention but results in anything but a bland, pasty mush. "It's a far superior flavor," said Peter Davis, executive chef of Henrietta's Table, who uses grits from Anson Mills in South Carolina. "We've had a lot of positive feedback on it."

Davis doesn't use grits as a mere side, but builds a dish around them: grit cakes topped with mushrooms, tomatoes, and a flageolet bean ragout.

While you would expect a place like Magnolia's Southern Cuisine in Cambridge, Massachusetts, to serve some variation of traditional grits, chef and owner John Silberman also uses them in a more elaborate way. His "Hoppin' Shavonne" combines stone-ground grits with black-eyed peas, Parmesan cheese, and marinated tomatoes in a twist on the classic Hoppin' John. Magnolia's also serves a braised lamb shank over grits.

Silberman buys his grits from Logan Turnpike in Georgia. "Ten or fifteen years ago it would have been difficult" to get them here, he said. "Now it's as easy as an 800 number, calling UPS, and a few days later it's here."

Artisanal or not, grits have long had a storied place in Southern culture. The singer Al Green has said he pursued religion and became a minister after a former girlfriend threw a boiling pot of hot grits on him. Jimmy Carter campaigned for the presidency with Walter F. Mondale on the "Grits and Fritz" ticket, a reference to Carter's Georgia roots and Mondale's nickname. More recently, a Christian rap group named itself after the grain.

"There are all these spinoff things," said Professor James C. Cobb, an expert on Southern culture at the University of Georgia. "Like grits as an acronym for Girls Raised in the South. It's become one of those things that's taken on a life of its own."

Quaker Oats, one of the largest producers of grits, sponsors the National Grits Festival in Warwick, Georgia, and the World Grits Festival in St. George, South Carolina. People from around the country come to compete in cook-offs, beauty pageants, and grits-eating tournaments. Every year, unique uses for grits come to light.

The contestants enter everything from new takes on the breakfast side to desserts. "They use shrimp, we had an ice cream—it was good—cakes, spaghetti, pies, desserts," said Ruthel Patrick, cook-off coordinator for the Georgia festival.

With restaurant chefs in Boston using them, will grits one day no longer be linked to the South? Not a chance, said John T. Edge, director of the Southern

Foodways Alliance. "The idea that grits are for the most part not served beyond the Mason-Dixon Line appeals to Southerners," Edge said. "I think many a Southerner would be happy to share grits with the great unwashed beyond, but it's part of our identity. I don't see grits goose-stepping across America, leaving oatmeal in their wake."

The Invasion of the Whores de Orvrays

Robert St. John

"They're gonna have Mexican prostitutes there," said Forrest.

"How do you know?" I said.

"I heard Mrs. Wagner on the telephone. They're bringing them in from some town south of the border. Mexico, probably. A town called Orvrays, I think it was."

"That's not necessarily in Mexico," said Chris. "Orvrays could be any Latin American country." Chris was our intellectual. His father was a college professor.

So began the most memorable episode of the summer of 1972—my sixth-grade year—the two-week period our entire neighborhood spent in anticipation of busloads of love-sick floozies invading our Mississippi town from somewhere south of the border.

The eavesdropee, Mrs. Wagner, was a native of Hungary. It was said that she came from the same town from which the Gabor sisters hailed. Even though she had lived in south Mississippi for eighteen years, her accent was thick and awkward. She pronounced "with" as "weet" and "the" as "dee" and had an affinity for goulash and paprika. Accent or not, there was no mistaking the word "whores." It was the world's oldest profession and along with it, the world's oldest pronunciation. There was no doubt in anyone's mind that they were talking about exotic and lustful Latin ladies, and they were probably en route to our town at that exact minute.

Being European, it was widely understood that Mrs. Wagner had a different sensibility than the other mothers in the neighborhood. "She's more open-minded," Chris said. "She has a laissez-faire attitude."

"You mean she likes girls?"

"No. She's liberal. And she asked who was bringing the whores de Orvrays. I heard it. She said 'de' but my sister said that 'de' means 'of' in Spanish. They're whores of Orvrays, Mexico, and they're coming to the Johnsons' party. Just think, Mexican hookers in our neighborhood."

"I wonder if Hugh Hefner will be there, too," I said.

"Are you sure she didn't say Norway?"

"Nope, she said Orvrays and they'll be here in two weeks."

The news spread from brother to brother, brother to sister, sister to mother, mother to father, and within a matter of hours word of the upcoming Johnson party had traveled to the outermost reaches of the Hillendale subdivision.

For the next two weeks, every woman in a twelve-block radius had a telephone cocked and loaded between her shoulder and ear, every father was meeting another father in the back yard, bridge clubs were abuzz, and beauty parlors were rife with scandalous scuttlebutt. All were covering the same subject: the painted ladies who were coming to the Johnsons' party. The Bible Belt gossip line in our small Southern town was on all-out full-bore ringing-off-the-hook red alert.

In a town where the local district attorney had banned *Last Tango in Paris* from being shown in local theatres, a busload of whores was a noteworthy event. At the grocery store, at the ballpark, and at church—male, female, young, and old—everyone was talking about the upcoming Johnson party.

Three days before the party, Mildred Baker passed away while sitting in the dryer chair at Marilyn's Beauty Parlor. She had gone under the dome around eight-thirty in the morning, had a massive coronary, then sat—stiff and unattended, beehive baking—until closing time when the nail girl realized Mildred "hadn't moved in a while." The coroner was never able to pinpoint the exact time of death due to the elongated exposure to the heat of the dryer, but most believe she passed sometime around nine-thirty after Celia Rhodes and Betty Chapel came in talking about the Johnson party.

The men of the neighborhood were uncharacteristically low key. There was a different air about them—a flicker of hope. Some publicly disparaged Mr. Johnson; some secretly wished they could trade places.

The event was turning out to be more scandalous than the Franklin Christmas Tree Controversy six months earlier. The Franklin family was from "somewhere up North," my mother used to say. I later found out they were from Kentucky, a Northern state to most in the area. On their first Christmas in town, the Franklins had committed the cardinal Yuletide sin: blue lights on a metallic silver Christmas tree. My mother wrote it off as the act of Catholics, others blamed the Franklins' Northern breeding, most chalked it up to a lack of good taste. Phones were busy for weeks.

Like the Franklins, the upcoming party's host, Dick Johnson, was an interloper. He had arrived two summers prior after being hired as the new marketing manager at one of the town's banks. "Marketing," my mother said. "He's probably from New York." He and his two sons moved into the old Tyler home two blocks from my house. The Tylers had moved out after getting the first divorce ever granted in Forrest County, Mississippi—an event, as it turned out, even more scandalous than a silver and blue Christmas tree.

Mr. Johnson was a Jack Cassidy look-alike who sported tiny Speedo bathing suits around the country club swimming pool, kept *Playboy* on his bedside table, and wore a goatee. His teenage sons tortured cats and shot at neighborhood kids with BB guns. Over the years, there had been rampant stories of wild key-parties, skinny-dipping, swinging, and all manner of sinful and hedonistic debauchery at the Johnsons'. Certainly a party with exotic Latin ladies of the evening shipped in from Mexico wouldn't be a stretch.

The Johnson party was a turning point in our adolescence. Until then the highlight of our hot Mississippi summers had been prank-calling neighbors on the telephone, the main victims being the family of a college professor named Dr. Orange. "Is Dr. Apple there?" we would ask, stifling giggles. "I'm sorry, you've got the wrong fruit," an Orange on the other end would reply. It was always good for a laugh, and I think for at least the first two hundred times, the Orange family got a kick out of it, too.

On the day of the party we awoke early and the entire day was spent in the neighborhood tree house across the street from the Johnsons'. We wanted to see the whores from Orvrays arrive, watch them pile out of the limousine and sashay half-dressed into the house. The music would then be turned up, the lights would be turned down, and all manner of sexual depravity would ensue.

As night fell, teenagers looking for action, frat boys in search of cheap thrills, and most of the uninvited men of the neighborhood loaded into jeeps, vans, and station wagons and cruised up and down the street trying to catch a glimpse of a real, live hooker. At seven-thirty guests had begun arriving and there wasn't a whore in sight.

Had we not gotten out of bed early enough? Had we missed the floozies' arrival the night before? Did Mr. Johnson smuggle them into the house in the catering van? At nine-fifteen we sent Chris across the street to get answers.

As he walked across the street, Chris recognized a catering waitress on a smoke break in the garage. He pulled the girl, a friend of his sisters', aside and whispered, "When are the whores gonna get here?"

"What?"

"The whores. Mrs. Wagner said that there were going to be whores from Orvrays, Mexico, here."

The caterer looked puzzled for a minute, paused, and then grimaced. "You idiot. What Mrs. Wagner said was: h-o-r-s (or) d-'-o-e-u-v-r-e-s (derves). Hors d'oeuvres, not whores de Orvrays, or whores from Orvrays."

"You mean they're not coming?" Chris said.

"Who?" said the caterer.

"The whores."

"No. You want a cheese straw?"

Chris wasn't listening. Despondent, he walked back over to the tree house and gave us the news.

The neighborhood slowly slipped back into its predictable routine. Ladies found new telephone-gossip topics, the Franklins fell into lockstep and switched to Scotch pine, and finger foods became finger foods again— although, for some strange reason, the term canapé fell into favor. My friends and I entered junior high at a new school and spent the next three years in search of female foreign exchange students from Mexico. Mr. Johnson took a job in Dallas and, according to Mrs. Wagner, abandoned the banking trade to become a male model—that, or a frail bottle.

For years afterward the men of the neighborhood could be seen cruising the streets at night in the family Chevrolet, always slowing at the Johnson house—a distant look of longing in their eyes—none ever stopped; they always kept on driving.

Tasty Tradition Rolls On

Bill Archer

Jesus told his disciples that if they had faith the size of a mustard seed, they could move mountains. For the past seventy years or so, the parishioners of a small Catholic church in southwestern Virginia have been putting their faith in small packages as well—the cabbage roll.

"During his message this morning, Father Gaudy (Gaudencio G. Pugat) said to imagine how many people that one little cabbage roll has brought together," Cindy Froy said. "There are people here today from as far away as Washington, D.C., and beyond. Several people from St. Michael's Catholic Church in Glen Allen, Virginia, are here helping us today."

Around the time of the Great Depression, parishioners of St. Elizabeth Catholic Church started hosting a Hungarian Cabbage Roll Dinner in the fall of the year as a fundraising activity, as well as to gather together in fellowship with family and friends. Although the church recreation hall is small and can only seat eighty at a time, hundreds of people turn out for the annual tradition that originated with the Hungarian families who came to the Pocahontas, Virginia, area to work in the coal mines.

"We have sold 125 carry-out meals in the first hour and fifteen minutes," Jimmy Johns said. "The recreation hall has been full the entire time. It's hard to wash the silverware fast enough to serve the people."

It's appropriate that St. Michael's in Glen Allen—a parish that serves about 2,700 people—has partnered with St. Elizabeth, a congregation of about twenty-five. Because of the concentration of Hungarian coal miners, the town of Pocahontas was called Little Hungary during its heyday. St. Michael's has a Hungarian connection as well. The church is located near the intersection of Springfield and Hungary roads in Glen Allen.

Several St. Michael's parishioners came to Pocahontas in October of 2007 as part of the church's Appalachian Ministry program and stayed for the Hungarian Cabbage Roll Dinner. "We thought it was such a good idea that we decided to host our own dinner in Glen Allen," Michael Smith said. "People from here at St. Elizabeth came down to show us how to roll the cabbage rolls. We came down today to help understand the flow of the dinner."

As he has for the past several years, Andrew Satmary served as the host but was really too busy to do much more than smile and direct the hungry diners to their seats.

"We say the cabbage roll dinner tradition is seventy-plus years, because Daddy's eighty-one years old, and he remembers attending the dinners when he was a little boy," Cindy Froy said of her father, Andrew Satmary.

In addition to supplying a helping hand, members of St. Michael's parish brought eight hundred coats to distribute to local families in need as well as eight hundred blankets and a trailerload of infant cribs and other items to help young families.

"There are two other churches in the area that we are also twins with," Smith said. "We came here to learn how we could help, and we found out about this dinner."

Smith said the St. Michael's members rolled eighteen hundred cabbage rolls under the direction of the volunteers from St. Elizabeth but turned right around and gave them to help Sunday's dinner.

"It was a blessing," Froy said. "We had all of our cabbage rolls done, but our freezer quit working and all of the rolls we had done were spoiled. We got a new freezer and went back to work and St. Michael's helped us out."

"We rolled five thousand more cabbage rolls the next Saturday," Smith said.

While the volunteers are one part of the story, the delicious cabbage rolls were another. When asked how good they were, Roger Mullins put his fork down long enough to raise two thumbs high and smile.

Good Humor

Devon Brenner

The square, white van cases the neighborhood
plastered with signs promoting the treats you slurped
   as a kid—
fudge bars and drumsticks, rocket pops and push-ups.
There's a strawberry shortcake bar and lemon ice in a cup,
a pink foot with a gumball toenail
and novelties for the newcomers—
not just the little kids who get Sponge Bob on a stick
and super-sour, color-changing Dora the Explorer twisting
   treats,
but also the immigrants—welcomed to the window
with a lime bar flavored with salt or guava or acai—
concessions sold in Tupelo, Mississippi,
along with Heath bars and plain old popsicles.
A speaker rings out "The Entertainer" and children
   come running,
bringing parents and cousins, fishing coins from
   their pockets,
as the driver doles out sweet trifles
and servings of trust
from the frozen chests of the ice cream truck.

The Liquid South

Early Times in Mississippi

Donna Tartt

Bourbon, for me, is a smell that goes all the way back to childhood and Christmas, the red-striped cocktail glasses at my grandmother's house, grown-ups in corsages and wearing their best jewelry, everyone laughing, the very smell of warmth and gladness on the breath of people I loved.

Even when I was tiny, I knew the sugary burn of its taste—in eggnog (of which I was allowed only a sip, once a year, in a painted cup from a doll's tea set), in the whipped cream my mother used on pecan pies, and in the boozy butter cakes with cherries and walnuts that we ate at Christmas. My family never called it bourbon, they only called it whiskey, and until I was sixteen or seventeen I believed all whiskey was bourbon. Even in desserts, it had a dangerous, grown-up taste, a hazardous smolder I associated with Christmas fireworks—possibly because, as it was explained to me, the proof of whiskey had been determined in the old days with a lighted match and gunpowder. Gunpowder, soaked in any liquor at least 50 percent alcohol, will flash up and ignite (or, as I imagined, explode, with the thrilling Roman-candle smell that drifted over the yards in the old part of town, at Christmastime).

I grew up in a dry county. The liquor store—a shack, in a field, just across the line into Yalobusha County, Mississippi—was discreetly called "the package store" by even the roughest and most incorrigible lushes. Apart from the occasional bottle of rum—which ladies used "as flavoring" in Bananas Foster and fruitcakes—bourbon was generally the only spirit that people had in the house, if they had anything. Beer was for hoodlums; gin was for Englishmen; wine was a rarity. When the adults of my childhood drank, they drank bourbon—Wild Turkey, Old Grand-Dad, Kentucky Tavern, Old Crow, even the names were sort of a poem—and they drank it not as a casual matter of the nightly cocktail, but only at parties or when they were ill or deeply distressed, so for me it was a sitting-up-late smell, the smell of gatherings and special occasions: of parties and hilarity but also of grief, emergencies, coughing and sickrooms, high fevers, lights burning late into the night. At my house, the bottle was kept under the bathroom sink, with the iodine and Band-Aids, like medicine.

Bourbon was what I drank on my first date with a boy, in the dark front seat of a Cadillac in winter, freezing to death in my silver-white evening dress. At school in New England, and in my early days in New York, I drank bourbon because I was homesick, and it smelled rich and warm like home. I've had some festive bourbons at Harry's Bar in Paris—also at the Grand Hotel in Stockholm, where Faulkner drank more than a few bourbons before he went in to deliver his speech and accept his prize. But as I've grown older, bourbon has become so freighted with the past that it's almost an unbearably sad drink: the smell of old men standing around after funerals. I almost never drink it now, for fear of being swamped by nostalgia. That particular dark sweetness reminds me too much now of lost friends, lost childhood, lost things in general. The last bottle of bourbon I can remember buying was years ago, during a sad autumn when I was living out in the country, in France: early October darks, vineyards in the rain and country roads littered with chestnut leaves, hunters' gunshots echoing through the woods with a lonely pang of my Mississippi childhood, rain and more rain and gusty nights, early dinners in deserted rural cafés, and a melancholy walk home to bed.

Before, in Paris, I'd been struck by all the bottles of Jack Daniel's left as grave offerings in Père-Lachaise and Montmartre, sitting atop the tombs amid dank bouquets and piles of rotting leaves, and I was left wondering if bourbon had some distinct funereal whiff that made it a pleasing gift to the dead, or if bourbon drinkers were simply more apt to be disconsolate and roaming the graveyards in a foreign city—which seems the more likely possibility, since bourbon drinkers are some of the saddest people I have ever known.

There are only twenty dry counties left in Mississippi. In the town where I grew up, there are now three liquor stores on the road to my old school, stocked with single-barrel bourbons unheard of when I was a kid. I can't say what happened to the shack in Yalobusha County, Brown's Package Store (or "Dr. Brown's," as it was picturesquely known to its customers), except that it is almost certainly gone now. With it has vanished—for better or worse—much of the secrecy and ritual that characterized bourbon drinking when I was a child, that sense of the Jim Beam hidden in the glove compartment, the uncles passing the bottle around out on the back porch. (My friends and I, when we were children, used to stumble across those flat pint bottles squirreled away in the oddest places: in old suitcases, in toolboxes and flowerpots in neighbors' garages, under beds and behind bathtubs, in the desk drawers of our parents' employers, inside the back panel of an old console stereo specially altered for the purpose—perhaps most memorably, under the front seat of the school bus. Our bus driver, Mrs. Trotter, when confronted with the discovery, commented: "Even old Trott needs her a little pickup now and then.")

But along with the danger—the cocktails in the car on the way to the country club, the drunken midnight drives home from dances in the Delta—a lot of the magic has vanished, as well. Gone are the dizzy Christmas parties of my childhood, with firecrackers, candy and cake, and fragrant old gallants in high-waisted suits (some of whom, after one too many snorts, could be persuaded by a pleading child to do their imitations of Al Jolson in *The Jazz Singer*, or stand on their heads in the corner).

Even now, the afterburn of those parties still glows fiercely in my vision, like the colored sparks that showered across my retinas long after the last fireworks had been shot, after the coats had been fetched and the last toddies had been downed and the guests—still talking loudly in the clear winter night—tromped out to their cars laden with presents, shouting their happy good-byes.

Sazeracs
I Take My Liquor Brown

Sara Roahen

My people drink too much, both geographical sets of them. In my birth home, Wisconsin, and my adopted home, New Orleans, I sometimes seem to be the only person who has a sense of this. I'm an incorrigible lightweight and a misbehaving drunk; I learned early, around eleventh grade, that these traits make a destructive combination. Aside from the two years I spent in high school under the spell of a boy who drank Mad Dog like soda, I've managed to maintain the status of soberest chump in the room.

I may as well have *DD* tattooed on my rear end, for "designated driver," and I often wind up paying more than my fair share of the bill, but as with food or friends or money, the less alcohol you have the more you appreciate it, and I have a lover's appreciation of a good cocktail. More precisely, a good brown cocktail.

When in Wisconsin, I covet a regional variation of the old-fashioned, the brandy old-fashioned sweet—a tawny concoction of muddled fruit, brandy, Angostura bitters, sugar, and either 7 Up or soda, or, less common, water. In New Orleans, it's the promise of a Sazerac, a not altogether dissimilar regional drink now made with rye whiskey, that teases me through the days.

There's no single supreme bowl of gumbo in New Orleans, no gold standard against which locals agree to judge oyster po-boys, no definitive recipe for shrimp rémoulade. I do believe, however, that there exists a perfect Sazerac, and I first drank it on Lundi Gras, 2003, in the bar at Clancy's Restaurant.

The perfect Sazerac is a foxy brown-red, the hue that rye whiskey attains when stained with a few dashes of Peychaud's bitters, a vital Sazerac ingredient first swallowed by New Orleanians in the early to mid-1800s. The perfect Sazerac is shaken or stirred to cool lightly and served up in an old-fashioned glass, a stout and comfortable shape for a stout and comfortable drink. Its raspy brown-liquor base smoothes out like melted chocolate with a touch of sugar and a swirl of breathy, anise-flavored Herbsaint around the glass; Angostura bitters add a warm, quiet spiciness. A twist of lemon, its essential oils releasing as you drink, is the Sazerac's versatile mediator, brightening the whiskey, steadying the sugar, and matching the bitters with its own dull bitterness.

When I pulled out my notebook and asked Clancy's bartender for his technique, he shrugged. "Just luck, I guess. Don't ask me for another one." Of course I asked him for another one. I may be a one-and-a-half-cocktails-a-night kind of gal, but my people north and south always ask for another one. I am loyal to both.

When you consider that brown liquor defined my childhood as much as, say, snow days and sunburns did, my predilection for the Sazerac begins to look predestined. My barely postadolescent parents made me and my sister, Stephanie, right about the time that their partying habits matured to include mixed drinks. Loving both kids and cocktails, they determined that the two were not mutually exclusive. They were correct. While the adults raged on Badger football Saturdays, Stephanie and I got to eat unlimited taco dip and monkey bread. Once, after I gorged myself sick on toffee bars, my Aunt Nancy set me up with a stiff shot of peppermint schnapps—not to drink, but to place on my bedside table as an aromatherapy treatment.

Much of my parents' early partying went down at the hilltop home that Nancy shared with my Uncle Larry, a man whose command of the brandy old-fashioned remains unparalleled, awing and intoxicating my mom's side of the family once a year at their Christmas party. Larry stirs his old-fashioneds with a cinnamon stick, which softens as you drink and slowly releases its spice. You're meant to leave the cinnamon stick in your glass to flavor the next one. Of course there's a next one.

No one but my kindergarten teacher flinched when, at six years old, I mentioned my desire to become a cocktail waitress when I grew up. The early parties marked me in so many ways. I still have a stash of purple velveteen Crown Royal bags in my underwear drawer. I don't know what to use them for, now that I no longer need a lightweight storage solution for Barbie clothes, but they hold too much sentimental weight to toss.

On either end of the Mississippi River, Wisconsin and Louisiana are in opposition, both geographically and culturally. Whereas the former excels at giant muffins, the latter bastardizes batter baking and prefers croissants; Midwesterners pass summers in basements, protected from the tornadoes that spin away entire towns, even as hurricane season keeps the Gulf Coast running for higher ground; whereas Wisconsin drove its Native Americans onto reservations, Louisiana gave them Houma and other integrated towns of their choosing. In spite of these differences, it was my brown-liquor-soaked Wisconsin upbringing that sensitized my booze antennae to the Sazerac's magnificence.

It may be that I lucked out, first trying the cocktail at Commander's Palace, the revered house of Creole cooking old and new where the kitchen occasionally slips but the bartenders never do. More likely it was the drink's inherent righteousness that spoke to me. The Sazerac is a cocktail so classic that it has never suffered a coming-of-age or a fall from grace. And unlike the Wisconsin brandy old-fashioned, whose history is so undocumented that it seems to have sprung from some country well, the Sazerac's noble past is one of immigration, entrepreneurship, and regulated debauch. Something like the origins of New Orleans itself.

The Sazerac's muse, if not its sole inventor, was just a child when his family, plantation owners originally from France, fled the colony of Saint-Domingue (now Haiti) during that country's long and violent slave rebellions. Antoine Amédée Peychaud grew up to be an apothecary in New Orleans. In 1834 he opened a storefront on Royal Street, where he ground roots and herbs and spices and barks, and administered his healing tonics to ailing customers. An empath, like all good bartenders, Peychaud realized that a spoonful of liquor helps the medicine go down; the running story is that he dribbled his bitters into *coquetiers*, hourglass-shaped eggcups that were the precursors to jiggers, filled with cognac. Thus one of America's first cocktails—and the French Quarter's first shots—was born.

Some histories, namely those of the New Orleanian persuasion, contend that Peychaud mixed *the* first American cocktail. The proof, they say, is the word *cocktail* itself, an obvious bastardization of *coquetier*. There exist other convincing theories about the origin of the American cocktail, but as none directly involves the story of the Sazerac, I'll let them be.

In Peychaud's time a taste for brown drink was ubiquitous in this port city, including at the French Quarter's Sazerac Coffee House (long not in business), a namesake of the French brandy Sazerac de Forge et Fils, and the location that's acknowledged today as the birthplace of the first cocktails that New Orleanians called Sazeracs. Eventually ingredients other than bitters and brandy entered the cocktail's mix; among them was French absinthe, that poetic, debilitating, naturally anise-flavored spirit that was banned worldwide by the early twentieth century—but not before New Orleans established itself as a grand place to lose a few days.

Absinthe was outlawed because of its reliance on the plant wormwood, a bitter herb with debatable psychoactive properties. A demand for absinthe was so strong in Europe and New Orleans at the time that producers soon improvised by making wormwood-free, anise-flavored pastis, such as New

Orleans native Legendre Herbsaint. Originally produced and bottled here, Herbsaint now comes from a distillery in Kentucky. I prefer it in Sazeracs to other popular pastis brands (such as Pernod and Ricard) for its local roots, its more aggressive herbaceous overtones, and its pretty olive-amber shimmer.

But while Herbsaint is preferable, the brand of pastis is not as important as its use. A Sazerac is no Sazerac without that trace of anise, a hauntingly irresistible bluish flavor to the black-licorice-inclined and a fatal repellent to all others. In a collection of her short stories, the New Orleans writer Poppy Z. Brite speaks for the world's Sazerac-averse through a character whose father "would give me a sip of his Sazerac to teach me not to be an alcoholic." The character, John Rickey, describes Herbsaint as "like the black jelly bean if you took the sugar out and replaced it with bug spray." I'm fond of this description because it's dead on, whether you love Sazeracs or despise them.

Recipe writers are divided on whether Sazeracs ought to include Angostura as well as Peychaud's bitters. Stanley Clisby Arthur, who wrote *Famous New Orleans Drinks and How to Mix 'Em*, included Angostura in his as far back as 1937. I follow his lead, and I don't doubt that it's because Angostura's warm, barky, cinnamon-like qualities remind me of home. In comparison, there's a more medicinal anise edge and a black-pepper duskiness to Peychaud's Shirley Temple–red tonic. The two bitters complement each other in a Sazerac, adding dimension without confusion, like the way you might fill out a gumbo with both powdered red pepper and liquid Tabasco.

At some point rye whiskey became New Orleans's brown liquor of choice, replacing brandy—perhaps around the time of the Civil War, when importing from France grew cost prohibitive. In *Famous New Orleans Drinks*, Arthur submits that exactly when the switch occurred is moot: "American rye whiskey was substituted for the cognac to please the tastes of Americans who preferred 'red likker' to any pale-faced brandy." The red-likker preference stuck fast in New Orleans: To the best of my knowledge, I've never been served a brandy Sazerac without asking for it. A few class-conscious bartenders around town do ditch the rye for high-end, woody, burnt-sugar bourbons, but these are too robust and wind up drowning the Sazerac's harmonious convolution of flavors. An economical Wild Turkey rye does just fine. Ordinary bourbon works in a pinch.

Martin Sawyer, an octogenarian who tended bar at the Rib Room in the Omni Royal Orleans Hotel for about thirty-four years (and for three decades prior to that in other French Quarter bars), paid homage to former and contemporary tastes by stirring brandy *and* rye into his Sazeracs. I wish I had tasted one. While he has reinhabited his flooded New Orleans East home, Sawyer retired after Katrina.

I can't explain why brandy has enjoyed more longevity in Wisconsin, where residents consume more Korbel brandy per capita than in any other state. Nor can I explain why brandy didn't make a significant comeback in New Orleans in later years, when the United States began to produce loads of it. Coming to know the Sazerac has, however, led me to formulate an unorthodox theory about the evolution of Wisconsin's brandy old-fashioned—a theory with holes but also intrigue. It begins with a Mississippi riverboat captain who took his Sazerac habit upriver but ran out of absinthe along the way (as anyone would). My Northern European ancestors, who would have received the captain, were an industrious people. I imagine they made do by adding a bit more sugar to his punch, a cinnamon stick for spice, and perhaps some canned fruit for color if the captain had drained his Peychaud's bitters. True to their Protestant temperance, they would have lengthened the drink with water, and later with soda. Voilà: the first Wisconsin brandy old-fashioned.

My fairy-tale history would have Wisconsinites and New Orleanians communing over brown drink not long after the pirate antihero Jean Lafitte (for whom one of New Orleans's oldest bars is named) was dealing in slaves and helping to save Louisiana from English rule. It certainly would spice up the history lessons in my home state, which when I was in school leaned heavily on my ancestors' angelic involvement in the Underground Railroad and their mastery of milk production.

No one has corroborated my upriver cocktail theory. I once cornered William Grimes, who wrote the terrific cocktail-history book *Straight Up or On the Rocks*, at a literary festival in New Orleans. Having listened to my theory/fantasy on the connection between Sazeracs and brandy old-fashioned sweets, he replied, "Unlikely." I took it with a grain of optimism. It wasn't a no.

I've since run the idea by other students of the cocktail, though more casually than I did with Grimes. Now I pretend that I'm mostly joking, and I don't work up the courage for that until cocktails have been served. "Unlikely" turned out to be generous—other people just numbly nod. Sometimes I ask myself why I persist in forcing connections between my two peoples. I found a home in New Orleans. I built a life here and discovered a cocktail to love. So why all the looking back, all the comparisons?

I suppose it's because the depth with which I felt instantly at home in New Orleans has never seemed entirely serendipitous. The tastes, the people, the places that touch me—on the surface they were exotic, different from anything I'd tasted or met or experienced before. But I often wonder whether they were wholly new or whether what resonates for me most deeply in New Orleans is the sense of home I had growing up, just in a warmer, more colorful disguise.

Is this why I find it additionally heartening to note that New Orleans's first cold cocktails were chilled with ice harvested from Northern lakes (including the Great Lakes around Wisconsin), the ice packed in sawdust and either paddled down the great river or sailed down the East Coast from New York and into the Gulf of Mexico? The transport and, later, production of ice forever changed the Sazerac, which, like all early cocktails, was first drunk warm. Some drink makers, such as those at Galatoire's Restaurant, still revel in the luxury of ice by lavishing their Sazeracs with cubes of it. One never scoffs openly at anything frozen in the subtropics, but I don't prefer rocks in mine. Too much cold dulls a Sazerac's thrilling points of flavor.

If it seems counterintuitive that a lightweight would find such an obsession in cocktails, consider the first drink—or, rather, the second drink. Aside from its ritualistic pleasures, isn't the second drink always a letdown? It's like the second kiss, or the second time in New York City, or the second breath after you've been underwater too long. All the warm fuzzies of intoxication and none of its evils are concentrated in that first drink, above all the first sip. There's a soft melancholy in drinking liquor, which I experience most strongly drinking the brown kind, which settles at once into the bones, a complete benign passivity. Long before drunkenness takes over, drinking offers the release of the final sob following some deep misery, when your body just can't cry anymore.

It's natural, then, that drinking became emotional first aid following Katrina, when tears fixed nothing. My husband, Matt, and I were visiting his mother and stepfather in Manhattan on the day of the hurricane; we didn't get to use our return plane tickets for a month. During those long days and nights in New York, I naturally yearned for a Sazerac. Because of the drink's claim on me, coupled with my lousy tolerance, I basically had given up drinking anything else in New Orleans. But even on the evening we visited one of those fashionable Manhattan bars where the "mixologists" specialize in resurrecting classic American cocktails—and account heartily for inflation when ringing up your tab—I couldn't bring myself to order one. Though my affair with the Sazerac had stifled my cocktail curiosity and biased my palate, it made no more sense to drink one outside New Orleans than to eat a po-boy. The French refer to *terroir* when speaking of the effects of a specific grape-growing region's climate and geography on the character of its wine. It's not the best association, as no Sazerac ingredient grows in New Orleans soil, but there is a sort of emotional *terroir* that can unite certain tastes to specific places. During our Katrina displacement in New York, I took up with the Manhattan.

Matt and I eventually used our return tickets before we were technically allowed back into New Orleans. His hospital ID was enough to convince a peach-fuzzed national guardsman to wave us over the Orleans Parish line. Before heading to our home in a sliver of Uptown that hadn't flooded, we checked on a few of our favorite food places. The vintage neon sign at Angelo Brocato Ice Cream & Confectionery had smashed to its Mid-City sidewalk; flies darkened the water-ruined ice cream parlor's windows from the inside. There was no movement, or turtle soup, at sodden Mandina's Restaurant around the corner. We rejoiced to see a few dirty men brushing themselves off outside Port of Call, a French Quarter burger joint—they told us they would resume grilling burgers as soon as gas and electricity were restored.

Our own block was silent—no kids, no cars, no electrical buzz, no birds—but for the small man who stamped down the street and asked for our credentials. Mr. Leo had been staying at his brother's (our neighbor's) house ever since warlike chaos at the Superdome "shelter" had driven him upriver. For the first few days after the hurricane, before the cavalry arrived, he performed boat rescue missions as far out as the Jefferson Parish line; he pushed Pedialyte in shopping carts ("borrowing" both supplies and cart from our officially closed neighborhood supermarket) to the dehydrated babies stranded downtown; he donated a generator to a nearby police station; he watched the gas tanks of every vehicle on our block get punctured and drained by a man desperate to escape the city; he cooked for hungry stragglers before he gave away the generator; he slept on his brother's porch, armed; and he mowed all of our lawns so they would look pretty when we returned. Mr. Leo told impossible stories. Over time, many of them checked out.

After he made sure, by checking our IDs, that we belonged to the house for which we had keys, Mr. Leo asked if we had thought to import some cold beer. Dang. Only momentarily disappointed, he offered to share the ice and juice a relief agency brought by his place every morning if we would bust out some of the spirited mixers in our liquor cabinet (he correctly assumed that we had a liquor cabinet). Then, cocktail in hand, he helped us clean the maggots out of our refrigerator, patch our wind-damaged roof, and feel at home again.

Of all the American things most New Orleanians in the city could not do for months following Katrina and the ensuing flood—make a phone call, take a warm shower, surf the Web, heat a can of beans, shop at Wal-Mart, go to work—catching a buzz was not among them. The everyday movement of the city had all but stopped, but the drinking never did. Mr. Leo had hit upon a six-pack of his favorite beer, Natural Ice, while browsing in the dark, unstaffed supermarket and had considered it a gift from God.

Once residents began to repopulate New Orleans, drinking calmed frazzled thoughts and fried emotions. Friends and neighbors toasted the relief at seeing each other again, and they toasted the sadness of innocence—and more than fifteen hundred people—lost. Our house sustained the sort of wind-related damage you expect from a strong hurricane: shredded roof, torn siding, a downed pecan tree crushing the backyard fence. We had no right to complain, given the hell others struggled to endure, but after a day of minor inconveniences—waiting with other heartsick people for an hour in line at the grocery store, arguing with insurance adjusters, breathing plaster dust, triaging curbside debris into tree remains, construction trash, and household garbage—Matt proclaimed that cold booze was more sanitizing than a shower.

I didn't notice a subsidence of alcohol consumption among my friends and neighbors as ordinary conveniences began to return, because the storm lingered. (New Orleanians use *the storm* and *Katrina* not only to indicate the primary meteorological incident, a hurricane, but also to encompass the levee breaches, the ensuing flood, the resulting deaths, the rescue efforts, the governmental blunders, our extended and sometimes permanent stays in the diasporas, the near death of our city, Hurricane Rita, which arrived three weeks after Katrina, and, in many cases, every single day that has passed since August 29, 2005. For the hardest hit, *the storm* and *Katrina* continue to define everyday life.) Depression and ways of coping with it, like drinking, became casual conversation topics. In June 2006, nine months after the hurricane, a cabdriver taking me to the airport commented, apropos of nothing—other than that we both were living in post-Katrina New Orleans—that he used to be a social drinker. "Now, I can't even eat until I've had a couple of beers," he told me. The following week, *The New York Times* published an article about the alarming suicide rate in our town. Overdrinking sounded like a responsible alternative.

When I wrote about New Orleans before Katrina, I resisted mentioning some of the obvious clichés: *laissez les bon temps roulez*, "the Big Easy," Goldschläger shots from a drive-through daiquiri shed, that kind of thing. Back then they seemed lazy and unoriginal, evoking an image of life in New Orleans that the city should perhaps try to shed. Now I long for lightheartedness to define us again one day. Certainly there were New Orleanians who drank to fill a void before the storm; I worry that most of us do now. Which is not the same as saying that we're a city of stumbling drunks. Most nights end soberly.

My Northern people are good-times drinkers. As far back as my memory reaches, I've been envious of my parents' ability to cut completely loose. As when they were raising me, their partying now appears to be pure enjoyment. And yet ever since Katrina did to me at thirty-five what I did to them in their twenties—turned me into an adult—I do wonder.

The Sazerac

Makes one cocktail.

2 ounces rye whiskey
3 dashes Peychaud's bitters
3 dashes Angostura bitters
½ tablespoon simple syrup*

1 tablespoon Herbsaint or other
  pastis
Twist of lemon

Fill an old-fashioned glass with ice to chill. In a cocktail shaker, combine
rye whiskey, Peychaud's and Angostura bitters, and simple syrup. Add a
few ice cubes and stir. Empty the old-fashioned glass of its ice and replace
the ice with the Herbsaint; swirl the Herbsaint around the inside of the
glass to coat, and pour out any excess. Strain the whiskey mixture into the
glass and twist the lemon over the top, dropping it into the cocktail as a
garnish if you wish.

*To make simple syrup at home, dissolve any amount of sugar into an equal
  amount of warm water, and chill.*

The Michelada
Getting to the Bottom of a Mysterious Texas Concoction

Francine Maroukian

It's rare to meet a Texan with an identity problem; these folks are loud and proud to let the world know exactly where they're from. But the lineage of the Lone Star State's quirky beer-over-ice concoction is a different story.

The Michelada—pronounced mee-cha-*lah*-dah—struggles with a murky past. Perhaps it was invented by a revolutionary general named Don Augusto Michel or came about when the Tecate Brewery encouraged drinkers to rub a lime and sprinkle salt on its newly introduced beer cans to diminish the tinny taste. Even though *Michelada* loosely translates as "my cold beer," maybe the name does refer to the days when the drink was made with Michelob. However, despite its questionable background, there's no mistaking the Michelada's link to Tex-Mex border culture. When the food is spicy and the sun is hot, it makes sense to keep your beer cold.

Unsure of its origins, the Michelada does what it can to fit in. Travel north and the mix includes tomato juice, according to Sarah Fisher, bar manager of the Hotel San José in Austin, where the Michelada is typically a lighter drink with a tart edge. But even when you settle on a style, it's tricky to pinpoint the proportions.

"We don't measure the ingredients. You have to feel the Michelada—make it by touch," Fisher says. "The mix is delicate, so tinkering with even one ingredient alters how the flavors interact. More Tabasco and your beer goes from picante to downright mean; the amounts of soy sauce and Worcestershire give the drink a savory richness. Make enough of them and you'll be able to tell if you have the right mix by the color and how the ingredients blend."

But there's one constant: The Hotel San José Michelada is always topped off with south-of-the-border beer. First-timers might want to start with a lighter beer, such as Modelo Especial. For a step up in flavor, Fisher recommends either Pilsener of El Salvador or Xingu, a Brazilian black lager with a rich, "roasty" flavor, medium body, and a clean, malty finish.

"We serve it on the side, giving each drinker the freedom to pour the beer into the mix exactly as he likes it," Fisher says. "That's very Texas."

The Hotel San José Michelada (an approximation)
Makes one drink.

A couple of dashes Tabasco
A couple of dashes Worcestershire
  sauce
Quick pour (¼ ounce) dark soy
  sauce

Generous pour (2 or 3 ounces)
  fresh lime juice (less if you like
  a meatier texture, more if you
  want a thinner drink)
4 to 6 twists of coarsely ground
  black pepper
1 bottle south-of-the-border beer

Rim a 20-ounce glass (with straight sides) with coarse salt. Fill the glass halfway with ice cubes; the denser the cube the better (melts slower). Add all ingredients except beer over the ice and garnish with a lime wheel. Serve with a stirring straw and beer on the side, adding beer to the glass according to individual taste.

Dr. Enuf
A New Age Nutraceutical with a Patent Medicine Pedigree

Fred W. Sauceman

We step into the sugar room. It's 112 degrees year-round. Next door, in the mixing room, the temperature drops decidedly. My students marvel at kegs of caffeine.

We've come, on a day in late fall, to learn the chemistry of Dr. Enuf, as my students explore the foodways of Southern Appalachia. The Tri-City Beverage bottling facility sits in a sparsely settled neighborhood at the foot of Buffalo Mountain on the south side of Johnson City, Tennessee, a soft drink city of nearly sixty thousand where Mountain Dew was first bottled. Marion, Virginia, farther north, claims the drink, too, and Knoxville, one hundred miles to the southwest, makes its own case for soft drink stardom, since two brothers from there created Mountain Dew as a chaser for whiskey.

Dr. Enuf is a Jekyll-and-Hyde drink. The sugar in the heated tanks is pure cane. The caffeine content is stiff. Yet the nation's first carbonated, vitamin-enriched soft drink, with a latent lemon-lime flavor, has always been promoted as a curative. Alongside the caffeine sit bins of B vitamins. Thiamine, niacin, and potassium share label space with caffeine and sugar. Dr. Enuf was created above the Mason-Dixon Line but is only sold below it.

According to corporate lore, Bill Schwartz, a Chicago chemist, developed the formula after hearing his co-workers complain of lethargy. Charles Gordon, back in Johnson City after military service during World War II, saw an ad in *Bottler's Gazette* magazine (forerunner to *Beverage World*) and bought the rights to the formula.

When it first came out, Dr. Enuf sold for twenty-five cents while other soft drinks were going for a nickel.

"People paying that extra twenty cents thought it was doing something wonderful for them, and it took off," says Pat Sturgill, the company's current vice president of local sales.

"My aunt had cancer, and during radiation and chemotherapy, it eased her stomach."

It's been hawked as a hangover cure, credited with mind-clearing qualities, and touted as a way to stay alert during college examinations.

"In college during finals, I took ten thousand milligrams of caffeine one week cramming for a test," says Sturgill, whose job is to keep area stores stocked with the drink. "If I survived that, I guess caffeine's not too bad."

Brides and grooms have ordered Dr. Enuf to be mixed into their wedding cakes. It's been stirred into clear mountain moonshine and swizzled into darker drinks like Jack Daniel's sour mash whiskey. Mainly, though, it's taken straight, as its creator intended.

Charles Gordon was a marketer ahead of his time. When his product debuted, he bought full-page ads in the region's newspapers—the *Elizabethton Star*, the *Johnson City Press-Chronicle*. Those were the days when paperboys tossed tightly folded squares of newspapers onto front porches. Gordon's ad was designed in the style of a news story, and he paid the paper carriers to fold the newspaper backward, fooling people into thinking this new drink had garnered front-page attention.

The evening before Dr. Enuf hit the store shelves, Gordon paid staff at Johnson City's Memorial Hospital to slap stickers onto the bumpers of physicians' cars: "Dr. Enuf is Here!" Folks headed downtown for a hot dog the next day at John and Olga Kovach's place inside the Trailways bus station couldn't miss a banner stretched across Main Street heralding the advent of the new drink. "The Dr. Has Arrived," it read. The drink was embraced so readily by East Tennesseans that it had to be rationed.

From the Truman presidency to the New Millennium, the company's advertising slogan, or positioning line in today's parlance, has always been, "The Original Energy Booster." The message held up well.

"We were the first energy drink on the market, fifty years before Red Bull," says Sturgill. "I see people paying a dollar ninety-nine for Red Bull, and I'm thinking you can pay ninety-nine cents for ours and get about the same pick-me-up."

However, except for Internet sales, that lemon-lime caffeine jolt is only available in stores located in seven East Tennessee counties; the Knoxville, Tennessee, area; Boone, Hickory, and Asheville in North Carolina; Greenville, South Carolina; and Danville, Abingdon, and several counties in Southwest Virginia. The counties of Carter and Greene, in East Tennessee, represent the drink's healthiest markets. Around three hundred cases of Dr. Enuf are trucked to Roan Mountain, near the North Carolina line, every week.

Ali Williams was assigned to a trash pickup detail for a service-learning class at East Tennessee State University in the fall of 2006. "Every other piece of trash I picked up on Roan Mountain was an empty Dr. Enuf bottle," she says.

"Back in the late 1980s, when we first started talking about Dr. Enuf as a 'new age' beverage, there really wasn't a name for us, a classification," says Sturgill. "Then the name nutraceutical came out to describe 'good-for-you' drinks."

The crossbred moniker, a marrying of "nutrition" and "pharmaceutical," entered the American lexicon. There is now an American Nutraceutical Association, and it publishes a journal.

According to the association's Web site, a physician, Dr. Stephen DeFelice, coined the term. He established the Foundation for Innovation in Medicine in Cranford, New Jersey.

DeFelice writes, "A nutraceutical is any substance that is a food or a part of a food and provides medical or health benefits, including the prevention and treatment of disease. Such products may range from isolated nutrients, dietary supplements and specific diets to genetically engineered designer foods, herbal products, and processed foods such as cereals, soups and beverages."

At least for now, the U.S. government takes no stance on what constitutes a nutraceutical. It is purely a marketing term and carries no regulatory controls, but Sturgill senses the impending grip of the government. "I think before long, they're going to make us list how much caffeine is in our drink."

In its marketing, Dr. Enuf targets the eighteen-to-thirty-four age group—males for the company's regular products, females for diet drinks.

The name Dr. Enuf can be easily punned and played upon. Sturgill says the company once launched an advertising campaign aimed at the twelve thousand students attending nearby East Tennessee State University. Ads asked the probing question, "Are you getting Enuf?"

"We tried that only once," he adds, "then decided we're not that type of company."

The type of company Tri-City Beverage does want to be is lean and regional.

"One thing I've learned in a small company is even though you have a high position, you've got to be willing to take on extra work," says Sturgill. "The 'not-my-job' theory doesn't work here. If we all had that, we would have been out of business. At Tri-City Beverage, we only have eighteen employees, and we make do."

According to the white imprint on the twelve-ounce souvenir bottle, Dr. Enuf contains 246 percent of the daily requirement of thiamine (B1), 85 percent of the niacin (B3) requirement, and 75 percent of iodine. Some theorize that the drink took off in Southern Appalachia because it provided vitamin content that was previously lacking in diets and did indeed make people feel better as a result. The drink's name echoes days when many mountain people distrusted medically accepted cures administered by physicians.

In *Now & Then: The Appalachian Magazine,* Johnson City bird watcher and librarian John Hart cited another reason for the drink's reputation in the mountains: "The rising popularity of Dr. Enuf in the face of shrinking sales for other independent bottlers nationwide is due to the native independence of the local people. Dr. Enuf drinkers like it not only because it's a quality drink, but because it is a chance to rebel against the corporate monotony of our age. It's a vote for cantankerous idiosyncrasy that flies in the face of high-tech marketing, million-dollar Michael Jackson ads [Hart was writing in 1988], and the homogenized, sanctified franchise mentality."

The company always sought to differentiate itself from the national soft drink conglomerates, and it did the same when "sports drinks" like Gatorade hit the market.

"Dr. Enuf is unique when compared to other sports and health drinks because of its light, lemon-lime flavor and carbonation which isn't flat or salty," Charles Gordon explained in a 1995 news release announcing a "new age" marketing push for the product. Gordon's eldest son, C. O. Gordon Jr., is the company's president and chief executive officer today.

In 2002, Tri-City Beverage expanded its line, and its color palette, with an herbal, ruby-hued version of Dr. Enuf. But unlike Schwarz's calculated blending in his Chicago laboratory, this drink was an accident.

"We thought we were running regular Dr. Enuf, but the person handling quality control for us at the time wasn't sampling the product," Sturgill recalls. "We ran one thousand cases, delivered them, and then started getting calls from customers asking us what we had done to their Dr. Enuf."

It turns out that cherry flavoring had been dumped into the lemon-lime. The company sent its delivery people back out into the field to pick up all the errant bottles, but reaction to the new flavor was positive.

Says Sturgill, "It's a fun business when little things like that happen."

In addition to fd&c Red 40 and a bit of Blue 1, Herbal Dr. Enuf contains ginseng and guarana, the ingredients imprinted in gold on the label. The company's Web page cites Mayo Clinic studies indicating that ginseng "fights fatigue, helps with concentration, and boosts the immune system—all things the Ancient Chinese have known for years. It also increases resistance to the effects of stress and improves circulation and mental functioning, while reducing the risk of cancer."

Ginseng has been treasured in the mountains of Appalachia for generations. Cherokees used the root to treat stomach disorders, convulsions, and headaches. Today, North Carolina ginseng diggers grind the roots into a powder and pack it into capsules. They claim the powder increases the body's tolerance for temperature variations.

Guarana, a small, fruit-bearing tree that grows in South America, supposedly possesses properties akin to caffeine, since its chemical composition is similar. "Guarana is acknowledged to increase mental alertness, fight fatigue, and to increase stamina and physical endurance," declares drenuf. com. Various Web sites describe guarana's supposed power to cure "bowel complaints."

Herbal Dr. Enuf's cherry flavor harmonizes with traditional Southern soft drink tastes. North Carolina's cherry-flavored Cheerwine has been bottled in Salisbury since 1917. And fizzy Cherry Lemon Sun-Drop, mixed at R.O.'s Bar-B-Cue in the Piedmont mill town of Gastonia, North Carolina, is ordered up as an accompaniment to the restaurant's slaw burgers. Tri-City Beverage, incidentally, was the first Cheerwine distributor outside the Carolinas.

Sturgill says Tri-City Beverage has no plans to follow the mass-market trends of the soft drink industry by using high fructose corn syrup.

"With all the negative press, we've stayed away from it, although sugar is much more expensive. We don't want to lessen the drink by putting corn syrup in it."

The company has considered a caffeine-free variety of Dr. Enuf, and officials believe it might work, since Dr. Enuf is viewed in Southern Appalachia as more of a soft drink rather than an energy drink. The drink's current caffeine content exceeds that of its sister beverage, Mountain Dew, but is less than an average cup of coffee. Dr. Enuf occupies a prominent spot on a Web site called "Bob's Caffeine Shrine."

The company continues to bottle in glass, which creates, Sturgill says, a better taste. At top capacity, 360 bottles are filled each minute. The lemon-lime mix is stored in 750-gallon tanks.

Bottling is done at thirty-four to thirty-six degrees, and then the product is warmed. Without that reheating, bottles would sweat in the boxes and drinks would fall through the soggy cardboard and shatter in convenience store parking lots.

Dr. Enuf is a survivor. It has straddled the decades from sales in slide-top coolers at weatherboarded country stores to bop-in-and-out convenience markets off interstate highway exits. It's an alcohol-free descendant of nineteenth-century America's exotic elixirs and patent medicines, and its claims of relief for "untold misery" have been embraced by old-timers and new-agers alike.

Its message has remained the same, from Charles Gordon's bumper stickers applied in a hospital parking lot to simulated soft drink bubbles on the Internet: relief from that tired, run-down feeling, no matter what the cause.

Have a Fried Coke— and a Frown?

John Kessler

It sounds like the fictional South run amok—a bad Jeff Foxworthy joke or another horror faced by the hapless canoe party of *Deliverance*. But, no, fried Coke is real, and it's here.

Beginning Saturday (April 12, 2008) at the Georgia Renaissance Festival, Atlantans will be treated to the city's iconic beverage transformed into a hot, crispy mass of caloric excess. Fried Coke.

This confection made a big splash (actually, a thud) at the Texas State Fair in 2007, where it won the "Creativity Award." Invented by Abel Gonzalez Jr., it consists of a Coca-Cola-infused batter topped with cola syrup, cinnamon sugar, whipped cream, and a cherry.

And the taste?

"Unequivocally disgusting," avers *Dallas Morning News* restaurant critic Bill Addison. "It sort of tastes like a Coca-Cola cake on steroids—sweet on sweet on sweet, unrelenting sweetness."

"Top Chef" contestant Richard Blais, known for his avant-garde cooking, hasn't tried fried Coke but says he'd rejigger the technique given a chance to fry his own Coke.

"I might make and then fry a Coke ice cream with liquid nitrogen. It freezes so quickly that it would keep its carbonation," says Blais. "So when you bit into it, it keeps the middle cold, refreshing, and carbonated."

"It's a novelty, something to try once," advises Addison. "I'm just not sure how many second takers there will be in the world."

Taste of Tradition
Iced Tea

Fred Thompson

My mother swears she didn't put sweet tea in my baby bottles, but the twinkle in her eye and the sly, sideways smile tell me she's probably not being truthful.

I can remember Mother letting me watch her prepare the tea when I was as young as five or six. She was meticulous in her method. A small (probably not even one-quart) saucepan's only job was to handle the making of tea. It had a black stain from the tea's tannins, and nothing else—not even dish soap—ever touched the pot's innards. (I am happy to report that this little pot now resides with me.) Six tea bags and two cups of water would work their magic to form the base for a half-gallon of tea. Sugar was poured up to about an inch deep—approximately a cup and a quarter, according to my recent calculations—into an old-fashioned glass pickle jar reclaimed for this use only. Slowly the warm tea concentrate filtered over the sugar. Why the jar didn't shatter, I'll never know. Mother would stir the black walnut-colored liquid until the grittiness of the sugar was gone. Then came six cups of cold tap water and another quick stir.

"Let's wait till it cools off to have a glass," she would say. I later discovered she didn't like how ice would weaken her glass of tea at this stage. And the cooling was never done in the refrigerator because it would make the tea cloudy.

Life was good with this daily ritual and a never-ending supply of sweet tea. Mother still insisted that I drink ample amounts of milk since I was "a growing boy," but a glass or two of "ice" sweet tea was inevitable. But just before Christmas when I was eight, Mother sat me down and said, "Daddy is in the hospital because his heart isn't working just right. Things are going to have to change when he comes home."

By *change*, I hoped she meant that my newly arrived sister would get returned to the store she came from. Never did I realize that sweet tea, the real stuff with sugar, was being taken off our home's menu along with fatback, bacon, and fried chicken. My farm-raised, Southern-cook mother had to struggle with new seasonings and vegetables as well as artificial sweeteners. Consequently, I relished trips to my grandmother's and later to any girlfriend's house for meals that were always accompanied with a large glass of *real* sweet tea.

I left for college at the age of eighteen, and on my first trip home, I found that Mother was a good cook again, at least for the weekend. By then, Dad was disciplined enough about his diet, so my homecomings became an event—a ham hock or two reappeared in the vegetables, and sweet tea, the *real* deal, was poured with gusto. In one of the few moments Dad ever talked of World War II, he told me how important tasting his mother's sweet tea was when he returned from postings in Africa and England.

"While I had watched the world change, that simple first sip of Mamma's tea told me I was home, that I was loved and respected for what I had done. Sugar was still rationed, son, but Mamma used it to celebrate my homecoming," Dad said as water welled in his eyes.

Since college begins the task of self-reliance, I knew I needed to learn how to feed myself. And the first recipe I acquired was the one for Mother's sweet tea. Easily made in a dorm-allowed, old-style electric popcorn popper (yes, this was a time before microwaves), it was the beginning of my exploration of Southern food.

Sweet tea has been called "the house wine of the South" and justifiably so. It blends with and complements so many Southern favorites. But iced sweet tea is also the sign of hospitality. It transcends race, religion, and politics because it truly welcomes all to the table and welcomes home those who have wandered to far-flung places—whether for college, war, or business. Sweet tea—your mother's sweet tea—means you are home.

Praise Wine

John Simpkins

I've been black since birth. I'm not sure how long I've been a Jew. "You're the only black person I know who can quote Woody Allen movies," said my Jewish friend, Peter, when I asked him to assess my Jewishness. "I only quote from the early good ones," I explained. "And those I love. In fact, love is too weak a word for what I feel. I more than love them. I 'lurve' them."

"Sammy Davis Jr. was your favorite member of the Rat Pack," Peter continued, pressing his case. "You even sent your three-year-old to summer camp at the Jewish Community Center. He recognizes the Israeli flag, can sing the dreidel song, and is constantly asking for challah. If you're not Jewish, Jonah certainly is."

Pete then reminded me how excited I was when he offered to read from the *Zohar* at my wedding. Then I remembered the frequent calls from my mother during my travels. "I'm just calling to see how you're doing. Oh, don't worry about me. I'm fine. I just thought I'd call since I hadn't heard from you in awhile. No, things are fine here. Don't worry about me."

I know why I'm black, but it was harder to figure out why I'm a Jew. As with so many voyages of personal discovery, the search for my Inner Jew begins with food and drink. For me, any discussion of food and drink has to include Sundays with my grandmother. Mama Sena's house in Lexington, South Carolina, was the Sunday dinner gathering place for the eighteen of us first cousins, who spanned a twenty-three-year range and felt more like siblings than cousins. Because she was a church lady, there was little work actually done in Mama Sena's house on the Sabbath. She even refused to allow anyone to wash clothes on Sunday for fear that "someone could be washed out of the family." It is primarily for this reason that I spent most of my childhood fearing washing machines as agents of death.

The fruits of the labors of the rest of the week, however, were in abundance. The standard Sunday menu featured cucumbers in white vinegar, macaroni and cheese, sweet potatoes, ham, rice, gravy, and stew beef, ending in a lemon chiffon ice cream love fest. Our drink of choice was either Coca-Cola or iced tea, except for the most auspicious dinners. On very special occasions— holidays, weddings, births—Mama Sena's table would include wine. This was the only alcohol I ever saw Mama Sena drink. Indeed it was her only vice. Except for smoking like a chimney and cussing like a sailor. But otherwise, her only vice. Though we had our share of alcoholics in the family, drinking hard liquor always seemed to be an after-hours activity.

And when Mama Sena served wine, she always chose kosher wine. Mogen David and Manischewitz provided me with my first taste of alcohol. This, too, marked the beginning of my transformation into one of the Chosen People. To me, wine had to have that "double triangle thingy" on it in order to be truly legit. It didn't hurt to have a bunch of bearded guys dressed all in black. Far more important than vintage were these things.

Exactly why my grandmother adopted kosher wine as our celebratory drink of choice remains something of a mystery. Theories abound, from the sweetness that surely appealed to infrequent wine drinkers, to price, to the fact that kosher wine frequently has been used in communion services in African American churches.

As a member of the Women's Missionary Society in our local AME church, Mama Sena would have been responsible from time to time for obtaining wine for the sacrament. She may have developed a taste for it in the course of carrying out her duties. Drinking kosher wine in the home was just another example of how African Americans deftly navigate the sacred and the profane, never allowing one to destroy their appreciation for the other. The journey that kosher wine took from the communion table to Mama Sena's table was in some ways no different than the musical wanderings of Aretha Franklin, Al Green, and Sam Cooke from gospel to R&B and back again.

In fact, one of the oldest of the eighteen first cousins still refers to kosher wine as "praise wine" and keeps a bottle of Mogen David hidden away in her pantry, as if to prevent it from contaminating the high-toned good stuff she so proudly displays in her fancy under-counter wine fridge. For her, it's a comfortable memory of our childhood. Or perhaps a constant connection to her own Inner Jew.

Ultimately, it matters little why Mama Sena and other African American church women developed a taste for kosher wine. In addition to bringing families together, "praise wine" has produced a generation of black oenophiles. It has propelled me to a global adventure of food and drink of all kinds. I've had wine from Bordeaux, Otago, the Okanagan Valley, and most parts in between. In each place I've found something worth savoring. Moreover, I've formed friendships that have outlasted any bottle. In addition to leading me to an appreciation for being a black Jew, praise wine has enriched my life in a profound way. In other words, it has been a mitzvah.

Butter

Elizabeth Alexander

My mother loves butter more than I do,
more than anyone. She pulls chunks off
the stick and eats it plain, explaining
cream spun around into butter! Growing up
we ate turkey cutlets sautéed in lemon
and butter, butter and cheese on green noodles,
butter melting in small pools in the hearts
of Yorkshire puddings, butter better
than gravy staining white rice yellow,
butter glazing corn in slipping squares,
butter the lava in white volcanoes
of hominy grits, butter softening
in a white bowl to be creamed with white
sugar, butter disappearing into
whipped sweet potatoes, with pineapple,
butter melted and curdy to pour
over pancakes, butter licked off the plate
with warm Alaga syrup. When I picture
the good old days I am grinning greasy
with my brother, having watched the tiger
chase his tail and turn to butter. We are
Mumbo and Jumbo's children despite
historical revision, despite
our parents' efforts, glowing from the inside
out, one hundred megawatts of butter.

Contributors

Elizabeth Alexander is a professor of African American studies at Yale University. She read her poem "Praise Song for the Day" at the 2009 presidential inauguration.

Brett Anderson is a James Beard award winner. He is restaurant reviewer and features writer for the *New Orleans Times-Picayune*.

Bill Archer, of Bluefield, West Virginia, has enjoyed a long career as a newspaperman. He and his wife, Evonda, have three children and six grandchildren.

Ben Barker is chef and co-owner of Magnolia Grill. A James Beard award winner (2000), a father of two, a grandfather of two, and a lover of pig, he is coauthor of *Not Afraid of Flavor*.

Lucretia Bingham has written about family for many magazines, including *Smithsonian, Conde Nast Traveler,* and *Saveur.*

Roy Blount Jr., who contributes columns to *Garden and Gun* and other magazines, is a writer and lover of food. His most recent books are *Alphabet Juice* and *Long Time Leaving: Dispatches from Up South.*

Devon Brenner teaches teachers to teach, specifically reading and writing, at Mississippi State University.

Kara Carden, a lifelong Tennessean, is a writer who now subsists on a vegan diet—no offense to egg fighters.

Margaret Carr, a staff member at East Tennessee State University, is a native of Carter County, Tennessee, where she resides with her daughter, Lydia.

Anthony Cavender is professor of anthropology in the Department of Sociology and Anthropology at East Tennessee State University.

Mei Chin, a recipient of the 2005 James Beard M. F. K. Fisher Distinguished Writing Award, is a writer living in New York. Her mother, Ann Ping, and her Aunt Yen recently attended their fortieth reunion at Douglas Southall Freeman High School in Richmond, Virginia.

Pete Daniel is a curator, author, and past president of the Southern Historical Association and of the Organization of American Historians. Among his many books is *Breaking the Land.*

Alan Deutschman is the author of four books, including *Walk the Walk* and *A Tale of Two Valleys*. He lives in Atlanta.

Charles C. Doyle, a native Texan, teaches folklore and Renaissance literature at the University of Georgia. His specialty is proverbs.

Crescent Dragonwagon's James Beard award–winning cookbooks include *Passionate Vegetarians* and *The Cornbread Gospels*. The former Arkansan now lives in Vermont.

Neely Barnwell Dykshorn is a freelance writer, editor, and stylist who lives and works in Richmond, Virginia.

Kathryn Eastburn is the author of *A Sacred Feast* and *Simon Says*. She lives in Galveston, Texas.

John T. Edge, director of the Southern Foodways Alliance, has written or edited more than ten books. He contributes regularly to a number of publications.

John Egerton, originally from Kentucky, is the author of the landmark book *Southern Food: At Home, on the Road, in History*. He now lives in Nashville, Tennessee, where he frequents meat-and-three restaurants.

Amy C. Evans is an exhibiting artist and oral historian for the Southern Foodways Alliance.

Beth Ann Fennelly is the author of four books, most recently *Unmentionables: Poems*. She lives in Oxford, Mississippi, and teaches at Ole Miss.

Marcie Cohen Ferris is an associate professor in the Department of American Studies at the University of North Carolina–Chapel Hill. She is the author of *Matzoh Ball Gumbo*.

Martha Hall Foose of the Mississippi Delta is a chef and storyteller. Her recent book, *Screen Doors and Sweet Tea*, won a James Beard award.

John S. Forrester is a columnist for the *Boston Globe* and a lover of grits.

Jeffrey Gettleman is a graduate of Cornell University and a columnist for the *New York Times*.

Jessica B. Harris is a food historian and cookbook author who lives in New York City and New Orleans. Among her books is *Beyond Gumbo*. Forthcoming is *High on the Hog*.

Michelle Healy is a writer for *USA Today*. She has a fondness for tea cakes.

Dan Huntley is coauthor of *Extreme Barbecue* and a former *Charlotte Observer* columnist who smokes meat and makes boudin in York, South Carolina.

Andrew Huse teaches and works as a special collections librarian at the University of South Florida in Tampa. He specializes in Florida foodways.

Rheta Grimsley Johnson is a columnist for King Features Syndicate of New York and the author of *Poor Man's Provence*, among other books.

Loyal Jones formerly directed the Berea College Appalachian Center in Kentucky and has published widely on subjects related to Appalachia.

Jennifer Justus writes about food and life for the *Tennessean* in Nashville.

Marilyn Kallet is the author of fourteen books, including *Packing Light: New and Selected Poems*, from Black Widow Press.

John Kessler is a staff writer at the *Atlanta Journal-Constitution*. He writes frequently about food and restaurants.

Barbara Kingsolver is an acclaimed writer whose work has won the National Humanities Medal. Her recent book *Animal, Vegetable, Miracle* chronicles a year of deliberate eating with her family on its southwest Virginia farm.

Corby Kummer is a senior editor at the *Atlantic* and winner of the James Beard M. F. K. Fisher Distinguished Writing Award. His most recent book is *The Pleasures of Slow Food*.

Carroll Leggett, a public relations professional, is a columnist for *Metro Magazine* who often writes about eastern North Carolina culture and foodways.

Edna Lewis was a noted southern chef and writer. Her published works include *The Taste of Country Cooking, In Pursuit of Flavor*, and *The Gift of Southern Cooking*.

Francine Maroukian, the author of numerous books, is a contributing editor for *Travel + Leisure, Garden and Gun*, and *Esquire*.

Anne Martin is a journalist based in Greenville, Mississippi, and a freelance writer for *Delta* magazine.

George Motz is a filmmaker in Brooklyn, New York. He loves hamburgers and is, by mere chance, the author of *Hamburger America*.

Joan Nathan is a James Beard award–winning author of numerous books, including *Jewish Cooking in America*.

Jack Neely is a *Metro Pulse* columnist who writes about Knoxville, Tennessee, and its history. His latest book, *Market Square*, is a history of that venerable institution.

Tore C. Olsson is a PhD candidate at the University of Georgia. His dissertation examines post-1965 immigration to the South and its impact on foodways and agriculture.

Molly O'Neill writes for the *New Yorker*. A longtime food columnist for the *New York Times Magazine*, she is the author of the forthcoming treatise on American cookery *One Big Table*.

Scott Peacock is a James Beard award winner and executive chef of Watershed restaurant in Decatur, Georgia. His fried chicken is fabled.

Kathleen Purvis has been a newspaper journalist since 1978 and has been food editor of the *Charlotte Observer* since 1989.

David Ramsey, who writes frequently for the *Oxford American*, is a writer and schoolteacher in New Orleans, Louisiana.

John Shelton Reed, a retired sociology professor, is coauthor, with Dale Volberg Reed and William McKinney, of *Holy Smoke: The Big Book of North Carolina Barbecue*.

Julia Reed of New Orleans is the food and drink columnist for *Newsweek* and the author of *Ham Biscuits, Hostess Gowns, and Other Southern Specialties*.

Sara Roahen is a writer, oral historian, and new mother living in New Orleans. Her first book, *Gumbo Tales: Finding My Place at the New Orleans Table*, is currently the focus for the One Book Greater New Orleans program.

Fred W. Sauceman, longtime administrator at East Tennessee State University, is the author of *The Place Setting*, a three-volume book series on Appalachian foodways.

Salley Shannon, the current president of the American Society of Journalists and Authors, is a freelance writer for many national magazines.

Susan Shelton, a graduate of East Tennessee State University, is writing her thesis on the folklore and foodways of corn.

Chuck Shuford is an occasional contributor to the *Daily Yonder*. A native of North Carolina, the author now fries his livermush in Knoxville, Tennessee.

John Simpkins lives in Charleston, South Carolina, and Vancouver, British Columbia. His work has appeared in the *Oxford American* and the *New Republic*.

Martha Stamps is a Nashville native, a former columnist for the *Tennessean*, and the chef-proprietor of Martha Stamps Catering.

Robert St. John of Hattiesburg, Mississippi, is a chef, restaurateur, author, food writer, and world-class eater. His latest book is *New South Grilling*.

Garland Strother, a native of Tensas Parish, Louisiana, is a retired librarian now living near New Orleans. His work has been published in the *Texas Review*, *Louisiana Review*, and other journals.

Donna Tartt is a novelist born in Greenwood, Mississippi. Her work has been translated into twenty-eight languages.

John Martin Taylor is a food writer and purveyor of stone-ground, whole-grain, heirloom corn products. He is the author of four cookbooks, including *Hoppin' John's Lowcountry Cooking*.

Sarah Anne Loudin Thomas is a native of West Virginia. She and her husband, Jim, now live in Asheville, North Carolina, where she works for the Presbyterian Home for Children.

Fred Thompson is the author of eight cookbooks, including *Iced Tea*. He is the publisher of *Edible Piedmont* magazine and a columnist for the *Raleigh News and Observer*.

Lee Walburn is former editor in chief of *Atlanta Magazine*. He received the Lifetime Achievement Award presented by the City and Regional Magazine Association.

Daniel Wallace is the author of four novels, including *Big Fish* and *Ray in Reverse*. He lives in Chapel Hill, North Carolina, where he teaches writing at the University of North Carolina–Chapel Hill.

Robb Walsh is the award-winning food critic for the *Houston Press* and the author of several food books and cookbooks. His thing is Texas food.

Ari Weinzweig is co-owner and founding partner of the Zingerman's Community of Businesses in Ann Arbor, Michigan. His most recent book, *Zingerman's Guide to Better Bacon*, was cured in a smokehouse to infuse authentic scent to the pages.

Katherine Whitworth, a freelance writer living in central Arkansas, believes the world could do worse than simply feed itself well.

Sylvia Woods, a native of Kentucky, teaches English in Oak Ridge, Tennessee. She writes poetry and fiction.

Marianne Worthington of Williamsburg, Kentucky, is the author of a poetry chapbook, *Larger Bodies Than Mine*, and editor of a music anthology, *Motif: Writing by Ear*.

Kevin Young is the Atticus Haygood Professor of English and Creative Writing and curator of the Raymond Danowski Poetry Library at Emory University. He lives in Boston and Atlanta. His latest book is *Dear Darkness*.

Acknowledgments

Unlike broth, books like this one benefit from many hands. I thank the Southern Foodways Alliance at the University of Mississippi for starting this series, the University of Georgia Press for embracing it, and the writers who have continued to enliven it by allowing their work to be included in this fifth volume of *Cornbread Nation: The Best of Southern Food Writing.*

John T. Edge, general editor of the series and director of the Southern Foodways Alliance, was an endless source of information and inspiration. His colleague Mary Beth Lasseter meticulously secured reprint permissions and biographical information on contributors. John Shelton Reed and Dale Volberg Reed, fellow East Tennesseans and the editors of *Cornbread Nation 4,* gave me insightful guidance over plates of barbecued fresh ham at our beloved Ridgewood in Bluff City, Tennessee.

I thank all the staff members at the University of Georgia Press who had a hand in the creation of this book—most especially Nicole Mitchell, Erika Stevens, Jon Davies, and John McLeod. Douglas Clayton skillfully and sensitively copyedited the manuscript.

Renna Tuten at the Richard B. Russell Library for Political Research and Studies at the University of Georgia and Rebecca Tolley-Stokes at East Tennessee State University's Charles C. Sherrod Library helped track down articles on subjects ranging from chicken mull to red velvet cake. Amy Evans of the SFA generously provided photographs to illuminate the foodways of immigrant groups in the South.

I am grateful to my employer, East Tennessee State University, for understanding that the study of Southern foodways is profound and for recognizing its rightful and overdue place in the academy by granting me time to complete this book.

Finally, I thank my wife Jill, who has taken this full-circle journey with me, from the soup beans and cornbread of our youth, detouring through the stews and composed rice dishes of Persia, and finally returning to the black-iron skillets of our Appalachian homeland.

The following is a list of permissions to reprint the essays and art that appear in this book:

"Why Study Southern Food?" by Marcie Cohen Ferris. Originally published in the *Southern Register*, Summer 2008.

"What Is Southern?" by Edna Lewis. This letter from Edna Lewis to Eugene Walter is reprinted with permission from the estates of Eugene Walter and Edna Lewis. Originally published in *Gourmet* magazine, January 2008.

"The Grace before Dinner," by Jennifer Justus. Originally published in the *Tennessean*, December 14, 2008.

"Gratitude: May," by Barbara Kingsolver. Originally published in *Animal, Vegetable, Miracle: A Year of Food Life*, copyright © 2007 by Barbara Kingsolver, Stephen L. Hopp, and Camille Kingsolver. Reprinted by permission of HarperCollins Publishers and Faber and Faber Ltd.

"Corn as a Way of Life," by Loyal Jones. Originally presented at the 2003 Southern Foodways Alliance Symposium, Oxford, Mississippi.

"Between the Rows with Both Hands: Bean-Picking in Northeast Tennessee," by Margaret Carr. Originally written as a piece for class, it is also printed in *Now and Then: The Appalachian Magazine*, Spring/Summer 2009.

"Field Pea Philosophy," by Scott Peacock. Originally published in the *Atlanta Journal-Constitution*, July 24, 2008.

"The Season of Fried Green Tomatoes," by Martha Stamps. Originally published in the *Tennessean*, March 2008.

"Onion Medicine," by Anthony Cavender. Published here for the first time by permission of the author.

"Coveted, French, and Now in Tennessee," by Molly O'Neill. From the *New York Times*, February 28, 2007. © 2007 The New York Times. All rights reserved. Used by permission and protected by the copyright laws of the United States. The printing, copying, redistribution, or retransmission of the material without express written permission is prohibited.

"Living through the Honey," by Daniel Wallace. Originally published in *Sweet Tea Journal*, Spring/Summer 2006.

"Capturing Summer in the Ice Cream Churn," by Dan Huntley. Originally published in the *Charlotte Observer*, June 10, 2004.

"Sweet Potato Pie," a poem by Marilyn Kallet. Originally published in *Now and Then: The Appalachian Magazine*, Spring/Summer 2007.

"Ode to Chicken," a poem by Kevin Young. From *Dear Darkness: Poems*, by Kevin Young, © 2008 by Kevin Young. Used by permission of Alfred A. Knopf, a division of Random House, Inc.

"Mulling over Mull: A North Georgia Foodways Localism," by Charles C. Doyle. Originally published in *Midwestern Folklore* 29, no. 2 (2003): 5–11.

"Some Like It Extra Hot," by David Ramsey. Originally published in the *Oxford American* 49.

"Victory or Supper: The Easter Egg Fights of Peters Hollow," by Kara Carden. Originally featured in *American Profile* magazine, March 10, 2002.

"There's a Word for It—the Origins of 'Barbecue,'" by John Shelton Reed. Adapted from *Holy Smoke: The Big Book of North Carolina Barbecue* (Chapel Hill: University of North Carolina Press, 2008).

"A Jewish Yankee's Quest for the Last Great Country Hams of Western Kentucky: How a City Boy Fell Madly for Country Ham and Wound Up Eating It Raw," by Alan Deutschman. Published here for the first time by permission of the author.

"Ode to a Catfish House," by Katherine Whitworth. Originally published in the *Oxford American* 57.

"Soft-Shell Science," by Carroll Leggett. Originally published in *Raleigh Metro Magazine*, October 2008.

"Humble Paddlefish Fulfills Southerners' Caviar Dreams," by Jeffrey Gettleman. From the *New York Times*, July 19, 2003. © 2003 The New York Times. All rights reserved. Used by permission and protected by the copyright laws of the United States. The printing, copying, redistribution, or retransmission of the material without express written permission is prohibited.

"Bayou Coquille," a poem by Garland Strother. Originally published online by *The Dead Mule School of Southern Literature*, June 2008. www.deadmule.com.

"USDA Approved: The Mark of Discrimination in Twentieth-Century Farm Policy," by Pete Daniel. Originally presented at the 2007 Southern Foodways Alliance Symposium, Oxford, Mississippi.

"So Long, White Lily," by Jack Neely. Originally published in *Metro Pulse*, June 25, 2008.

"What Happened to Poor Man's Pâté?" by Chuck Shuford. Originally published in the *Daily Yonder*, November 6, 2007.

"Friends and Fancy Food," by Rheta Grimsley Johnson. This version of the syndicated column appeared in the *Knoxville News-Sentinel*, January 4, 2009. Reprinted by permission from King Features Syndicate.

"Eating My Heart Out: The Good and Bad of the Meal of a Lifetime," by Beth Ann Fennelly. Originally published in the *Oxford American* 57.

"Funeral Food," by Kathleen Purvis. Originally published in *Edible Lowcountry*, Fall 2007.

"Sad Streaks and Weepy Meringues," a poem by Sarah Anne Loudin Thomas. Originally published in *Appalachian Heritage*, Summer 2006.

"Malabsorption Syndrome," a poem by Marianne Worthington. Originally published in *Literary Lunch*, edited by Jeanette Brown with Flossie McNabb (Knoxville, Tenn.: Knoxville Writers Guild, 2002).

"African American Foodways: Food, Fear, Race, Art, and the Future," by Ari Weinzweig. Originally appeared in *Zingerman's News*.

"Juneteenth Jamboree," by Robb Walsh. A version of this article was originally published in *Gourmet* magazine, June 2007.

"The Sacred Feast," by Kathryn Eastburn. Originally published in *Saveur* 94.

"Open City," by Jessica B. Harris. Originally published in *Saveur* 115.

"Red Velvet Revisited," by Neely Barnwell Dykshorn. Originally published in *Virginia Living*, April 2007. Reprinted with permission of Cape Fear Publishing.

"The Food and Music Pantheon," by Roy Blount Jr. Originally published in *Gastronomica*, Spring 2008.

"A Fine Virginian," by Lucretia Bingham. First published in *Saveur* 99.

"Chapel Hill Eats and a Chef Remembers," by Ben Barker. Originally presented at SFA's Camp Carolina, September 2007.

"Purdue," by John Martin Taylor. A version of this article first appeared in *Charleston* magazine, December 2004.

"Platters and Permanence Walk and Talk A-Plenty at Spartanburg's Beacon," by Susan Shelton. This piece was originally part of an oral history project for The Foodways of Appalachia course at East Tennessee State University, Fall 2008. Published in *Now and Then: The Appalachian Magazine*, Spring/Summer 2009.

"The Restaurant That Time Forgot," by Lee Walburn. Originally published in *Atlanta* magazine, February 2008. Reprinted by permission of *Atlanta* magazine.

"Miss Congealiality," by Julia Reed. A version of this article was published in *Ham Biscuits, Hostess Gowns, and Other Southern Specialties* (New York: St. Martin's Press, 2008).

"Opinion Stew," by Salley Shannon. Originally published in *Saveur* 87.

"This Recipe Is Remembrance," by Michelle Healy. Originally published December 19, 2006. Copyright 2006, *USA TODAY*. Reprinted with permission.

"Knowing," a poem by Sylvia Woods. Originally published in *Now and Then: The Appalachian Magazine*, Spring/Summer 2008.

"Muffulettas and Meringue Pies: The Immigrant Experience in the South," by Amy C. Evans. Images previously published online at www.southernfoodways.org as part of the SFA Oral History Initiative.

"Your Dekalb Farmers Market: Food and Ethnicity in Atlanta," by Tore C. Olsson. Originally published in *Southern Cultures* 13, no. 4 (2007).

"Descendants of Greek Immigrants Aren't Pining for Pita," by John T. Edge. Originally published in the *Atlanta Journal-Constitution*, March 27, 2008.

"From Barbecue to Baklava: The Delta's Culinary Crossroads," by Amy C. Evans. Originally published in *Delta Magazine*, September/October 2006. Reprinted here by permission of the author.

"The Delta Hot Tamale: Save Those Coffee Cans," by Martha Hall Foose. From *Screen Doors and Sweet Tea: Recipes and Tales from a Southern Cook* by Martha Hall Foose, © 2008 by Martha Foose. Photographs copyright © by Ben Fink. Used by permission of Clarkson Potter/Publishers, an imprint of the Crown Publishing Company, a division of Random House, Inc.

"In the Doe's Kitchen with Aunt Florence," by Anne Martin. Originally published in *Delta Magazine*, September/October 2006. Reprinted with permission of *Delta Magazine*.

"Home Cooking: East Meets South at a Delta Table," by Joan Nathan. From the *New York Times*, June 4, 2003. © 2003 The New York Times. All rights reserved. Used by permission and protected by the copyright laws of the United States. The printing, copying, redistribution, or retransmission of the material without express written permission is prohibited.

"Virginia Is for Wontons," by Mei Chin. Originally published in *Gourmet* magazine, October 2008.

"Bozo's," by George Motz. Originally published in *Hamburger America: One Man's Cross-Country Odyssey to Find the Best Burgers in the Nation* (Philadelphia: Running Press, 2008).

"Currying Flavor," by Brett Anderson. © 2008 The Times-Picayune Publishing Co. All rights reserved. Used with permission of the *Times-Picayune*.

"Cooking for a Sunday Day," by Corby Kummer. Originally published in the *Atlantic*, June 2008. Reprinted by permission of the author.

"Welcome to Cuban Sandwich City," by Andrew Huse. Originally published in *Cigar City Magazine* 1, no. 2.

"Global Cornbreads: The Whole World in a Pan," by Crescent Dragonwagon. Originally featured in *The Cornbread Gospels* (New York: Workman Publishing, 2007).

"Demystifying Grits for the Northern Palate," by John S. Forrester. Originally printed in the *Boston Globe*, March 8, 2006. Reprinted here by permission of the author.

"The Invasion of the Whores de Orvrays," by Robert St. John. From *Deep South Parties* (New York: Hyperion, 2007).

"Tasty Tradition Rolls On," by Bill Archer. Originally published in the *Bluefield Daily Telegraph*, October 27, 2008.

"Good Humor," a poem by Devon Brenner. Published here for the first time by permission of the author.

"Early Times in Mississippi," by Donna Tartt. Originally published in *Garden and Gun*, Holiday (November/December) 2007.

"Sazeracs: I Take My Liquor Brown," by Sara Roahen. From *Gumbo Tales* by Sara Roahen. Copyright © 2008 by Sara Roahen. Used by permission of W. W. Norton & Co., Inc.

"The Michelada: Getting to the Bottom of a Mysterious Texas Concoction," by Francine Maroukian. Originally published in *Garden and Gun*, November 2008.

"Dr. Enuf: A New Age Nutraceutical with a Patent Medicine Pedigree," by Fred W. Sauceman. From *The Place Setting: Timeless Tastes of the Mountain South, from Bright Hope to Frog Level—Thirds* (Macon, Ga.: Mercer University Press, 2009).

"Have a Fried Coke—and a Frown?" by John Kessler. Originally published in the *Atlanta Journal-Constitution*, April 11, 2008.

"Taste of Tradition: Iced Tea," by Fred Thompson. Originally published in *Taste of the South* magazine, July 2008.

"Praise Wine," by John Simpkins. Adapted from a presentation at the 2008 Southern Foodways Alliance Symposium, Oxford, Mississippi.

"Butter," a poem by Elizabeth Alexander. Orginally published in *Body of Life* (San Fernando, Calif.: Tia Chucha Press, 1996).

The Southern Foodways Alliance

The Southern Foodways Alliance (SFA), an affiliated institute of the Center for the Study of Southern Culture at the University of Mississippi, celebrates, teaches, preserves, and promotes the diverse food cultures of the American South. Along with sponsoring the Southern Foodways Symposium and Southern Foodways Field Trips, we document Southern foodways through oral history collection and archival research.

Established in 1977 at the University of Mississippi, the Center for the Study of Southern Culture has become a focal point for innovative education and research by promoting scholarship on every aspect of Southern culture. The center offers both BA and MA degrees in Southern studies and is well known for its public programs, including the annual Faulkner and Yoknapatawpha conference and the Conference for the Book.

The fifty founding members of the SFA are a diverse bunch: they are cookbook authors and anthropologists, culinary historians and home cooks, chefs, organic gardeners and barbecue pitmasters, food journalists and inquisitive eaters, native-born Southerners and outlanders too. For more information, point your browser to www.southernfoodways.com or call 662-915-5993.

SFA FOUNDING MEMBERS

Ann Abadie, Oxford, Miss.
Kaye Adams, Birmingham, Ala.
Jim Auchmutey, Atlanta, Ga.
Marilou Awiakta, Memphis, Tenn.
Ben Barker, Durham, N.C.

Ella Brennan, New Orleans, La.
Ann Brewer, Covington, Ga.
Karen Cathey, Arlington, Va.
Leah Chase, New Orleans, La.
Al Clayton, Jasper, Ga.

Mary Ann Clayton, Jasper, Ga.

Shirley Corriher, Atlanta, Ga.

Norma Jean Darden, New York, N.Y.

Crescent Dragonwagon, Eureka
Springs, Ark.

Nathalie Dupree, Social Circle, Ga.

John T. Edge, Oxford, Miss.

John Egerton, Nashville, Tenn.

Lolis Eric Elie, New Orleans, La.

John Folse, Donaldsonville, La.

Terry Ford, Ripley, Tenn.

Psyche Williams Forson,
Beltsville, Md.

Damon Lee Fowler, Savannah, Ga.

Vertamae Grosvenor,
Washington, D.C.

Jessica B. Harris, Brooklyn, N.Y.

Cynthia Hizer, Covington, Ga.

Portia James, Washington, D.C.

Martha Johnston, Birmingham, Ala.

Sally Belk King, Richmond, Va.

Sarah Labensky, Columbus, Miss.

Edna Lewis, Atlanta, Ga.

Rudy Lombard, Chicago, Ill.

Ronni Lundy, Louisville, Ky.

Louis Osteen, Charleston, S.C.

Marlene Osteen, Charleston, S.C.

Timothy W. Patridge, Atlanta, Ga.

Paul Prudhomme,
New Orleans, La.

Joe Randall, Savannah, Ga.

Marie Rudisill, Hudson, Fla.

Dori Sanders, Clover, S.C.

Richard Schweid, Barcelona, Spain

Ned Shank, Eureka Springs, Ark.

Kathy Starr, Greenville, Miss.

Frank Stitt, Birmingham, Ala.

Pardis Stitt, Birmingham, Ala.

Marion Sullivan, Mt. Pleasant, S.C.

Van Sykes, Bessemer, Ala.

John Martin Taylor, Charleston, S.C.

Toni Tipton-Martin, Austin, Tex.

Jeanne Voltz, Pittsboro, N.C.

Charles Reagan Wilson,
Oxford, Miss.

ABOUT JOHN T. EDGE

John T. Edge (www.johntedge.com) is the director of the Southern Foodways Alliance. He writes a monthly column, "United Tastes," for the *New York Times*, is a contributing editor at *Garden and Gun*, and a longtime columnist for the *Oxford American*. His work for *Saveur* and other magazines has been featured in six editions of the *Best Food Writing* compilation. He has been nominated for four James Beard Foundation awards, including the M.F.K. Fisher Distinguished Writing Award. In 2009, he was inducted into Beard's Who's Who of Food and Beverage in America.